The Ten Commandments of Wealth Creation

Your Road to Riches Blueprint,

for the Success you truly deserve!

By Praveen Kumar & Prashant Kumar

Table of Contents

Table of Contents

Author's Note

This book is about 'Ten Commandments of Wealth Creation' that reveals 10 fundamental truths or principles about how to create wealth.

Am I Moses to whom God has revealed the truth? The simple answer is a definite 'No'. I am just an ordinary guy who rose from poverty and through my experience and experiments stumbled upon these truths in the process of creating wealth. The best part is that like many people I was oblivious of the fact that lack of financial security was the root cause of my misery.

I am fortunately blessed with a keen analytical mind that yearned to find fundamental truth about permanence happiness in life. I never let that spark die even when I was poor and struggling. My intense search led me to understand the fundamental principles of wealth that anyone can apply to his life to become wealthy.

The fact that you are reading this book is because you have that spark within to expand from your current situation and become greater than what you are today. You don't want to suck up to your boss, live in a place that is dictated by your current financial circumstances, you have the strong desire to give financial security to your loved ones, travel to exotic places and meet exciting people.

To fructify your dreams you need money but don't know how to go about it. You watch rich and the famous on TV or video clips and read about them in newspapers, books and magazines. Their stories are inspirational but how they got there is bit of a mystery to you. Only if we could be like them....

This book will teach you how to generate cash for investing, how to use leverage the right way to compound your wealth, create multiple streams of income for financial stability and also wealth protection strategies on how to keep wealth within your family for generations. If you have a sincere desire to improve your financial wellbeing and that of your loved ones, then this book will hopefully show you the path. It will save you from making mistakes and accelerate your path to a more fulfilling life.   •

This book will show you how simple it is to create wealth. All you need is an understanding of the principles and application of them in your daily life.

When you read a book about wealth creation, you must always inquire about the author. Is he genuine and does he have the experience?

I have read many books on wealth creation that talk about 'No money down deals' or 'Leveraging.' Reading about these concepts is very exciting for people who wish to become rich in no time, with little effort and no money of their own. However, most of these authors never explain the pitfalls of nothing-down deals and excessive leveraging - which make me believe that they lack the experience it takes to execute the same in real life.

I am blessed to be able to reside in New Zealand; one of the most beautiful countries in the world. However, my story began halfway around the globe, in a nondescript town in India. I was born to a family of veterans- who for generations served as soldiers in the armed forces- completely oblivious to the world of financial planning or wealth building.

Life in India, in the sixties, was tough with little or no prospects. And to make matters worse, I was abandoned by my father at the young age of 14 years. On my young shoulders, fell the responsibility of my mother who was just a high school graduate with no job prospects, an unmarried sister and a younger brother. I was ill-prepared and confused.

We found support and solace, in that tumultuous phase, in my grandfather's presence. He was a man of limited means but of great heart and wisdom. He inspired us by saying "Eat only half a slice of bread but never give up on your education or dreams."

I joined the Navy at the tender age of fifteen. The academy was a place where a roof over the head and free rations were guaranteed. My dreams were limited to survival in those days. I was a depressed and troubled soul...scrutinizing why life was so cruel to me. I contemplated suicide on several occasions but had too many responsibilities to give up on life. The intense physical routine at the National Defense Academy also helped me from getting into mischief. When you run ten miles every morning, go for horse riding and do drills under the hot, scorching Indian sun, there is very little energy left to tie yourself to a ceiling fan.

To address pain within, I turned to philosophy. I read every philosophical text I could lay my hands on Plato, Socrates, Spinoza, Voltaire, Kant, Schopenhauer, Spencer, Lau Tzu, Nietzsche, Freud, Carl Jung to name just a few. I was devouring books morning, evening, night and even on the shit-pot so as not waste time to get to the bottom of that deep sorrow that engulfed me. Although I got some insight into my problems, bouts of depression continued to haunt me.

To understand the cause of my suffering, I turned towards religion. My intense spiritual quest lasted for well over a decade. During this period, I neglected the material side of life in order to enlighten myself. In any case, I had no money because I was sending every rupee I earned back home to support my family.

One day my spirit would soar heavenward, but the next day I would be depressed again. Slowly through daily meditation and yoga, my mind became steady and the fluctuations reduced. Then one fine day it dawned on me that 'life is' and the spiritual and material world are closely interwoven. The spiritual side cannot exist without material well-being.

I decided to give up on my celibacy vows. I was honest enough to recognize that suppressed sexual thoughts were acting counter productively towards my spiritual growth. However, getting married is easier said than done.

 Finding a suitable wife posed a huge problem for me. I was fairly good looking and had a good personality thanks to the countless hours of drills at the Academy. Girls would find me alluring as I could play the guitar and sing, in addition to being a good dancer. But when it came to committing, I could always sense a hesitation. In those days, I was very proud of my new-found spirituality and boastful of my non-materialistic approach to life. I was the quintessential 'philosopher fool' who knew much of the inner self but nothing about what motivates young girls of marriageable age.

When all attempts at organic love fail—family relations come in handy, in India, in the form of an arranged marriage. They found me a beautiful girl who was equally non-materialistic and clueless about money matters. We were a match made in heaven. Our bank balance was zero, but this did not trouble either my wife or me.

Our motto in the Navy was 'Either you can be an officer and a gentleman or be rich.' I proudly chose to be an officer and a gentleman. Fortunately, I kept away from liquor which was another requirement to prove my competence as a non-caring, happy-go-lucky officer who was ready to die for his country at the drop of a hat.

Both I and my wife lived in our blissful non-materialistic state, till a reality check arrived in the form of our two beautiful children.

At this point, even impractical philosophers like me are forced to become practical. When you look into those innocent eyes and feel the touch of those little hands holding your fingers, your heart melts. I love my children deeply and did not wish them to suffer the same fate that I did.

My financial security was my job in the Navy, and I tried to excel so that I could get promotions and plum postings. Hard work pays off and all bosses are not bad. I was lucky to get an overseas posting to Mauritius which opened my eyes to the world of finance for the first time in my life. I met with people who were making huge sums of money through currency transactions, and by being the middlemen in the trade with South Africa (trading with India was banned due to Apartheid.)

Lest I was left behind, I purchased 20 volumes of Business Management books and read them several times to fill in the gaps in my knowledge. Although I had a grasp of economics, personnel and financial management, I was still clueless as to how I may use this knowledge in real life to make money.

I got into real estate investing perchance. When I returned back to India from my overseas sojourn to my horror, I found that my sister's marriage was in trouble. She asked me to help her out and invest in a boutique shop in Delhi from where she could run her garments business. With my wife's consent, we put our entire savings from the 3 years overseas tenure and purchased a small retail shop. My legs were shaking when I closed the deal. Family and friends told me I was a fool and that I had paid too much for the property. Funnily, my critics had never purchased an investment property.

In the next five years, the price of the property we purchased went up by five times. Such ridiculous price increases happen only in India. We were luckily caught in a vertex of an upward property cycle. From being ridiculed to becoming an investment genius—my friends and family were now seeking investment advice from me. I was equally clueless. The only thing I had done was to act, despite my fear, motivated by my desire to help my sister.

This little deal was an eye-opener. I understood the power of real estate investing and whenever I found little money, I started buying real estate. In those days there were no books or seminars on real estate investing in India. I was a street-smart investor aided by a competent broker who gave me one advice that I have not forgotten to date. He said "You should only buy cows that give milk. There is no point in buying a calf that you have to nurture for years before it gives milk." This one advice has kept me out of trouble in turbulent financial times.

I applied for a premature retirement from the Navy in the mid-nineties. By that time, my real estate income had sufficiently replaced the stipend I received from the Navy... I thought to myself, "If I could do this well as a part-time investor then I will be able to accelerate my growth by removing those shackles of the Navy where making money was looked down upon."

I was in for a rude surprise soon after I left the Navy. Real estate market, after a bull run since I started investing, went into a nosedive when the Indian Government, in all its wisdom, decided to carry out a nuclear test. Economic sanctions were imposed by most countries and businesses around the country started going bust. My properties became vacant, and cash flow dried up.

Having been a master of good times, I was clueless about what could be done. In panic, I sold a large number of my properties at a loss. To generate cash, I founded a security agency that was partially successful, but I found it to be very stressful to run. I quit that business as I was not happy doing it. The failure was due to the fact that I did not have the mindset for business, although I did not realize it at the time. I went back to sea stationed as a Captain in Merchant Navy. The good old sense of job security takes over when there is panic; my dreams of being an entrepreneur lay in shambles.

Stressful financial conditions forced me to start looking for answers. I was struggling with my real estate business when a friend of mine recommended 'Real Estate Riches' by Dolf De Roos—this book was an eye-opener! It was the first book I read on investing. I became an avid reader and read everything I could lay my hands on. Entrepreneurial spirit, once again, rose within me. It was like the good old days when I was devouring those books on philosophy.

During this period, we migrated to New Zealand. I was excited because Dolf De Roos belonged to that country and had written that it was "a haven for property investing with no capital gain tax, stamp duty or estate taxes."My true education in business and investing kick-started after my arrival in New Zealand. I had very little capital to start with;the value of money shrinks dramatically when you convert rupees 50 to a dollar.

Only a migrant can understand how tough it is to start all over in a new country, especially when you are on the wrong side of fifty. Being a submarine captain is perhaps one of the most difficult jobs in the world—it made me resilient but I had no real-world skills for a job, apart from some experience in real estate investing. I decided to become a commercial real estate consultant as that would give me the opportunity to learn in an area where I wanted to start my business.

It was a steep learning curve. Fortunately, my job made me interact with multi-millionaires who were buying hotels, commercial buildings, shopping malls, warehouses and businesses. I would discuss investment and business strategies with them for hours and learn the basis of their decisions. To my surprise, I found that these millionaires were always willing to talk about their stories on how they built their wealth.

To expand my knowledge, I started attending paid seminars not only in property investing, but business building and internet marketing. I spent thousands of dollars which paid me rich dividends when I started my own investment company.

I multiplied and grew my investments…then came the big financial crash of 2008. Businesses were collapsing and there were mortgagee sales all around the country. I was better prepared this time because of my experience in market crash in India at the turn of the century.

A large number of my clients went bankrupt because of cash flow problems. On the other hand, few smart ones multiplied their wealth ten times over. I realized that great wealth is created in downturns. I also realized the difference in being rich and wealthy for the first time. Wealthy people don't work for money. Instead, they make their money work for them in diverse ways. Many rich people, on the other hand, make huge sums but their money and lifestyle can vanish because they do not understand the fundamental principles of wealth creation and protection. You can read numerous stories on sports, lottery winners, music and movie stars who go bankrupt despite earning millions of dollars.

This book is based on my journey from having a 'job safety' mentality to being self-employed, and eventually transiting to owning my own business. I took a decision a couple of years back to change my active income to passive income. I decided to work on projects that need my effort once but pay me repeated income for the rest of my life. It was the best decision I ever made.

We diversified our income sources to include digital publishing and affiliate marketing alongside our real estate business.

Today both me and my wife are retired and enjoy the fruits of our labor and continue to grow our passive income. We may not be rich by some standards as money is just a relative figure. We consider ourselves wealthy with multiple streams of passive income that support our lifestyle, whether we work or not.

Poverty and poor mindset are the greatest evils on the planet that force people do mean and evil things in spite of their best intentions. The good news is that with knowledge and little effort, anyone can become wealthy. I am a living example and proof that it can be done. My net worth today would have been at least fifty times more, had I possessed the knowledge that I have now. I don't want my readers to make the same mistakes I did in my younger days that set me decades back.

It is inspiring to read biographies of Steve Jobs, Bill Gates, Warren Buffet and other remarkable billionaire wealth creators. There is no harm in trying to achieve those lofty heights. However, most ordinary folks find taking those first few steps towards wealth creation overwhelming when starting out. Hopefully, simple principles that I enunciate in this book will help them get started on the journey.

There are people who question me, "why should I learn about investing when I don't have any money to invest?" I tell them, "You don't have that money because you have not invested any time and effort in getting financially educated." Money is never the issue. It is a faulty mindset that holds people back.

I would like to thank multitudes of mentors in my life who have helped and influenced me directly or indirectly by expanding my mind-state. These include: Purshotam, Dhir, Kewal Ahuja, Robert Kiyosaki, Robert G Allen, Brad Sugars, Raman Sarin, Phil Jones, Tom Hua and Anik Singal, to name a few amongst many.

I would also like to thank my wife, Rachita, and my two children, Nandita and Prashant, who have been my inspiration and rock, by my side, through thick and thin. I promised them light at the end of the tunnel when we were working hard as a family to build our wealth—they joked about the tunnel but never lost faith in me, and I am ever grateful for their support. Wealth building process at times feels like being inside a dark tunnel as it takes a bit of hard work and time at the beginning, but once you exit the tunnel, you will be greeted with the brightest of sunlight—take the first step, and you will never regret it!

Preface

Have you ever wondered what separates school dropouts, wealth creators like Bill Gates and Thomas Edison, from the highly educated professionals who rent their brains to the highest bidder?

Specialized knowledge is amongst the most plentiful and cheapest form of service which may be harnessed! If you doubt this, refer the payroll of any university.

Knowledge one needs to create wealth is totally different and must never be confused with the formal education offered in schools and colleges. Thomas A Edison had only 3 months of schooling during his entire life; he did not lack education, nor did he die poor. The same is true for Henry Ford and Dhiru Bhai Ambani (a grass root Indian entrepreneur,) whose son Mukesh Ambani, may soon be challenging Bill Gates for the title of the richest man.

Why is it that we have such a limited number of wealth creators? What holds us back? The problem lies in our educational systems, society and family beliefs that were created during the industrial age. In those days, wealth remained in the hands of powerful governments or a very few rich people.

The education system in the industrial age was designed to cater to industries working towards mass production. People aspired to work for the government or in a corporation. In the industrial age, the concept of professional education to find jobs became popular. The idea of 'job security' or 'one job for life' took root. You worked your way up the corporate ladder and once you retired, the company or the government took care of your needs. The standard of living went up for most people. Remember the Sixties…we lived in a dream world…then, man stepped on the moon and everything seemed possible. Unfortunately, the party did not last for long.

The Industrial age systems took a couple of centuries to formulate. The information age has crept up unsuspectingly and has taken hold of our lives. It started with the advent of personal computers—and the internet has created a virtual world where thoughts, ideas and information fly across the globe with the ease of a click.

Exchange of ideas that ushered the industrial age due to the advent of the print media is now happening at over a billion times faster pace due to the internet. The new information age has completely changed the rules of the game; one that lasted for centuries. Knowledge knows no international boundaries, nor does capital. It flows to wherever the economic environment is more favorable and there is possibility for money to be made.

Corporations of the past are downsizing, reducing their workforce and hiring consultants/ temporary workers to cut down on costs. Workforce has become very mobile and long-term relationships between employers and employees are a thing of the past. As a result, more and more people are being forced to take responsibility for their financial futures and security. This is causing an unbearable amount of stress on people not adapting to the change.

The gulf between the rich and the poor is widening; the middle-class-which grew as a result of the industrial age-is rapidly vanishing and slipping into the abyss of poverty. They cannot make their ends meet and are confused.

The ever-increasing pace of technology is reducing product life cycles. Robots are replacing humans; jobs are becoming redundant.

To survive in this rapidly changing world, there is a need to continually reinvent oneself.

With advancements in medicine, health standards improved. Infantile death rates went down, epidemics were controlled and lifespan increased. This had a dramatic effect on the ratio of the retired population to working population that paid taxes to support the social security system. The governments and corporations no longer have the money for the social security system that they created.

The choice before us is either to learn and adapt or perish in this new world.

The good news is that we live in one of the most exciting times in our history. With the dawn of the information age, old rules have given way to the new. It no longer takes 'money to make money.' In this new world, 'money is just an idea.' Ideas can be converted to money, very much like Einstein's famous equation wherein matter can be converted into energy.

It takes 'value addition' to create wealth. The cost of material in a plastic micro-chip is only 0.1% of the selling price. This is true for any high-tech product or service. It is knowledge that gives value addition.

People who have grasped this essential change are the new wealth creators. Bill Gates, a boy from a middle-class family and a college dropout, was one of the first to understand this paradigm shift and act on it – no wonder he became the richest man in the world! A generation of billionaires and millionaires followed suit.

In the new world a millionaire is being created every 60 seconds. There are hundreds of self-made billionaires who are in their twenties and thirties. This pace will only hasten as it is just the beginning of the new age.

The next 50 years will give rise to a new generation of wealth creators who will overtake the giants of today. Are you the next millionaire or the next billionaire? It has never been simpler.

Information age makes it possible to start a new business or convert an idea into money with relative ease. But unfortunately, most of us are still saddled with the old mindset. It is the age of new thoughts, ideas and wealth creators. Those who do not grasp this new knowledge will be left behind.

This book is about adjusting to a paradigmatic shift. It is designed to draw you out and develop you from within. It is about removing chaff from the wheat and going right into the heart and fundamentals of wealth creation as a process which will help you become an enlightened millionaire whether you are in business or an investor or aspire to be one.

The book is organized in ten chapters. Each chapter explains a fundamental truth; these are the Ten Commandments of Wealth Creation. The first three commandments relate to internal principles of wealth creation. The balance seven commandments deal with external principles of wealth creation. Without understanding and incorporating the inner principles, it is not possible to apply the external principles of wealth creation in a sustainable way. Once you understand the Ten Commandments, there is nothing stopping you from achieving your destiny.

There is no greater creativity or nobler cause than becoming an enlightened millionaire. The good news is that anyone can do it without exception, even if you don't have a dime in your pocket. By creating wealth, you change not only your future but that of those you love and the ones who come in contact with you. Statistics show that one millionaire creates 10 jobs directly or indirectly, and a billionaire 10,000 jobs. There is no greater charity or worthier cause than trying to become an enlightened wealth creator.

Once you understand the principles and acquire the right mindset of a wealth creator, you will be like a magnet attracting riches. Money will come to you so quickly and in such abundance that you will wonder as to where it had been hiding during the lean years. So, start now—take one step at a time. A long march of thousand miles starts with the first step.

As you read this book, engrave 'The Ten Commandments of Wealth Creation' not on any stone–but in your heart and mind.

Thou Shall Sow the Seed of Wealth in Your Mind

> *"If you want to change the fruits, you will first have to change the roots. If you want to change the visible, you must first change the invisible"*
>
> — T. Harv Eker

The first commandment is perhaps the most important; without comprehending this in full measure, the other commandments won't work.

Every beautiful poem that was ever written, a great work of painting or sculpture that captivated you, a song or a book that captured your heart and mind, started as a simple thought in someone's mind. Just look around you – the bed you sleep in, the computer you work on, the shoes you walk in, the car you drive and the house you live in, or the stylish clothes you wear – everything was brought into existence with an idea that made money for its author.

It is the impulses of thought that have created air planes, space ships, skyscrapers and every invention you see on this planet. There was no nuclear power until someone visualized it. There was no radio or television until the time someone tapped onto radio waves. There was no electric bulb before Edison invented it.

Nietzsche rightly put it, *"Everyone thinks that the principal thing to the tree is the fruit, but in point of fact, the principal thing to it is the seed."* It is always the seed that precedes the tree and the fruits. We run after the fruits but the actual thing is the seed.

According to the Upanishads (ancient Hindu text that was written thousands of years ago,) even the universe was created when God had an idea. He said, *"I am one, let me be many."* The universe was thus created. This is supported by the Big Bang theory that the scientists have propounded of late; even they do not understand what caused the Big Bang! Is the world around us a manifestation of God's thought process? These are philosophical questions which all of us ponder when we search for answers. There is a lot of merit in this argument.

Thoughts are indeed the most powerful instrument of creation. Napoleon Hill, in his book *Think and Grow Rich* writes, *"Truly, "thoughts are things" and powerful at that, when they are mixed with definite of purpose, persistence, and a burning desire for translation into riches, or other material objects. All earned riches have their beginning in an idea."*

If you want to have a bite of the 'rich fruit,' then you have first to change the roots that nourish the tree and the fruit; what is visible is just a manifestation of what is not visible. Your wealth is the extension of your thought process. If you have the mindset of a millionaire, you will become a millionaire. Once you expand your mental state to be that of a billionaire, then there is nothing on earth that will stop you from becoming a billionaire.

There is no doubt that starting point of all riches is in the seeding-the thought process- that, *'I will be Rich.'* The important part is to know how to select the right seed, to plant it, give it a proper nurturance, and grow it into a healthy strong tree so that it can start bearing the right kind of fruits and in lots of quantity.

We are what we are because of the seeds of thought we have planted. If we want to be rich, we have to plant the right seed; the seed of mango will not produce an apple. For a harvest of riches, we have to plant the seed for being rich in our minds.

Oops! I forgot. Before we select the seed and plant it, we have to prepare the soil to receive it. Without the soil preparation, the seed will die. So, let us start from the very beginning. Initially, it is the soil preparation that matters.

Prepare the Soil for Seeding

It is our attitude to wealth which holds us back. In the majority of the cases, it does not provide the right kind of soil to plant the seed of wealth. Most of us aspire to be rich but it is our outlook that keeps us poor.

Wealth comes to those who become wealth-conscious. Failure to acquire riches comes to those who are not money conscious. Why do we harbor such a poor attitude towards wealth when we aspire for riches? This is mainly due to how our brain computer was programmed when we were young.

The memory chip in our mind records everything – it records every event, experience, thought, dream or feeling we have ever had. It is an amazing machine. It simultaneously records millions of inputs from our five senses nonstop, 24 hours a day. They are stored in layers and layers, buried deep within our subconscious. Each new layer buries the preceding layer deeper into our subconscious.

Bigger the event, deeper the impression it leaves on our mind. Even the most insignificant of events are recorded and stored; many believe that impressions of our past lives are passed on to us through the genetic code. We are what we are because of the sum total of those past impressions and our personalities and attitudes are defined by these past impressions that are buried deep within our subconscious.

Most of these impressions were recorded when we were very young and had little or no control over them. They were recorded by individuals who had their own limitations of knowledge and human prejudices. They left an indelible mark on our mind because we loved and respected them. They were our parents, teachers and friends whom we trusted because their love for us was unconditional.

Events and thoughts mixed with emotions create the deepest of impressions. It will be wrong to suggest that everything we were taught and all that we experienced in our respective childhoods was wrong.

Some of the knowledge that we gained is invaluable to us. Nothing can substitute the feeling of love, care and concern that was transmitted to us that brings us joy today. But it is wise to know that impressions that form our attitudes today were based on imperfect knowledge.

Another important thing to remember is that the processor in our brain, that interprets the incoming data before recording, was not fully developed when we were young. In many cases, we recorded the wrong results simply because of our faulty interpretations of the events around us.

We judge new events in our lives based on the imperfect information stored in our memory. Our brain processor becomes tainted when it compares new events with our not so perfect recorded data of the past.

Our emotions are the sum total of impressions caused by thoughts and feelings stored in our subconscious, and they are undeniably powerful. It is our feelings, dominated by the subconscious, that lead to action. While making financial decisions, we are torn between logic and emotions. It is mostly emotions that win.

When feelings become strong within us, they force us to act. Finally, it is action that leads to wealth creation. If we are able to change our thought process, then we can change the outcome of our future. Our destiny is in our hands and we cannot blame it on others.

Limiting Beliefs

Now, let us examine some of the myths about money that were drilled into our subconscious when we were young. You may relate to some of them:

- Money is the root of all evil.

- Behind great wealth there is a crime.

- It takes money to make money.

- Money can't buy you love.

- Money isn't everything.

- It takes hard work to make money.

- The best things in life are free.

- It is easier for a camel to go through the eye of a needle than for a rich man to enter the kingdom of God.

- You can either be an officer and a gentleman or rich.

- Wealthy people are snobbish.

- Money does not grow on trees.

- Money can't buy happiness.

Whew! Even if you believe in a few of them, they are designed to keep you poor for life. In fact, you might even decide to get rid of whatever little money you might have.

Let us examine some of these limiting beliefs to know if they are correct. At one point of time, people believed that the earth was flat. This belief made people behave as though it were flat. As a result, it limited exploration and expansion. Only when it was known that the world is round did Columbus set out to find a sea route to India and in the process discovered America.

The same is true for our limiting beliefs regarding money. So long as we believe in them, they will restrict us in our imagination.

Is money the root of evil?

The answer is a definite no. In most of the cases, it is extreme poverty that drives people to steal, become dishonest and even resort to violence to survive. Money is neutral; it is neither good nor evil. It is, however, a very powerful commodity. When in the hands of the right people, it can do a lot of good or it can become a destructive force when used wrongfully.

It is extreme lust for money that can sometimes make people go wrong. If anything, it is poverty that is evil. It makes people do things that they otherwise will not do. We have to rid the world of poverty from this planet to make it a better place to live in.

Behind great wealth there is a crime

In the initial stages of wealth creation, we do not have access to the right advice as we do not have sufficient money to buy it. Also, at times, our haste to get rich quick makes us cut corners which leads to problems with the taxman or law.

At some point during our growth, dawns the wisdom, that the best and fastest way to create wealth is through a legitimate route. A crime behind every great wealth is a very sweeping statement. In every great endeavor, mistakes are made and a majority of them happen to be genuine.

It's hard to believe that wealth creators like Edison, Carnegie, Warren Buffet, Steve Jobs and Bill Gates had anything to do with crime. This is also true for 99% of the wealth creators who do not fall in the same league.

Money does make money when invested sensibly, but it is only a very small aspect of wealth creation. It is ideas and an educated mind that create wealth and not crime. There are criminals who succeed in the short run but the law invariably catches up.

"Money can't buy me love..."

If there's one thing that stills hums in my mind, it's the lyrics made popular by the Beatles number. Ask any sensible girl – who is also honest – if this assumed correlation between money and love holds true. You will get the right answer.

Someone rightly said, '*Whoever said money can't buy you love doesn't know where to shop.*' The love you have for another, when expressed through something that only money can buy, can bring love in return. Make no mistake on this one.

Money isn't everything

I fully agree with the statement: 'Money isn't everything." There are much more important things in life than money: our families and friends, health, spiritual wellbeing, pursuit of art and culture are definitely more important, amongst many other things. However, money makes it possible to pursue these important things in life. Money provides the freedom to pursue your dreams.

It takes hard work to make money

The rich and the poor have the same number of hours to work. It definitely does not take extraordinary hard work to become rich. Even the poor work hard at what they do, in fact, people who are relatively poor work harder than the rich. The rich because of knowledge work smarter than but not as hard as the poor.

The best things in life are for free

This is very true. Some good things in life do come for free. Like the beautiful sunset or the fresh air we breathe. However, some of the most delightful things in life that we as humans enjoy come with a price tag.

Having money at our disposal does not mean that we cannot enjoy the free things that God bestows on us. With money, we have the power to enjoy both.

It is easier for a camel to go through the eye of a needle than for a rich man to enter the kingdom of God

I will take the privilege to have my own story account for this; I have seen such extreme poverty which I hope no one ever gets subjected to.

Was I ready for spiritual development in those earlier years of poverty? The answer is a definite no. In those initial years, I was just fighting for my survival. God was absent from my conscious mind. I started on my spiritual quest once I was settled in a regular job and had some kind of an income.

My spiritual development has progressed along-with my material advancement. It is never the material world – of being rich or poor – that comes in the way of our spiritual advancement, but the attachment to the material world.

Heaven is not for you, in so far as you're attached to your few possessions; person with an enlightened view to wealth has better chances of making it to heaven.

You can either be an officer and a gentleman or rich

I was invariably imbued with this ideology during my training at the military academy. I instantly identified myself as an officer and a gentleman. This one belief kept me poor for the larger part of my life.

Wars are about financial control and power. Once this knowledge dawned on me, I decided to apply for a premature retirement from the military to follow my destiny.

Wealthy people are snobbish

I have met some of the nicest people who are wealthy. However, it is true that anyone who values their time may appear snobbish when they do not give us adequate attention. Approach a wealth creator with a brilliant thought or an idea and see how attentive they get.

Most enlightened wealth creators are exceedingly humble—they have a spark in them that will kindle a spark in you provided you have the right mindset.

The fault can also lie in our judgment stemming from our own insecure self.

There is a saying, "***When the shoe fits - the shoe is forgotten, when the belt fits - the belt is forgotten, and when the mind is right - for and against are forgotten***." Before passing judgment on others, it is imperative that we have our hearts and minds in the right place.

Money does not grow on trees

On the contrary, money does grow on trees as you further your reading and increase your financial knowledge. The only thing needed is to prepare the soil, plant the right seed, nurture the plant through the initial stages. Once it grows big and strong, it will not only give you all the money you need, but also new seeds to plant more money trees.

Money can't buy happiness

This is very true because happiness is a state of mind. Money, however, can provide you with the freedom to pursue whatever field of activity you may choose, which in turn, helps create a happy state of mind.

It gives you the freedom to travel, go on holidays, get involved in charities, learn new hobbies, indulge in personal development and spend more time with your family. The choice is entirely yours according to your definition of happiness.

Stress-filled, unhappy moments in my life have been – when I could not meet my financial commitments – like paying bills or providing for the basic needs of my family.

The list of attitudes that hold us back from getting rich, discussed in the preceding paragraphs, is not comprehensive. I am sure if you look back at your life, you can compile your own list and find out what holds you back.

Compiling this list may not be as easy as it may seem because we do not understand how our mind works and the power of our attitude. Our inner nature or attitude built over the years resists change. It likes status co to remain and holds us back.

We have layers, and layers of impressions buried deep within our subconscious. Our subconscious guides us what to do. We are like prisoners of our inner nature. If we want to try out new things the data stored in our memory bank tells us this is not possible. It has never been done before. Our teachers and parents warned us against this. If you try this, there is a considerable risk involved. We can't change in spite of our best efforts. We get paralyzed.

If we wish to be successful: managing and training the mind are the most crucial skillsets that are required. We will need to free your perspective from the prejudices of the past.

How to Change your attitude

How do you change your attitude? How do you go from 'stay poor' printed in your subconscious to becoming a go-getter who says, "Being rich is your birthright?" Yes, you were born to be rich and it is your birthright.

To make this quantum change in your attitude, you have to take few simple steps. The first thing to do is to become aware of your inner thought process. And how does one become aware? It is simple... meditate!

Please, don't freak out. Most people get confused. They think— to meditate is to get into some tremendous yogic posture and concentrate on the problem till you get the answer to the problem. Nothing can be further from truth.

Meditation means a reversal of the thought process. Our minds are overloaded with continuous inputs from our five senses, 24 hours a day. Even while sleeping, it works all the time chiming in dreams. It is burdened to the extent that it can't think straight.

It is high time you go to a quiet place where there is no disturbance, sit down quietly and turn off your five senses. Now drift inwards towards your mental space and observe what is happening there. Initially, you will see only the top layers - consisting mainly of pressing issues and problems that are worrying your mind.

It takes patience, practice and courage to unravel the inner workings of your mind. To uncover the layers of your mind, you have to become non-judgmental and fearless. The mind will try to put brakes on the flow; there is much fear, hurt and guilt there. It is very hard to uncover memories that cause so much pain. It will need great courage to command the mind to let go of the brakes and allow the buried impressions flow out from the mind.

While reflecting, do not sit in judgement, because you were not responsible for most of the impressions recorded in your subconscious. These events occurred when you had no control over them. They happened during your childhood. Let your thoughts flow out with one part of your mind as a mute witness. It may not happen in the first sitting, but in due course even the most deeply buried impressions will begin to appear.

This is why writers, musicians, painters and other creative people are given such a high pedestal to stand on. It is because each creative idea involves the reversal process of the mind. The creative people can invoke and have access to the deep recesses of their minds, and sometimes, even beyond the mind as we shall learn later.

Our awareness level increases when we start observing our thought process. We begin to understand that most of our actions are as a result of our previous programming. As our level of consciousness increases, we are freed from our pasts and start living, and making decisions in the present.

Increase in awareness will lift the lid on buried emotions, hidden fears and deep-seated myths that you have about money. You will understand the subtle influence that money exerts in each of your relationships, even with your nearest and dearest ones.

Money is the currency of power: it is used to manipulate and control. The person with greater resources uses his or her assets to control the behavior of the other person—whether they are friends, parents, children or spouses. In most cases, this happens at a subconscious level with none of the players fully aware of what is happening. Deep resentment develops in relationships as a result of this gameplay. Money matters are shrouded in mystery and there are layers of emotions that cover our motives.

Some reflection will prove that money is central to all our relationships. It influences many of our choices ranging from whom we marry, our choice of job, where we live to what we wear, eat and experience.

In our society, money is the metaphor for success and achievement. Having it can make us feel worthwhile and not having it can make us feel worthless. We are what we are because of the money we have. Somerset Maugham, put it rightly when he wrote, *"**Money is like a sixth sense without which you cannot make complete use of the other five.**"*

Further reflection will show that men may feel threatened if they earn less than their wives. Men associate money with success, prestige, risk, power and excitement. If a man loses his job, his shoulders will drop as though he has been emasculated and lost his manhood.

A man normally measures his worth to his wife, children and society in purely economic terms. Unemployment can lead to depression, low self-esteem, anger and perceived loss of power. Women on the other hand, look at money as a form of security that gives them freedom and independence. Change in relative earning capacities results in a shift of power dynamics, spending patterns and bedroom politics.

Another area where couples display a wide range of differences is in their ability to tolerate debt. Intimacy is stifled by financial conflict. If there is power imbalance in your financial relationship, there will surely be a similar imbalance in your sexual relationship. In extreme cases, this results in marital tension and relationship breakdowns.

You will be surprised to learn that there are more divorces due to money problems than there are because of sexual ones. Money, not sex, is the last taboo and an intensely private matter. People will discuss their problems of sex openly but when it comes to money they will clamp up even with their spouse. This is because money is power and any discussion regarding money threatens to change the power dynamics in relationships.

In many cases, love becomes a financial transaction. Parents are conditioned to believe that buying things for children is a measure of their love for them. Women feel loved only when their husbands shower them with gifts. Cutting financial resources is a tactic frequently used to establish control in relationships.

Many people offer financial help to gain power and status over others. The recipient, on the other hand, tends to become subservient and in emotional debt. Many people don't even spare themselves and go into a buying spree if they are lonely and depressed.

You must have heard of money strings—they are everywhere and mostly invisible!

Now reflect on your work scene; your financial security depends on your job. If you are fired it, will create havoc for your family. You are forced to succumb to every unreasonable demand of your boss. You cannot speak your mind freely or you may not get the next promotion.

I excelled in my naval career because the driving force there was my financial insecurity. My wellbeing, and that of my family, depended on my doing well in service. I could never speak my mind; deference was a sure way of getting written off. Only when I had built substantial residual income through my real estate investing could I freely express myself. I think I became a much better person and an officer once I gained a sense of financial security.

Money forces us to make compromises at every turn in our lives. Unfortunately, some people cross the barrier and break the law. They steal, don't pay taxes, become corrupt and in extreme cases, even resort to violence and murder. Money corrupts like nothing else.

Reflect on another scenario: what happens if you fall sick or become incapacitated to work? How will you cope? For how long will your insurance pay up? What happens to you or your family that relies on your income? Still many people say that, "money does not matter to them."

Most of us fail to realize that money has a powerful influence on us starting from the moment we're born till we die. We spend most of our waking hours trying to earn a living away from our loved ones. Our free time is spent in thinking about money: How to pay our bills? How to allocate the limited money we have? Whether to buy a new car or a house, go on a holiday, buy new clothes, send our children to better schools or look after our aging parents?

Conflicting requirements and lack of money causes anxiety in the deepest recess of our subconscious. Insecurity and financial pressures make us think and act in ways that are detrimental to those we love and the society at large.

The idea behind silent reflection is to increase awareness regarding money matters. It is to understand that money is the undercurrent of life that drives us. Our physical and spiritual wellbeing depends on it. Decision to acquire wealth and riches is a noble act towards not only us and our families, but the society at large.

Imagine the power of money in enlightened hands and the amount of good it can do: it can provide physical, mental and spiritual freedom. It can free the planet Earth from the ills of poverty that bind millions to a life of misery.

There is no nobler pursuit than the creation of wealth that is done in an enlightened way. It is the forerunner to spiritual development. In fact, spiritual progress is not possible without passing through the material phase and satiation of the basic human needs—which only money can provide.

Look at any religious organization, including the church; they thrive on patronage of the rich. Success in the material world is a prerequisite to entering the spiritual world. So, don't be afraid- it is your destiny to be rich.

There is an energy flow in silent meditation and stillness. Wherever you direct this energy, results will show. It is your mind's energy that decides your destiny and its flow can be controlled through mindfulness and silent observation.

Triggers that Work the Mind

There are principally two triggers that work the mind when it comes to acquiring great wealth. There may be slight variations but fundamentally there are only two triggers.

It is important to understand these triggers because all wealth is generated due to these two triggers. You will need to understand and use these triggers skillfully in order to create wealth. The two triggers are the 'pain' and the 'pleasure' triggers.

Pain comes from deprivation of basic human needs like food, shelter and love. Even the very thought of pain and deprivation can become great motivators that can get us started towards the process of wealth creation.

Pleasure, on the other hand, is fulfillment of desire unsatisfied. Even the thought of pleasure can get our minds excited with all kinds of possibilities and is an equally great motivator to get us started.

Pain pushes us whilst pleasure attracts us towards acquisition of riches. You have to understand what trigger drives you—it can be a bit of both. A little bit of meditation and awareness will help you identify triggers that work your mind. Meditation is nothing else but consciously observing your thoughts without judgement. Once you understand the inner thought process, you will be able to make sound choices in the present and not be driven by programming from the past.

In my case it was extreme poverty that drove me into the arms of spiritual quest to find the answers to my miserable state. For some reason, I bypassed the material stage only to realize at a much later date that my development was incomplete. This realization set me on the path towards attaining material success.

In some ways I am happy that I understood the spiritual values before embarking on the wealth creation process even though it set me back by a couple of decades. Money has given me great satisfaction- to educate my two children in the best of colleges that money could buy. It enabled our family travels around the world and expanded our horizons.

The greatest thing about money is the freedom it provides. It gives the freedom of time to explore relationships. Freedom of movement allows us to explore new thoughts, ideas and develop our unique genius. To become an enlightened wealth creator is to have freedom to do what you desire as long as it hurts no one and helps others.

Charity means to help others grow and make them stand on their feet so that they can hold their heads in dignity. Knowledge, education and health are the keys.

Education and the pursuit of knowledge has been the only difference between me and the poor village in India from where I emerged. I hope to acquire all the riches in the world and go back someday to set up an educational system that will empower others to do better than me.

My triggers of pain and pleasure may be different as compared to yours because your circumstances and experience of life are different. Your triggers and dreams are equally worthy. Take time to find them and focus on them.

Final Thoughts

Do not run after the fruit without sowing the seed first. In doubt- read a little, reflect a little, meditate a little and become aware of the power of the money in your life and the triggers that drive you.

The seed will engender the tree and the fruits, and not the other way round. You are destined to great riches. Being wealthy is your right—you may or may not realize this fact. The world is moving towards materialistic progression. Sooner you understand this fact about money, faster the manifestation of affluence and power will happen in your life.

Make a decision at this very moment that: "I will be rich and enlightened," and you shall be rich and enlightened. Your journey to financial freedom will begin as soon as you sow the seed of prosperity and becoming rich in your mind. It is as simple as that.

Even if one understands the importance of money, it is fear of the unknown and the risky that holds us back. No one has ever succeeded in life or created wealth without taking risks. Whether it is the decision to get married, start a business, invest in a property or choose a career; there are anticipation of the unknown. A sports person or an artist has to decide if they have sufficient talent to pursue their dreams or join the rest of mankind by taking a less risky option.

There is 'fog of war' in every decision in life. No one has a crystal ball to see the future. The worst thing in life is to freeze because of that fear of the unknown. When it comes to money and our financial future, this fear becomes irrational. In the second commandment of wealth creation, we shall examine the nature of fear and how we can overcome it to become truly rich.

Thou Shalt Burn Thy Fears in the Fire of Knowledge

If you have read the first commandment thoroughly, then having the desire to create wealth is only the first step in the right direction to become rich. However, the seed to creating wealth – that you have planted in your mind – has to be given the right nourishment to grow. It has to sprout, become a plant and then grow into a strong tree that will bear fruits of wealth for you. It is vulnerable initially to many negative forces from within and outside. We have to protect and nurture it through the initial stages.

Fear is your biggest enemy

That fear festering in your mind is the biggest threat to the seed of wealth creation that you have planted in your mind; it is like a weed that has to be removed before you can succeed.

Fear is a distressing emotion aroused by impending danger, evil, pain, etc., irrespective of whether the threat is real or imagined.

Fear is a hard-wired emotion, triggered by our subconscious. As human beings, we naturally fear everything that is unfamiliar to us and anything from our past that has resulted in feelings of pain. These feelings signal our brain, which drives our actions in such a manner that causes us to avoid pain at all costs. We will instinctually go to great lengths to prevent circumstances that bring about fear and the stress that is created within us through that fear.

We are afraid of fear because we are afraid of pain. This creates a very real problem for us, in that, we are instinctively driven away from just about everything that would result in the creation of our own financial independence.

Fear will always overwhelm everything that might bring about real change in our lives- it is unavoidable. It is in the nature of our brains to protect us from pain unless we make a conscious choice to achieve greater reward than the resulting pain brought about by what we fear.

DOUBT, FEAR, and ANXIETY are the three demons that bring our progress to an abrupt halt, right at the point when we are about to make a decision that has the potential to change our lives. Doubt creeps in and causes the fear, which in turn, causes the anxiety. The three can strike at lightning speed and freeze our decision-making capacity.

The demon of fear is, without a doubt, the biggest obstacle in our minds that does not allow us to nourish the seed of wealth. It is the fear of failure of losing all that we have achieved so far. It is the fear of criticism and ridicule. It is the fear of losing love and respect of our near and dear ones. It is always this irrational fear that holds us back from achieving greatness and financial success.

What is the source of this fear?

What is it that causes us to freeze and lose our senses, rationality and the power to act? The primary cause of this debilitating demon is ignorance. Knowing this truth will set us free. That, in itself, is a beautiful truth.

You must understand that there is only one thing to be set free from and that is ignorance. If you analyze carefully, it is always the lack of knowledge, and the understanding of things and situations that causes fear. Let me explain: prior to the age of Enlightenment, thunder and lightning, like most unknown forces, were misunderstood and proved to be a source of great fear in the minds of people. Tumultuous nights usually scared people out of their wits, they did not comprehend what was happening. They would believe the Gods to be angry and felt guilty of their wrongdoings. It left a very deep impression of fear on their minds.

These days when science has explained the true nature of thunder and lightning, occurrences and fluctuations in weather do not cause any anxiety or fear in our minds. It leaves no impression whatsoever. We go about our daily works as if nothing has happened. It is a non-event. *Fear burns in the fire of knowledge*. Likewise, if you have the right financial knowledge, you will not suffer from fear of failure.

Similarly, our fears predominate due to the layers and layers of wrong inputs and impressions stored in our subconscious. These impressions were formed as a result of the education system that was designed in the industrial age: designed in an age where only few were privileged and the rest were trained mentally and professionally to be at their service.

Our parents and teachers, whom we loved and admired, were part of the same education system. They unknowingly passed the same knowledge down to us: become professionals, become doctors, engineers, accountants and lawyers. Get a job in a good company, work hard and be successful. No one taught us to be wealth creators. No one taught us the skills to be wealth creators.

Even the media, influencing public opinion profoundly, is a product of that old thought. We can't blame them. They were educated in the same school of thought as most of us. They imbibed the fear of

God into us. The economy is going downhill. Next year, there will be a recession: they rattle rising unemployment figures, oil prices, inflation rate, foreign debt, national debt and make comparisons with the great depression of the thirties, when everyone seemed to have lost their homes and jobs.

Fear, greed and sensationalism sells—rationality does not. No doubt we're so afraid! Who would like to jump on to the bandwagon of uncertainties? Why take risks when you can get a decent job and survive? Fear is programmed in our memory chip in form of a blueprint that dictates our financial lives.

How to Overcome Fear?

We have to erase and rewrite that program if we have to succeed. Knowledge helps us to examine these fears and erase them from our systems.

Now look at the facts: our mindsets were created in a world that was poor. This was a time when there was a distinction between the privileged and the poor. These economic positions in life seldom changed. Either you were born rich or you worked for the rich. This has all changed now.

The world is moving forward at an unprecedented pace. Despite the doomsayers' prediction by the media, the world is on a projected trajectory of great material advancement. You have to just assess history, starting from the industrial revolution, to understand the financial progress made by mankind. This pace has accelerated in the past 50 years and will increase in manifolds as the information age progresses.

There might be slight aberrations but the writing is on the wall for anyone to see. The wealth of the world is about to explode as never seen before—are you going to be a part of this expansion or get left behind?

At present, there are less than 0.1% wealth creators on this planet. This is going to change very rapidly because this advancing information age makes it possible to impart knowledge. Are you ready to acquire that new knowledge that will burn your fears and set you on path of great wealth?

Expand Your Mind State

You have made a decision to become an enlightened wealth creator; else you would not be reading this book. This is great...but be warned! Your inner nature is very powerful and strong; it is fortified by millions and millions of past impressions.

Our minds are like an elastic band: if the new force is not applied, it will try to snap you back and restore to its original position. You will need to keep applying the pressure of knowledge and burn your fears till you break free.

This is the stage where permanent transformation takes place and you do not go back to your original position. It is as though the rocket fueled by knowledge puts you into outer space beyond the pull of gravity. There is a saying that, *"Once your mind expands it never goes back to its original state."* You will have to keep applying the pressure of Knowledge incessantly, till you find yourself in an expanded state of mind.

A rocket burns 90% of its fuel during its take off stage: once it defies gravity, very little energy is needed to keep it running. The same is true for a mind that wants to grow to an expanded state to create wealth.

All information that is recorded in our memory passes through a processor in our minds before it is recorded. The previously stored data that is recorded in our systems interferes with the processor as it analyzes incoming data. We have the capacity to change our blueprint by first erasing the old blue print by burning it in the light of new knowledge.

As the old data gets progressively removed from our systems, its interference reduces, and the capacity of our mind's processor improves. The process is very slow as there are layers and layers of files accumulated in our system. Some of these are like viruses that continuously affect the capacity of our processor to analyze data correctly.

It is a catch 22 situation: our processors are affected by the same files it is trying to analyze, which makes the task very slow and tedious. However, we can make a quantum jump in our processing capability by upgrading our processors, by increasing our financial, emotional and spiritual intelligence.

Financial Intelligence

An intellect that is honed financially, helps one see opportunities that they otherwise would have not. These opportunities are seen with the mind. An unknowing fool will throw a gem away thinking it is another stone; a wealth creator will see an opportunity to make money which an untrained mind cannot see.

Financial Intelligence is the third eye which opens doors to opportunities where none exist. It creates new opportunities. That is why they say 'rich invent money.' An untrained mind, on the other hand, can create extreme poverty that lasts generations by teaching it to their families.

Financial intelligence not only creates wealth, it sustains it. There are innumerable stories of professional sportsmen who made millions during their playing years only to become bankrupt within a decade. Mike Tyson, a heavyweight champion, is one such example. He earned millions during his lifetime but is now bankrupt.

You must have also heard about lottery winners who are back to where they started within five years of winning the lottery ticket.

I was recently reading an article on the descendants of Hyder Ali and Tipu Sultan who are today penniless. They are members of families who ruled over half of India few generations ago. Why is it that these families lost their wealth? There are other families who not only sustain but grow their fortunes over generations.

The world changes, markets go up and down, technologies change, economies boom and crash. The families who survive are those that make the efforts it takes to develop their financial intelligence, which allows them to adjust to the changes and also helps find new opportunities to succeed in this changing world. They also take the trouble to teach and transmit this intelligence to their younger generations and hence, are able to sustain their wealth for generations to come.

What is Financial IQ?

There are many facets of financial intelligence. It is about understanding assets and liabilities, capital growth and cash flows, passive income as against earned income, good debt and bad debt and making money work for you instead of you working for money. It is also about tax savings and protecting your assets including intellectual property rights.

Let us examine some of these aspects in greater detail.

Assets and Liabilities

An asset, as explained by Robert Kiyosaki in his book 'Rich Dad Poor Dad', is something which puts money into your pocket and liability is something that takes money out of your pocket. By this definition your house, car, boat, golf set and other luxury items that you buy (thinking they are assets) are in actual fact liabilities. All these so-called assets take money out of your pocket. Most of these depreciate in value (except may be your house,) and are high maintenance items that cost money out of your pocket.

Most of us think that we are buying assets, but in actuality, we buy liabilities that keep us poor. This does not imply that one should not buy these things that make us feel nice and good about life: one must buy them only once sustainable wealth has been created by first purchasing income-producing assets.

The real assets are businesses, investment properties, shares, bonds, etc., that put money into your pockets and also appreciate in value. To create wealth is to buy income producing assets such as real estate, businesses and paper assets.

Capital Gain and Cash flow

Wealth is created through a combination of capital growth and cash flow. Capital growth creates long-term wealth whereas cash flow sustains it in the short term and a balance between the two is needed to sustain and fuel the growth.

Short-sighted people only go for cash flow to fund their current needs. On the other hand, there are long-term investors (especially those who invest in properties) who get into serious trouble by not understanding the importance of cash flow. A sensible combination of the two is needed to grow financially.

Good Debt and Bad Debt

People are scared of taking debt for business expansion and investments as it causes a lot of stress. At the same time, they are not afraid of taking loans to buy cars or to go on a holiday.

Financially intelligent people know that creating debts for buying income-producing assets is a prerequisite for growing rich. A good debt is when money is borrowed to create money. Just like the bank: banks take money deposits from us at a lower interest rate and loan it back to businesses or for purchasing properties at a much higher interest rate. They make money on the difference, as can anyone.

The simple trick is to borrow cheap and create an asset that pays more. Bad debts are the ones that you borrow at high interest rate and use for buying assets that depreciate or produce less, or no income.

Make Money Work for You

The best definition that defines being rich is: *"In case you stop working today because of ill health/ accident or voluntary retirement then for how long will your savings sustain your current life style."* In some cases, it may be just a few days or at best a couple of months- this means you are poor.

In other cases, it may be a couple of years. A tad better situation but is certainly not a healthy one! You will be rich if you can sustain your lifestyle adjusted for inflation, indefinitely.

The super-rich can not only sustain their present lifestyle but they make it better, and also have surplus income to reinvest so that their net wealth increases with each passing year.

This can only happen when you have a large component of your money coming from passive income in the form of rents from commercial/ residential real estate, dividends from shares, intellectual property rights or interest earned from deposits. In other words, it is money working for you even when you sleep or are on holiday. In case of a job, the money will stop flowing the moment you stop working.

Saving on Taxman's Dollars

You may or may not realize this, but the most outflow of money from your pocket, during your lifetime, is the money paid in taxes. In many countries, taxes can be more than 50% of the income earned. These include the GST, Income Tax, Custom Duties, Excise Duties, Service Tax, Sales Tax, Capital Gains Tax, Stamp Duties and Estate Duties etc.

You may not even be aware of some of the taxes you pay because they are cut at the very source—before you get paid or they get added to the price of goods that you buy on a daily basis. If you add them all up, taxes can take away anything ranging from 40-75% of all that you earn.

Financially intelligent people use investment vehicles and tax saving strategies to save on these taxes. Money saved from taxes through proper planning and invested sensibly can make even a modest earner into a millionaire many times over.

Most financially uneducated people will try and hide their income to save on taxes, and eventually, get in trouble with the law. They will try and save dollars by not consulting an astute accountant and setting up proper structures to save legitimately on taxes.

To grow financially, one has to provide their income details and their turnover: when you do that, you become liable to pay tax. Proper tax planning – not tax avoidance – is the route financially intelligent people take.

Structures for Asset Protection and Tax Planning

This is a very important component of financial intelligence. You should protect your wealth even as you earn. Things, sometimes, can go wrong even with the right knowledge and intentions because no one can have full control over their environment or future events. There is an unknown element in each financial decision we take.

Rich people set up proper structures for asset protection and tax planning before they start. Yes, there is a cost involved in setting up these structures at the beginning, especially at a time when the business or the entity is not generating any income. Normally the cost involved is very small and will pay itself hundred times over if set up correctly. It will also make you sleep better at night.

Risk and Risk Management

Most people refrain from starting a business or investing somewhere because they feel that there is a huge risk involved. What appears like a risk to an untrained mind is like a cake walk for the financially intelligent. This is because they understand those risks and take adequate steps to insure that risk.

I sailed around the world in a 40 ft. yacht. My friends and family thought I had put myself at great risk in such a small boat but I had trained hard and was a knowledgeable sailor. I understood and respected the sea in all its moods. To me, sailing that boat was safe and an enjoyable experience that enriched me as a person.

Life itself is a risk! The fact that we are born and continue to live is a risky business. We travel by cars and airplanes that can meet with accidents. The human body is fragile. It can give in to cancer, heart failure or a stroke at any stage.

Then there are natural disasters that can strike us at any moment: earthquakes, tsunamis, volcanoes, fires or even a strike from an asteroid can take our lives away in an instance.

Added to this, man has created enough disasters for himself in the form of wars, nuclear power, global warming and terrorism. We cover our risks in daily life by taking prudent decisions and by insuring our health, life and property.

The same can be done in our financial lives. In today's world, every financial risk can be insured. There is a premium involved but this can be an expense that can be taken into account into the cost of running a business or investment. Financially intelligent people not only take out insurances, but also have an exit policy in place for every decision they take. They have business structures in place so that their personal wealth is not touched even if businesses or investments fail.

Robert Kiyosaki rightly put it: "*It is never the business or an investment that is risky. It is always the businessman or the investor who is the risk*." It is our lack of financial knowledge that causes the risk. We get carried away by our emotions of fear and greed, which cause the risk. Risk can be controlled and even eliminated through proper knowledge and insurance.

The biggest risk in life is to remain poor and to have no assets. An even bigger risk in life is to think that someone else will come to our rescue in the hour of need: be it the government, family or friends.

The best thing in life is to rely on our own strength and take steps to become not only financially secure but rich. We have a responsibility towards our family and loved ones to cater for their wellbeing, growth and emergencies in life. The real risk is in not taking timely action to make them financially secure. Avoiding risks to improve one's financial future is just an excuse.

Key Skills of Financially Intelligent People

Financially intelligent people have certain key skills that make them rich. Unfortunately, these key skills are not the focus of what is taught in our schools and colleges.

Creative Thinking

We live in an information age. Most of the times, our minds are overloaded with information; be it the television, the internet, mobile phones or many books and magazines. There is so much information available and very little time to process and digest it. Creative thinking suffers as a result.

A problem solving and creative mind knows where to look for information, and process the data towards a predetermined useful end. An undisciplined mind will waste hundreds of hours in non-productive conversation over the phone or surfing the net lacking focus.

Discipline and focus release the mind from information overload. Only a restive, inward looking and a meditative mind can think creatively and solve problems.

Negotiating

In life, to get what we want, we have to negotiate. We have to get the other party to agree to our terms and conditions. We have to have the skills to change their initial responses: from a "No" to a "Yes." We have to learn the art of compromising for the betterment of both parties.

Communicating

There can be no successful business transaction without proper communication skills. Forget about business development, even marriages and friendships rescind when there is a communication breakdown. You will not achieve your desired results, so long as you are not able to communicate your point of view.

Selling and Marketing

For most people, selling a product or an idea has horrible connotations. It involves rejection, which most people find hard to swallow. The basic truth is that there can be no wealth creation without selling a product or an idea. Profits are generated and encashed once they're sold.

You cannot be successful in any walk of life without being skilled in selling. When you walk into a job interview, you are selling your skills, talents and personality. Even successful dating involves selling your charm, beauty, inner qualities and character.

It is not selling that is difficult: it is the fear of rejection that one has to conquer. Ask any successful entrepreneur and he will tell you that marketing and selling together constitute the oxygen of any business.

Mathematical Mind

Investment and business is about numbers. Basic knowledge of mathematics and accounting is essential to develop a financial mindset. There is no calculus or higher mathematics involved, but basic knowledge is essential.

Emotional Intelligence

We are human beings and emotions play a big part in how we react to the events occurring in our lives. Unfortunately, we cannot control everything that is happening in the world but we can control our reactions to the events that affect us.

Money can be a very emotional thing. If you don't believe me, just visit a stock exchange market and dispassionately observe people and their behavior. How fear and greed take over our rational thinking, how jealous and angry we can get when it comes to money!

Lack of an emotional intelligence causes internal friction in our minds, which saps our energy to do more productive work. There is an internal dialogue which takes place within our minds continuously. There is strife and irritation in our heads if our internal value system is in conflict with our conscious mind. It is only when both are in tune that there is peace within, and our energy levels explode.

What is Emotional Intelligence?

Our emotions emerge from the subconscious. Emotional intelligence accounts for our ability to change unconscious reactions to a conscious response. It means: to perceive and understand emotion, integrate emotion to facilitate thought, and to regulate emotions to promote personal and financial growth.

There is a verse in the Upanishads (sacred Indian text) that states, "If you know a lump of clay then you will know about all the clay in the universe." This means that if you know and understand your own mind, then you will understand all the minds in the universe. All minds function in a similar manner. All our basic human and emotional needs are the same.

To improve our emotional intelligence, we have to bring more and more of our subconscious into conscious examination. Knowledge of the self is the most important step towards improving our emotional intelligence.

Wealth Creation is 90% psychology and only 10% strategy. We have to make internal changes and adjustments to our thinking process that is governed to a very large extent through our emotions, before we can go out and start making money. Changing our psychological foundations is the difficult part, once that is done, creating wealth is a cakewalk.

Spiritual Intelligence

It is essential to understand that we do not live only on one plane of existence. Firstly, there is the material world which we can see, feel and understand. This is the gross or outer cover of life. We aspire for material success and possessions in this world.

Then there is the mind which has two parts: the conscious and the subconscious part. We can't see it, but we know it is there because we can think and dream. The reality of this mind can be entirely different from the real world because it can imagine, dream and be creative.

Finer still is our spirit. Science can't prove it, but we know it is there. It is the unifying force of the universe. It is the underlying principle of life and existence. It unites and not divides. It connects everything in this universe.

At the level of the spirit, we are all one without any differentiation. It is an all-knowledgeable force that permeates into every living or non-living thing. It is also the source of all joy and bliss in this universe. You may call it soul, God or by any other name. It is a reality we cannot deny because at some level we can sense it.

Human spirit is the creative life force of this universe. Most people do not realize that whatever happens in the material world is the printout of the happenings in our spiritual and mental world. Creative people understand this fact and they dip their minds into the cosmos' intelligence to solve their problems and get new ideas.

What is Spiritual Intelligence?

The best definition of spiritual intelligence that I have found is by Frances Vaughan, who states:

"Spiritual intelligence is concerned with the inner life of mind and spirit and its relationship to being in the world. It emerges as consciousness evolves into an ever-deepening awareness of matter, life, body, mind, soul, and spirit. Spiritual intelligence, then, is more than individual mental ability. It appears to connect the personal to the transpersonal and the self to spirit. Spiritual intelligence goes beyond conventional psychological development. In addition to self-awareness, it implies awareness of our relationship to the transcendent, to each other, to the earth and all beings. Spiritual intelligence opens

the heart, illuminates the mind, and inspires the soul, connecting the individual human psyche to the underlying ground of being. Spiritual intelligence can be developed with practice and can help a person distinguish reality from illusion. It may be expressed as love, wisdom, and service."

There are two important things to understand: even the subtlest of movement in the spiritual mind can change things dramatically for the better in the subconscious and the conscious mind, with a resulting effect in the material world.

A thought impulse originating from the spirit can change our whole life. We only have to learn how to trigger that impulse. Secondly, as we gain spiritual intelligence, it harmonizes us with the rest of nature because it a unifying force. This is very important to us in the material world.

It is our sense of conflict in the material world that saps our energy. If we are in harmony then a powerful energy source explodes within us. This has as huge impact on our success in the material world, which is why developing spiritual intelligence is so important to our success.

Abundance of the Universe

Most people feel that to become rich you have to compete for the limited resources that are available in the material world. The act to acquire something in the material world means that you are denying something to the weaker. They abhor the idea that the rich exploit the helpless poor to build their financial empire, which creates a feeling of guilt that holds us back from becoming rich.

Many politicians have won elections exploiting this feeling of guilt and using the theory of social injustice. There is nothing further from the truth because the universe is not limited but abundant. There is no shortage. It is limited only by our restrictive minds.

Our universe is fundamentally abundant. It holds not millions, but billions of undiscovered thoughts, ideas and resources. Each thought, each idea can find resources that are worth billions of dollars.

Just look at the past: there was no television, radio or telecommunications industry before radio waves were discovered. Today, these are huge industries churning out billions of dollars and providing millions of jobs. The person who discovered this one idea – uncovered one secret of the universe – made millions of people wealthy. He did not take anything from the poor but elevated many from the poverty trap.

The same is true of nuclear energy, internet and thousands of new technologies and millions of ideas that are yet to be discovered. Even a very small idea can generate millions for us. We have to open our minds to understand the abundance of the universe.

> *"Out of abundance he took abundance and still abundance remained."*
>
> — Upanishads

The only truth about the universe: it is abundant!

If we embrace such an attitude, blessings and opportunities will follow. It is only limited minds that think that we compete for resources. It is the crab mentality that insinuates pulling others down to succeed.

In fact, truth is just the opposite. We succeed when we help others to succeed. There is abundance in this universe.

Darwin's theory of 'Survival of the fittest' only applies to the animal world. We humans have risen from rest of the animals because of our ability to co-operate and form societies for greater good. It is only fools who think that we are fighting for limited resources in order to survive.

Understanding abundance grows our financial, emotional and spiritual intelligence.

Honesty and Integrity

It is impossible to create long term wealth through dishonest means. The moment you become dishonest you fall out of sync with humanity and the rule of law. You will waste your creative energy fighting with your business partners, competitors, taxmen, customers and employees. Lies breed more lies. Truth and law will eventually catch up with you.

By being honest and leading a life of integrity, you will not only avoid any potential conflicts but generate goodwill that will have a multiplier effect in your wealth creation process. It is difficult to understand why people cheat at times and get violent and get in trouble with the law. In the process, they get entangled in fights, time consuming and expensive law suits, when it takes only miniscule effort to be honest and develop a financial intelligence to create wealth.

Getting Out of the Comfort Zone

To become rich is not easy and convenient. Getting rich can be very hard work. *If you are willing to do only what is easy, life will be hard. But if you are willing to do what is hard, life will be easy.* The rich are always willing to take difficult decisions and act on them whereas the poor take the easy and convenient way out.

To become rich is to step out into the unknown and conquer fear. Exploring new thoughts and ideas and incorporating them into our lives means getting out of that comfort zone we are accustomed to.

Each time you step out of your comfort zone, you conquer uncertainty and fear. This expands the size of your comfort zone. The size of your 'comfort zone' equals the size of your 'wealth zone'. By expanding your comfort zone, you will expand the size of your income and wealth.

The more comfortable you are in your little cocoon, fewer risks you will be willing to take and fewer opportunities will come your way. The more contracted you become with fear, fewer people you will meet, and fewer new strategies will you try.

If you are willing to stretch and expand your financial, emotional and spiritual intelligence, the size of your comfort zone will increase and you will attract and hold more income and wealth. The minute you become comfortable, you stop growing.

A moment of fear freezes you for eternity. Being comfortable and fearful has killed more ideas, opportunities, more action and more growth than everything else combined.

The human mind is the greatest soap-opera script writer in history. It plays and replays the greatest dramas—full of tragedies and disasters that never happened and probably never will. Mark Twain said it best: ***"I've had thousands of problems in my life, most of which never happened."***

Training and managing our minds out of fear and worries is the most important skill that we will ever develop. We have the power to run our thoughts. We will turn into a failure if we allow our uncontrolled thoughts to dictate our actions.

We have the ability to cancel any thought that does not support our growth process. We have to choose and install self-empowering thoughts. We have the power to control our minds and choose the actions that make us mentally, emotionally, financially and spiritually strong.

Robert Allen said something very profound: *"No thought lives in our head rent-free."* This means if we have fear and negativity in our minds, we will have to pay in terms of money, in energy, in time, in health and in happiness. If we have to move forward then we have to control and expand our mental state. We have to overcome our hesitancy and fears and re-write the script that governs our life.

You can be a millionaire in the next 24 months or sooner, if you can overcome the fear that holds you back.

Can We Totally Eliminate Fear through Knowledge?

The answer is no. The process to perfect our financial, emotional and spiritual intelligence may take years. Our knowledge and training can reduce fear to a very large extent but cannot totally eliminate it.

There will always be grey areas in our knowledge and fear of the unknown will make us hesitant from taking an action.

Act we must, despite our fears, because without action there is no wealth. Every decision in this world is taken with incomplete knowledge. We may try and cover most ground to reduce risk but complete knowledge of the future events and forestalling results is impossible.

We have to make decisions that affect our financial futures in spite of the fear that shackles our minds. This is where the leap of faith comes in: our spiritual intelligence gives us that faith. Courage means to act in spite of fear.

President Franklin D. Roosevelt said it best in his inaugural speech of 1933: *"The only thing we have to fear is fear itself."*

Fear is a natural emotion, and one which we experience with any endeavor we make, as long as we are alive. However, the choice to overcome that fear is ours to make, and will be the determining factor as to whether we fail or we succeed.

I remember seeing a war film wherein a soldier approaches his officer and confesses: **"Sir, I am terribly scared of going into combat."** The officer gives the soldier a knowing look and says so wisely, **"They must have forgotten to tell you in training school that courage only comes after you face your fears."**

Where there is success, there will always be the threat of failure. You can't have a victory when there is no threat of defeat—that's just reality. If this was not true, there would be no such thing as competitive sports: there would be no Olympics, there would be no Super Bowl, and there would be no Heavyweight Champion titles. Success is about defeating failure.

Knowledge is a big help in eliminating fear. But no one acts out of perfect knowledge. There is an element of uncertainty in every decision we make. It is not necessary to try and get rid of fear; success is about acting in spite of our fear.

Final Thoughts on Fear

Fears, when examined in the light of knowledge, are no longer fears. The impressions of financial fear and loss that are so deeply embedded in our hearts and mind begin to reduce with an increase in our financial, emotional and spiritual intelligence. Once this irrational fear is removed from the heart and the mind, the path for gaining riches is cleared.

It can take years to first erase and then rewrite the script in our subconscious that will set us onto path of wealth creation. Our fears and attitudes come in the way of our knowledge progression because they contaminate our processors.

If we had better attitudes and fewer fears, then our mind's processor will not be tainted; acquisition of new thoughts and ideas will be that much better. Once we have more knowledge, then we can better understand our attitudes and fears that cause hindrance in our journey of becoming rich.

The endless cycle of filtration and purifying of knowledge continues: we move from less knowledge to more knowledge and break one chain at a time that ties us to poverty. This can take an awfully long time. Fortunately, there are ways and means to short cut the process if we make a conscious effort to hasten the process. The third commandment will clarify this principle.

Thou Shall Re-write the Script of an Enlightened Millionaire on Thy Heart and Soul

The first step to becoming an enlightened millionaire is to get the mindset of a millionaire. **Process of wealth creation is 90% psychology and only 10% strategy**. Most people fail to become rich because they want to learn the strategy and not focus on changing their psychology.

To be a winner, you have to have the mindset of a winner. The inner change has to precede the external outcome. We have known this since the time we were kids: a certain set of rules enlisted by our parents, teachers and peers need to be followed. We believed in them because they were given to us in love and in good faith. Some of the rules that were ingrained in us were from people whose mindsets were steeped in poverty. We can't blame them because one or two generations back, most of our families were poor and struggling to survive.

As the world moves towards greater prosperity, we have to learn the new set of rules that govern the rich. The new rules are easy to learn only if you have an open mind to learn and succeed. We have to rewrite the script, or order a new set of rules that govern our lives.

It is not sufficient to get rid of the old impressions from our minds – it is only the first step. The old script was a baggage that held us back from becoming rich and forbade us from living life to its full potential.

To succeed, we have to re-write the old script to that of the 'Enlightened Millionaire' in our minds. This is the inner principle of wealth creation. Once the new script is written, it is a point of no return. You can never be middle-class or poor again even if you lose your entire wealth and have to restart from a scratch.

The millionaire mindset once achieved, is a non-destructive commodity. It stays with you for life. You can lose your millions but you will always bounce back. You are a millionaire because of your mindset.

Re-write the Script from Your Heart

The motivation to re-write the script has to originate from the heart because the mind has its own set of limitations— it is always the heart that rules. Whenever there is a conflict between the heart and the mind, it is always the heart that wins. A transformational change can occur only if it comes from the heart. Incremental increase of knowledge can take place in the mind but transformation of the mind can take place only if the heart is involved.

The heart, as we know it, is our subconscious. How can we involve our subconscious into the wealth creation process? To do that, we have to understand what triggers our heart and soul. We have so many desires buried within our subconscious. We have to simply uncover and trigger one or more of these desires into the wealth creation process.

To involve the heart means to find the predominant motivating triggers and activating them. You cannot live someone else's dream—you have to find your own.

The secret of wealth creation lies in finding your own triggers that drive your heart and soul. The nobler your trigger, the greater are your chances of success. A higher and better cause gets more people involved and your chances towards success increases exponentially.

A callous desire normally results in conflicting situations with a lesser chance of success. However, there is nothing wrong in following any of your dreams because once a dream is satisfied; there is always a next dream that will trigger you towards greater cause and effect. It is an evolutionary process. It is however, prudent on what you set your heart on and as Emerson rightly pointed out, *"it surely will be yours."*

To understand our triggers, we have to apply the *S.S.S* formula explained by Ron Holland in his book Talk and Grow Rich. According to him, to understand our subconscious we have to follow **SILENCE, STILLNESS AND SOLITUDE**. The secret to understanding these triggers of our mind lies in meditation – in silence, stillness and solitude or the S.S.S. When you become quiet, it just dawns on you.

Sometimes, an external stimulus is needed to activate the internal process... much like the process of falling in love. It is the beauty of an external person that activates love and desire in our hearts.

Similarly, experience of suffering can ignite compassion in our hearts. At times by putting ourselves in situations and gaining the right stimuli, we can understand the triggers that operate within our subconscious.

You will be able to re-write the '**enlightened millionaire**' script much faster if you understand your dreams and inner motivation. So take time out to understand these dreams and write them on a piece of paper—it will hasten the process. If you know your objective, then the path to success becomes easier to tread on.

The Butterfly Effect

To bring about internal change in our attitude, we have to understand the butterfly effect. The phrase refers to the idea that the flapping of a butterfly's wings might create tiny changes in the atmosphere that ultimately cause a tornado to appear (or prevent a tornado from appearing.)

The flapping wing represents a small change in the initial condition of the system, which causes a chain of events leading to large-scale phenomena. This implies that a small change in the initial condition may produce large variations in the long-term behavior of the system.

We do not have to do anything spectacular to help change our script to an 'enlightened millionaire's mindset,' but we can make small changes to alter the initial condition that can change the long term trajectory of our lives. In the succeeding paragraphs we will discuss some suggestions that can trigger a butterfly effect. You may apply some or all of them to change the outcome of your life.

Control the Inputs to Your Mind

To change the script of our life, we have to understand how the script is written in the mind. The script in the mind is written through thoughts, words, feelings and actions. Each one of them is very important as they leave indelible impressions on the mind. If we can learn to control our thoughts, words, feelings and actions in the present, then we have the power to change our future.

Power of Thoughts and Words

Thoughts are subtle but important because they are the starting point of the process. But once they become words, they have tremendous impact on both our internal and external reality. If you don't believe me, just call someone a bastard and your teeth will come out. Similarly, words of love and kindness will evoke a totally different – but positive – response.

Words, both written and oral, have tremendous power. They leave a deep impression on the mind. We are responsible for our thoughts and words and have to learn to control them. To have the millionaire's mindset, we have to snap out of any negative thought or action.

We have to read or listen to the words of successful and enlightened wealth creators. We have to place ourselves in their company and associate with them so that their words may influence us and change our script.

To illustrate this point: write down the names of five people with whom you spend your maximum time. Now, study their profile. Are they rich... entrepreneurs? Are they wealth creators? Or are they limited in their vision of job security? If you hang around with poor, negative and unsuccessful people then that is what the future beholds for you. You are writing the script of poverty.

To write the script of an enlightened wealth creator, you have to seek the right company to influence your mind. You have to change your reading habits and listen to lectures and tapes of highly successful people. You have to learn to speak the language of the rich.

Your script change will gain added momentum when words of success and positivity start flowing from your pen and mouth. The words you think, write and speak have greater impact on your mind than the words you receive from others.

Initially, the control of thoughts and words will look artificial and irksome. It may not come naturally but it can be done. It has to be a conscious effort. You have to start by watching our thoughts and words, and speak with good purpose only.

Through a change in your reading habits and allowing your mind to be influenced by the right associations, you can accelerate the process and completely change your script to that of an enlightened millionaire. It is a small change in the initial condition that is required to create the 'Butterfly Effect'. And once the effect takes place, it becomes a part of your inner nature.

There can be no Change without Action

Thoughts and words have to manifest into action lest there will be no change. Moreover, action and events in the external world leave a far greater impact on your mind than thoughts and words.

Thoughts are the starting point. They are subtle but create the least impact. Once they manifest into words, they create a much greater impact on the mind. And once words manifest into action, they have the most powerful impact on our minds and the outer world.

To understand this point, let us take the example of an inventor; he thinks of a new invention or product. It is just a concept in his mind. He does not wish to pursue the idea further. It dies a natural death. If he decides to writes a paper on the subject and speak at a few seminars, it not only clarifies his thought process but also starts influencing the minds of others. Now if he takes action to create the new product, then it will impact his future in financial terms but will also leave an impact on those who use or associate with the product.

Actions, though a result of thoughts and words, can prove to be a more powerful instrument of change, as they have a greater impact on the script.

A huge number of people, who read the right kind of books, listen to tapes and attend seminars but take no action. They wish to acquire complete knowledge and eliminate risk before embarking on the process of wealth creation. That perfect situation never comes because what future beholds, no one knows—it is always full of uncertainties.

An educated mind can eliminate some eventualities but, "the fog of war will always remain." All successful commanders know when to act despite being provided with limited information on the enemy. Inaction certainly leads to defeat. The same is true in the world of finance.

If you do not act then you cannot make any money. There is saying: *"once you put your money in line, knowledge will come that much faster."* There is no faster way to rewrite the enlightened millionaire's script than to take action. There is no teacher like experience. Think big but start small. Learn to take a few successful steps before you can start to run.

Knowledge + Action = Wealth

Action is the key. Without action, all your knowledge turns to waste. Be bold and take action. Boldness has genius, power and magic.

Whatever your inspiration or dream—act on it. The most fundamental principle of wealth creation is to take action. No one can ever reach the stage of complete knowledge to overcome fear.

All wealth creators have to learn to manage fear. In every decision you take, there will be an element of uncertainty. There has to be a leap of faith as the information required for decision making is never adequate. Act, you must, in good faith and intelligence! Inaction will keep you tied to poverty.

Once you start taking action, your experience and confidence will increase. There is no better teacher than experience. A few successful steps will change your future. You will rewrite wealth script ten times faster with action.

Feelings make your Words and Actions Stronger

Words when spoken with feelings are a hundred times stronger than those spoken with no heart in them. Have you enjoyed a song that has been sung with passion? It takes a totally new dimension. The same is true for action when it is backed by positive emotion.

When there is joy in action, there is no burden on the task at hand. If the heart is not there, it becomes a tedious job. To rewrite your script your heart has to be in it. Without feelings, there will be no joy or beauty in your script. It will be very difficult to rewire.

Uncovering the power of your emotions will release a tidal wave of change in your life. When there is feeling of love in your words and actions, you will be transformed.

To understand your genius and passion, you have to be still. Through silent introspection, self-reflection and meditation you increase your self-awareness. As your self-awareness increases, you will understand what your heart really wants. Don't chase the artificial or what the world wants you to be. Be true to yourself and your inner beliefs and success will follow you.

Clarity of Purpose

There has to be clarity of purpose when rewriting your script or it will be unintelligible. If there is no clarity then you yourself will not be able to read your script, let alone understand it.

Firstly, there has to be a decision that resonates with: "*I will be an enlightened millionaire.*" Then, you have to state your intention and commit it in writing. Writing your statement brings more clarity to your thought process.

Lastly, you have to announce it to the whole world that you are going to be an enlightened millionaire by a particular date—tell your friends, family and the whole world about your intentions. It will put pressure on you; instead it will keep you focused. You have to burn your bridges behind you to succeed. Without commitment, there is no clarity.

Goals are very critical to your success. They have to be clearly defined and practically achievable. To keep yourself balanced, you can record different goals in major areas of your life like health, relationships, intellectual, spiritual and financial goals. You have to write them, read them, see them and talk about them in every waking or dreaming moment of your life. You will then see your goals magically materialize into your life.

To become an enlightened millionaire you have to make a decision, state your intention and set goals. You have to live from your goals and think about them day and night.

Clarity and focus in your script will accelerate your pace of growth like nothing else. Can you imagine writing an article without a topic or a heading? The article will be confusing to the readers – it will be unintelligible. Similarly, without stating your goal and intention, your life script will be full of confusion.

To gain clarity you have to state your goals and put them in writing. You have to view and repeat these goals on a daily basis to stay on track and in focus. It looks simply but you will be surprised to learn that over 99% of the population has no stated goals and as a result, drift along in life. To be successful, you have to state your goals clearly and stay focused.

Be Congruent

There is a difference between a goal and an agenda: you can have a clearly stated goal but your hidden agenda can often sabotage that goal.

Our hidden agenda is normally driven by our ego, deep seated prejudices and value systems. Our hidden agendas are like saboteurs who are out to destroy our most well laid plans. We have to find these little saboteurs and convert them to our side.

To succeed you have to be congruent. You have to align your mind, body and spirit to a single purpose. Ask any top athlete. At the crucial point of winning-losing, they have their mind and body dissolves into one. There is no thought but only singularity of purpose. This singularity of purpose makes them champions.

The greatest loss of energy takes place because of attrition in the mind. When there is conflict of goals with our value system the script gets corrupted. We have to turn deep within ourselves to understand our hidden prejudices and value systems. We have to either bring in change to our inner attitudes or modify our goals to bring them into alignment with our core values. Without this, we will be working at cross purposes that will be deterrent to our success.

By little observation you can find out if there is a conflict within your mind and belief system.

People who complain of lethargy usually suffer from some kind of an inner conflict. One way to resolve such a conflict is through understanding the flow of energy. When everything is in alignment, there will be no noise and friction in the mind. If you are congruent, there will be explosion of energy within your system. Your script will then have clarity and sense of its purpose.

Transformational Change

Here we are not talking about increments in your script – we are talking of how you can achieve a quantum jump that can transform you instantly. It is transformational learning as against informational learning that is predominant in our educational system that defines our script.

Informational learning is passive; teachers talk and students listen. It is about memorization, examinations and grades. Teachers talk about subjects on which they have theoretical knowledge, but lack practical experience—such an education can never be inspirational.

Transformational learning is about self-discovery. The student is given an inspirational stimulus by a mentor who has traveled the path and has discovered the answers to the problems through his experience.

All the knowledge to become a millionaire is already within you. No one can teach you how to become rich. Someone can only inspire you to awaken every cell in your body that will cry out that you were born to be rich and free, and to live a life of abundance. It is your natural state.

Transformation occurs when the right stimulus is given to awaken what is inside us and our script changes instantaneously.

Mentors

The shortcut to transformational knowledge is to find a mentor; they are invaluable! They have travelled the path and they have the knowledge. They will stir you in their presence. A word of advice from them will transform you. It will be a life changing experience that no book, DVD or tape can provide.

Where can you find Mentors?

The truth is you cannot find a mentor until you are ready. The day you are ready a mentor will appear. A little preparation is required at your end to receive a mentor.

No one can inspire you until you are ready to be inspired. No one can change you until you desire the change. No one can make you rich until you want to be rich. When this happens, a mentor will appear in your life and take you forward in leaps.

There are mentors all around us but we don't see them because we are not mentally prepared for them. We associate ourselves with losers, time wasters, frivolous and non-productive people. How can we eject magnetic waves to attract successful people?

To gain some magnetic power, we have to initially force ourselves to the presence of people who emanate powerful doses of the magnetic energy we want. Association is a very powerful thing. If you associate with the right kind of people, you will be subjected to the right kind of energy fields. This will transform you. You will also become a magnet attracting the right kind of people. There is nothing new in it – it is the basic law of attraction.

"The soul attracts that which it secretly harbors, that which it loves, and also that which it fears. It reaches the height of its cherished aspirations. It falls to the level of its chastened desires – and circumstances are the means by which the soul receives its own."

— As a Man Thinketh by James Allen (1864 - 1912)

A mentor carries a hundred times stronger energy field. He can transform us to a different level instantly. However, we will receive the energy only once we are mentally prepared to accept the energy.

Thoughts have an energy that attracts like energy. A mentor will come to us when we are ready and not a day before that. We have to develop our thoughts (conscious and unconscious,) emotions, beliefs and actions to a certain level in order to attract the positive energy from a mentor.

If you study the lives of wealth creators, you will find they have been mentored not by one but several mentors at different periods of their lives. A mentor will not only fill the gaps in your knowledge but will inspire you to new levels of achievement, which you think is not possible. They will change your thought process and internal script.

Is it expensive to get mentors? Not necessarily. If you are serious and dedicated, you can get mentored for free. All masters take on assistants to do their 'grunt work,' so that they can leverage their time. You can volunteer to become their apprentice.

There is a Chinese proverb that goes like: *"A single conversation across the table with a wise man is worth a month's study of books."* You can invite a mentor to a meal—it works like a charm.

The Millionaire Mind-set Scripts

We do not have to do anything spectacular to change our script to an 'enlightened millionaire's mindset,' but make small changes to alter the initial condition that can change the long-term trajectory of our lives.

T. Harv Eker in his brilliant book, Secrets of the Millionaire Mind, has written about wealth files or scripts for mastering the inner game of wealth. Some of the scripts are discussed in the succeeding paragraphs. These scripts are very powerful and can cause a 'Butterfly Effect.' You may apply some or all of them to change the outcome of your life. Please study these scripts carefully and start applying them gradually to your daily lives.

Rich people believe 'I create my life'. Poor people believe 'Life happens to me'

Enlightened millionaires take responsibility for their life and actions. They do not blame others when things go wrong. On the other hand, poor people think they are the victims and are experts at the 'blame game.' They blame the government, the economy, their bosses, friends and family when they fail. Blaming others for them is like a stress reducer. Complaining and justification are like pills they become addicted to.

You can either be rich or a victim—it depends on what script you choose. You slit your financial throat each and every time you choose to blame others. So choose to stay above the line. At the end of each day, carry out a complete debrief and write down each situation and how you handled it. This will dramatically change the outcome.

Rich people play the money game to win. Poor people play the money game not to lose

In sports, you can never win a game by playing defense; you have to be offensive and score if you have to win. I once saw a table tennis match—a really good player playing offence was matched against a defensive opponent and I had never seen a defensive player of his caliber. He was a virtual returning machine: he would stand twenty feet away from the table and continue returning the smashes from his opponent. It forced the smasher to make mistakes as he was the aggressor. The crowd cheered for the defensive player as he was unique or probably they identified with him. The aggressive player made several errors and lost points, but in the end, he won handsomely to the disappointment of the crowd.

I was in the Navy and in every war game we played offensive tactics to beat any purely defensive strategy. We also found that it was nearly ten times cheaper to build or buy an offensive weapon platform – like a missile boat or an aircraft launched missile – than to provide a credible defense against the threat.

The same holds true for the money game: truly rich people go on the offensive. Their goal is to acquire massive wealth. They shoot for the stars. Poor on the other hand, want to be comfortable. They never want to stick their necks out or pick up a challenge. They are always on the defensive, acting within their comfort zone. Security is of paramount concern to them. As a result, they never win and never get rich.

Rich people are committed to being rich. Poor people want to be rich

The number one reason most people don't get what they want is that they don't know what they want. Rich people are totally clear that they want wealth. They are unwavering in their mind and are fully committed to creating wealth. They will do whatever it takes, as long as it is moral, legal and ethical.

Based on the Laws of Attraction, the universe will conspire to help them achieve their goal because the message the rich send out to the universe is very clear – they want to be rich! The poor on the other hand, send out confused messages because of the negative wealth files. "What if I can make money and then lose it all? I'll be in the highest tax bracket and will have to give away half the money to the government—it's too much work. My health may suffer. I will have no time for my family. I'll never know if people like me for myself or my money…my kids could be kidnapped."

Most poor people want to be wealthy but have a confabulating script and a vague desire to be rich. This is why they do not succeed. The rich on the other hand have a script that is fully committed to creating wealth—devoid of any confusion whatsoever. They want to travel, have time on their hands, provide best possible things to their loved ones or help others and give money to charity. If you want to commit, then put your goals in writing and read them morning, evening and night. Announce your commitment to the entire world. Be congruent in thought, emotion and action. Clarity of purpose leads to success.

Rich people think big – Poor people think small

The difference between the rich and the poor is only a couple of zeros behind their incomes and net worth statements. It is as simple as that.

There is a saying: "Size of the question determines the size of the result." If you ask yourself a question: "Can I earn $30,000 doing this?" Then you will get the wrong result. If you ask yourself the question "How do I create or earn a million dollars?" Then your mind goes to work in a different direction. It wants to find a solution and works ceaselessly to find a satisfactory answer.

Most people fail to ask the big question – they choose to play small. They are frightened of failure and even scared to death of success. Our life is not about shrinking and feeling insecure—life is all about expansion and discovering our true worth. As we expand and liberate from our fears, our very presence liberates others from their small attitudes. Think big; there is no greatness in being small.

You will be a millionaire if you start thinking like a millionaire. Want to be a billionaire? Then learn to think big like a billionaire—it is all in the mind and beliefs you have.

Rich People focus on opportunities. Poor people focus on obstacles

Rich people see opportunities – poor people see obstacles. Rich people see potential growth – poor people see potential loss. Rich people focus on rewards – poor focus on risks. The mindset of the poor is, "It won't work." The mind-set of the rich is, "It will work because I will make it work."

What you focus on expands. If you focus on opportunities, they will expand. On the other hand, if you focus on obstacles, they will look insurmountable. If you want to be rich, focus on making, keeping and investing your money. If you want to be poor, focus on spending your money.

Rich people see an opportunity, jump on it and get richer. The poor look at the obstacles and keep preparing to overcome them. They never take action, which is why they lose.

Action always beats inaction. Rich people get started after understanding the risks; they make adjustments and corrections as they move along. If you want to be rich, focus on opportunities and take action.

Rich people admire other rich and successful people. Poor people resent rich and successful people

One of the surest ways to remaining poor is to resent the rich. Most poor people are conditioned to believe that one can't be both rich and spiritual simultaneously or be rich and a good person.

There can be nothing further from truth. To create wealth, certain human characteristics are needed. One has to be intelligent, hardworking, reliable, focused, determined, persistent and positive. Moreover, the person has to be a good communicator with a high degree of human skills and integrity. Without some of these skills coming into play, it is impossible to become rich in the first place.

There may be a few exceptions wherein people have become wealthy through ill-gotten means. However, in my experience such wealth never lasts for long. Seek inspiration from the enlightened rich who are, by far, some of the nicest people. They have reached where they are because of their expanded mental state and positive attitude to life.

Practice the Huna philosophy which states, *'**Bless that which you want'**.* Write a letter or an email to someone successful you admire. Tell them how much you admire and honor their achievement. You will develop an instant connection to success.

Rich people associate with positive, successful people. Poor people associate with negative or unsuccessful people

Easiest and fastest way to create wealth is through association. Be with the rich and learn how they became rich and mastered the game of money. 'If they can do it, I can do it'.

You must have heard the old adage: "Birds of a feather flock together." This is very true because most people earn within 20% of the average income of their closest friends. If you want to soar, fly with the eagles and don't get stuck swimming with the ducks.

Being in company of negatively minded people can be infectious. You can get measles of the mind. Instead of itching, you get bitching and instead of irritation, you get frustration.

It is not your job to reform negative people. You must keep away from them. Once you develop the positive energy field around you, they will get influenced by it but not before that.

In the initial stages, you must charge your energy field by hanging around with winners. Read biographies of the extreme rich and successful: Warren Buffet, Bill gates, Steve Jobs, Donald Trump, Andrew Carnegie and the likes.

Join clubs which the rich frequent. Identify friends and family who pull you down and stay away from them. Stop watching trash television and stay away from bad news that could potentially pollute the mind. ***Rich people hang around with winners. Poor hang around with losers***. Never forget this basic principle.

Rich people are willing to promote themselves and their value. Poor people think negatively about selling and promotion

People who have issues with selling are usually broke – it's obvious. How can you create a large income in your business, or as a representative of one, if you aren't willing to let people know that you, your product, or your service exists? Even as an employee, if you are not willing to promote your virtues, someone who is willing will bypass you on the corporate ladder.

Poor have the fear of failure and rejection. They feel it is impolite to blow one's own trumpets. The world has so many products and services that nobody has the time for you or your product if you are not willing to step up and project yourself.

The poor have an attitude that makes them naively believe in their uniqueness. Hence, promotion is beneath them. Poor believe that because they are so special, someone will find them ultimately. They remain broke because of this attitude.

You may have the best talent and the product but no one will know of it if you are unwilling to promote. This is because everyone in the world has an information clutter and no time for you. You have to rise above the clutter and make yourself be heard.

Rich people are always excellent promoters. They know how to package their ideas, products and skills and they promote them with enthusiasm and passion. Robert Kiyosaki, author of the best-selling 'Rich Dad Poor Dad' series of books calls himself the "best-selling" and not the best writing author.

Every business depends on selling. Money is made only when something is sold in the market place. To become rich, you have to learn the art of promoting with 100 percent integrity. This can be done through courses in marketing and sales or reading books on the subject. People who shy away from this vital aspect cannot hope to amass wealth.

Rich people are bigger than their problems. Poor people are smaller than their problem

Poor people want to run away from problems – they don't want hassles and headaches. They will sweep them under the carpet or close their eyes like ostriches to wish them away. Problems have a habit of rebounding with a great vengeance. The more you try and avoid them…the poorer, broke and miserable they will keep you.

The secret to success is not to try to avoid or get rid of or shrink from your problems; the secret is to grow yourself so that you grow bigger than the problem.

The rich are problem solvers. They make money by identifying a problem and find a solution for it. People will pay money to solve their problems.

If by training you become level-10 problem solvers, do you think a level-5 problem will cause any worry or stress to you? The secret is to grow bigger than the problem.

The first step is to write down all the problems you are having in your life and then list actions to resolve them—this simple exercise will make your growth process to become bigger than your problems.

Your income will directly relate to the level of problem you are willing to solve. If you are an employee, you are solving a problem for your boss. You will get fired once you become a problem for the organization. If you are in business, you are solving problems for your clients. Be it servicing a car, providing plumbing services or pulling out a tooth. The quality of service and level of problem you are willing to solve will determine success of your business.

Rich people are excellent receivers. Poor people are poor receivers

For every giver there has to be a receiver, and for every receiver there must be a giver. One of the reasons why poor remain as poor is because they are poor receivers. They may or may not be good at giving but most certainly, they are poor receivers.

This holds true in every walk of life. To be loved, we have to know how to receive love. The universe has infinite abundance of wealth—it has to go somewhere. There are trillions of dollars floating around. If we are not ready to receive our share, it will go to someone who is willing to receive.

Being open to receiving is absolutely critical to creating wealth. There are times when money flows into our lives, we should accept the blessing of the universe gracefully and accept it as a gift. Once you learn the art of receiving, you will become a money magnet and start attracting money.

Rich people choose to get paid on results. Poor people choose to get paid based on time

The thumb rule to becoming rich is: "*Never have a ceiling* on your income." *Poor people trade time for money. The problem with this strategy is that your time is limited. This means that you are breaking the fundamental rule of becoming rich which means having no ceiling on your potential income.*

Rich people prefer to get paid in results. If they run a business, they get paid from the profits. Alternately, they prefer to work on profit sharing, stock options or commissions.

In the financial world, rewards are proportional to the risk one is willing to take. What the poor do not realize is that job security comes at a price and that price is wealth. You can make a small start by requesting your employer to pay you partly based on the results. Another option is for you to set-up your own small business or consulting company, or to join a network marketing company and become result oriented.

Rich people think ''both.'' Poor people think "either/or."

Rich people live in a world of abundance and poor people live in a world of limitations. Both live in the same physical world, but the difference is in their perspectives. Poor people think that either I can be rich or be spiritual.

Rich people think they can be both. Poor people think that either they can spend time with their families or work hard to become rich. Rich people think they can balance both.

Rich people believe "*You can have your cake and eat it too*." The middle-class people believe "*Cake is too rich, so I'll only have a small piece*." The script of the rich is to be creative and find ways for having "both."

The rich focus on their net worth; the poor on their working income

The vocabulary of the poor consists of: "How much I earn" or "How much I make." The rich, on the other hand, think of their net worth' and "How much profit I made." *The true measure of wealth is net worth, not working income.*

The words that write your script define your future. If you think in terms of 'earning' as opposed to 'net worth,' you will stay put in your job of trading time for money. *Where attention goes, energy flows and results show*. So, focus your attention on the right script to increase your income. Simplify your life style to reduce your cost of living and invest the savings or surplus amount. Create a net worth statement and revise this statement every quarter to help analyze your progression.

Rich people manage their money well, Poor mismanage their money well

Rich people are good at managing their money though they are not necessarily smarter than the poor; they just have a different approach towards money.

This small difference in habit makes the biggest difference in the financial outcome of being rich or poor. Poor people either mismanage or they avoid the subject of money altogether. The excuse generally given is either, "It restricts our freedom" or "We don't have enough money or time to manage."

Nothing can be further from truth, because managing money allows financial freedom. *The habit of managing your money is more important than the amount.* Until you learn how to handle what you've got, you are most likely not to get any more.

Rich people have their money work hard for them. Poor people work hard for their money

Most of us are programmed *"to work hard for money."* The rich on the other hand, reprogram themselves "**to make their money work hard for them.**"

Working hard has never made anyone rich—working smart is the way to riches. The more your money works, the less you will need to work.

The definition of financial freedom is the ability to live the lifestyle you desire without having to work or rely on anyone else money. Therefore, to become free you will need to earn money without working. To do this you will need to create a passive income wherein money keeps flowing in whether you work or not.

The sources of passive income working for you can be either financial instruments like stocks, bonds, mutual funds or businesses working for you that are in confluence with: real estate, royalties from books, music or software, licensing your ideas, network marketing etc.

These will be discussed in depth later in the book. In simple terms: poor people work hard and spend all their money, which results in them having to work hard forever. Rich, on the other hand, work hard, save and then invest their money so they never have to work hard again.

The key is to change the money blueprint from immediate gratification to thinking long-term. Balance your spending on enjoyment today with investing in freedom tomorrow.

You will need to change your "Material gratification" files and replace them with "Financial freedom" files. Change your focus from "Active income" to "Passive income." List out strategies you can put to work to generate passive income.

Rich people act in spite of fear. Poor people let fear stop them

Fear freezes us to act and our well laid plans fail to manifest; thoughts lead to feelings, feelings lead to actions and actions lead to results.

We may have all the right knowledge but unless we act, there can be no wealth creation. *Action is a bridge between the inner and the outer world*. Rich and successful people have fear; they have doubts and worries like the rest of us but they do not allow these fears to stop them.

Poor people on the other hand, allow their fears to limit them. To change our scripts, we have to break the habit and make a conscious effort to act in spite of doubt, in spite of worry, in spite of uncertainty and discomfort. We have to learn to act even if we are not in a mood to do so.

Rich people constantly learn and grow whereas poor people think they already know.

The three most dangerous words in English are "I know that." So how do you know if you know something? It is simple. If you live it, you know it. Otherwise, you heard about it, you read about it, or you talked about it, but you do not know about it. To know about it, you have to live it. If you are not really happy, there's a good chance you still have to learn about money, success and life.

Poor people generally try and prove that they are right and they have got it figured out; it is just a stroke of bad luck or a temporary glitch that has them broke and struggling.

There is an excellent saying by Jim Rohn that makes perfect sense here: ***"If you keep doing what you've always done, you'll keep getting what you've always got".*** If you are unsuccessful and not willing to change your life script or take the trouble to educate yourself, then you will keep getting the same results again and again. Someone rightly said, ***"Definition of madness is to keep doing the same thing again and again and expect a different result."***

There is a constant need to learn and grow; everything alive is constantly changing. If a plant is not growing, it is dying. It is true for every organism including human beings. If you are not growing, then you are dying.

Author and philosopher, Eric Hoffer, has rightly said, ***"Learners shall inherit the world while the learned will be beautifully equipped to live in a world that no longer exists."*** This means that if you are not constantly learning and growing you will be left behind.

Poor people usually complain that they do not have either the time or the money to get educated—these are plain excuses. The only thing normally lacking is the commitment to learn and change. Rich people, on the other hand, relate to Benjamin Franklin's famous quote: *"**If you think education is expensive, try ignorance**."*

Poor people seek advice from relative and friends who are equally clueless. This keeps them entangled in the web of poverty. The most expensive advice you can ever receive is free advice from an ignorant person.

Rich, on the other hand, continuously read books and attend seminars to improve the skills and strategies they need to accelerate their income, manage their money and then invest it effectively. They learn the game of money from those who are the masters in the field and have success become a corollary of it.

Your income is directly related to your inner growth, which includes: financial, emotional and spiritual IQ. You must commit to your growth and consider hiring personal coaches to keep you focused and on track in the various aspects of your life, including health.

The outer world is merely a manifestation of your inner world. There are outer laws of money that entail: business knowledge, money management and investment strategies.

Equally important are the inner laws, or the script that defines you as a person. It is not enough to be at the right place at the right time. You have to be the right person in the right place at the right time.

Fear, which is the biggest enemy of wealth creation, can – to a large extent – be controlled by expanding our financial, emotional and spiritual intelligence. The internal change in the script is critical before we can learn about the outer laws of wealth creation which in comparison are very easy to master. Once the internal transformation is complete, there is no force on earth that can stop you from becoming a millionaire.

Motivation for Creating Wealth

What drives you to create wealth is a very important factor that will determine your success. Deeper your motivation, stronger will be your foundation to create wealth.

If your desire to create wealth is motivated by external factors – such as buying a luxury car, going on a holiday, or moving into a larger house – then they are not formidable enough to take you very far. There is nothing wrong with these desires, but they can be satisfied soon enough. Money can buy you things, but not happiness.

Similarly, if acquiring wealth is motivated by greed or fear then it will not bring you happiness. These motivations are non-supportive and therefore, not deep enough to create sustained wealth.

To create long-term wealth, you have to be driven by an inner drive that is hard to satisfy. These may include: search for freedom from a job you do not like, to pursue your passion, your hobbies and sports. One of the great internal motivations can be the pursuit of personal growth including health.

The strongest innate motivation is the desire to help others—elevate them from their sufferings or teach them, using your own example as muse, how to create enlightening wealth. By pursuing a deeper cause, you will not only bring about transformational change within yourself but also the ones around you.

There are always challenges in creating wealth. It is easier to overcome those challenges once you motivation level is deeper than superficial.

Certain actions and changes in your everyday life may act as stimulus to understanding your deeper motivation. Firstly, give more value than you take from others: when you give value to others, you improve your own life. Wealth created by exploiting others never lasts long, and does it provide any internal happiness.

There should be a high level of integrity in your everyday actions. You cannot cheat your way into any meaningful wealth. Your mind is a great powerhouse; keep it pure and creative. Don't waste your energy in the pursuit of wealth through shortcuts and by causing harm to others.

The deeper and nobler your cause, greater will be your wealth. Such wealth will also provide you with inner happiness and peace.

Inner transformation always precedes wealth creation. I failed in my first few attempts at business not because of lack of hard work or effort, but because I was not adequately mentally prepared for business.

I hope that the first three commandments help you with the basics of inner preparation. Awareness of these principles is one small step and transformation will not happen overnight; combing action and experience will speed up that process. Constant education, associating with the right groups of people, and deep reflection will play a huge role if you wish to progress on the path of acquiring a wealthy mindset. Try and seek mentors at each stage of your growth—it will hasten your growth process. Make small changes in your life and observe the butterfly effect play out.

Fourth Commandment onwards, we will examine concrete steps that will help you with the process of wealth creation. Whether you are an employee, self-employed, an investor or in business— the principles enunciated will help you grow financially in each stage of your growth.

Thou shall Compound Thy Way to Riches

Albert Einstein, arguably one of the smartest men to have lived, is reputed to have said, "The most powerful force in the universe is compound interest." He called it the *"Eight Wonder of the World"*. However, it is baffling that so few of us fully comprehend the dynamics of compounding, its application and the paramount power it generates. We were taught how to solve compounding problems at school—and back then we were completely oblivious to its awesome power... Our teachers would have been millionaires had they understood its power. Unfortunately, like us, they only knew how to solve textual problems without being fully aware of the magnitude of it; when applied correctly- it has the capacity to change our financial future.

Understanding the Power of Compounding

For the ease of understanding let us take an example: Imagine you could invest one dollar at the beginning of the month—now imagine that one dollar in saving double with each passing day for an entire month.

On day two your investment will double to $2, on day three it will be $4 and on day four it will amount to $8, so on and so forth. I have plotted weekly graphs below to show you how your investment will increase. Allow these graphs to impinge on your mind, heart and soul because they hold the fundamental principle for you to become rich.

First Week

Investment Growth during the First Week

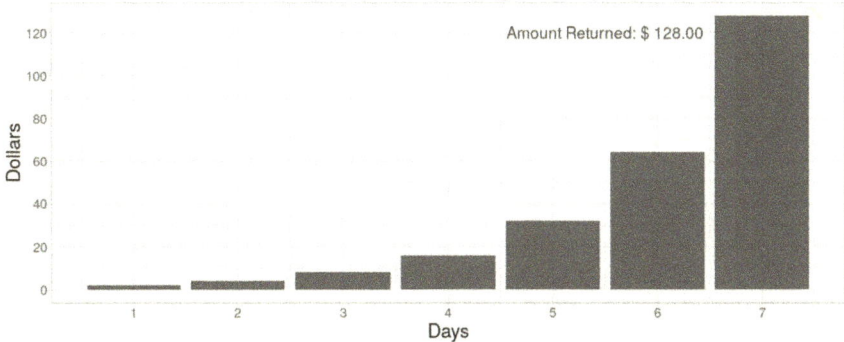

If you observe the graph above, you will notice that on day seven your initial investment will be worth $128. Nothing too inspiring, right?

Second Week - After the end of two weeks (fourteen days-see graph below) your investment would have increased to $16,384. I'm sure it is still not exhilarating. .

Investment Growth during the Second Week

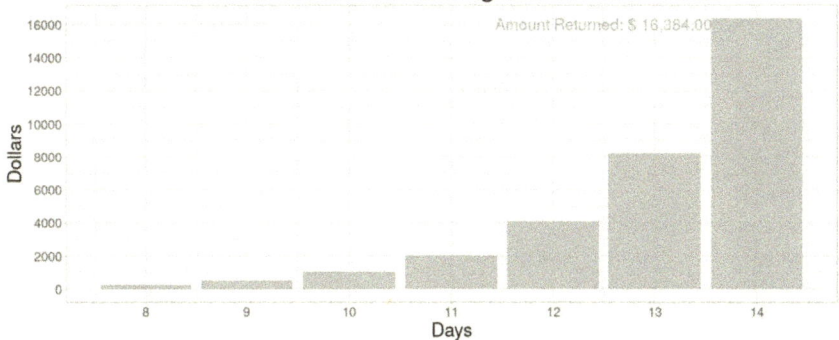

Third Week

On completion of three weeks (21 days), your investment would have grown to over two million as depicted in the graph below. Now things are starting to get interesting.

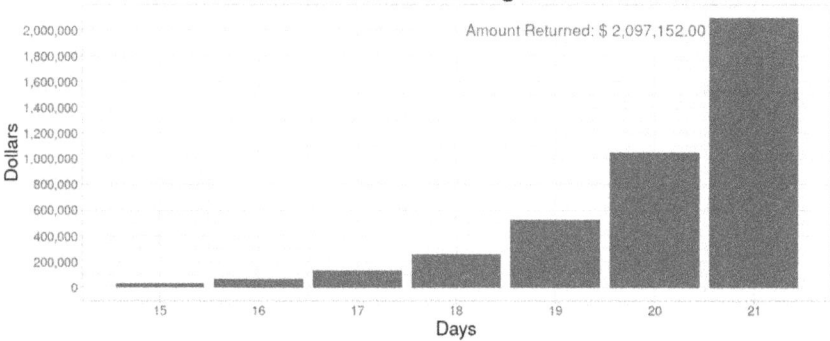

Investment Growth during the Third Week

Last 10 Days

At the end of four weeks (28 days), your one-dollar investment will now be worth over two hundred and sixty eight million dollars. Wow, this is getting interesting.

The fun is not over. In the next three days: 29th, 30th and 31st, your net worth will be over two billion dollars ($2,147,483,648, to be exact). In the last three days your investment multiplies nearly 10 fold. See how your money increases in a matter of four days (28th-31st), on the chart below.

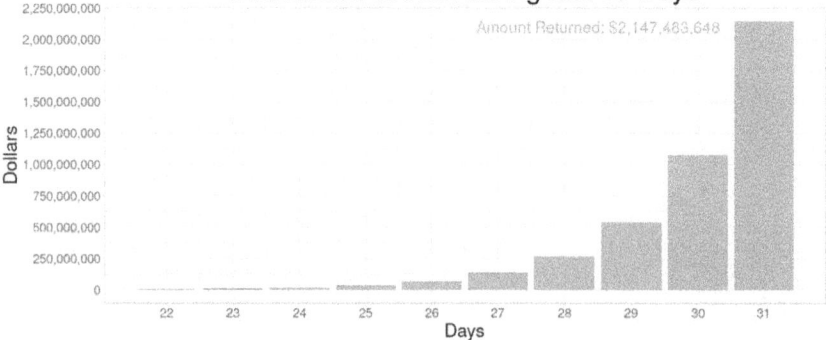

Investment Growth during last 10 Days

Graph Depicting the Entire Month's Growth

To help put your investment into perspective– observe the graph below that depicts how your investment will grow during the month. You will notice that during the initial period (up to the 22nd day, to be precise) your growth is not even visible on the chart. This is called the *'Tunneling Effect'* that I will describe in the succeeding paragraph.

Investment Returns in a Month

These graphs have been included to highlight the simple truth that *"With compounding your money multiplies exponentially if you give it time."*

If you were to wait just one more day—that is the first day of the following month, then your net worth will double to $4.3 billion. Moving forward with the passage of each successive day, your net worth will continue to expand at a mind-boggling pace.

The Tunneling Effect

When you first start out investing using compound interest, all the hard work takes place upfront, in the beginning. You have nothing to show for your effort.

This is called the 'Tunneling Effect'; it causes a lot of dismay and most people give up at this point because they do not see any tangible results for their sacrifice, hard work and effort.

If there is a confluence of patience and perseverance at this stage, then there is not only light at the end of the tunnel—there's an illuminating Sun shining in all its glory for you to bask in. Anyone who has become wealthy has passed through this dark tunnel. There is no escaping it.

"Nothing in the world can take the place of persistence. Talent will not; nothing is more common than unsuccessful men of talent. Genius will not; unrewarded genius is almost a proverb. Education will not; the world is full of educated derelicts. Persistence and determination alone are omnipotent."

— Calvin Coolidge

Warren Buffet, one of the richest men in the world, remarked about his wife when he was building his wealth *"**Susie didn't get very excited when I told her we were going to get rich. She either didn't care or didn't believe me - probably both, in fact.**"* You can read the biography of any wealth creator, and you will find in it the universal truth of the 'tunneling effect' and how they wanted to quit but didn't.

Critical Mass

If you persist and as the time goes on the critical mass kicks in and things begin to get better. Your investment becomes self-perpetuating; it starts growing under its own steam. The challenge at this stage is to not change course

The problem with the human mind is that it loses its focus rather easily; it diverts its attention to other thoughts and ideas. It will eventually start looking at other options. The key here is to maintain focus. Compounding is boring— B-O-R-I-N-G. It is boring until the money starts to pour in; compounding becomes very interesting hereon. In fact, it becomes downright fascinating! Compounding, if allowed to continue, catalyzes the expansion of your wealth to unfathomable levels.

The principle of compounding is also applicable to other forms of investment like: real estate investments and network marketing. Ninety percent of people drop out of network marketing because they do not fully appreciate the power of compounding. They feel discouraged once they face, and have to endure that tunneling effect, and quit. They fail to see the light that is just around the corner; dogged persistence is a great quality to have if you want to succeed.

Compounding Only Works in Time

The great thing about compounding is that anyone can do it. Compounding is the royal road to riches. Compounding is the safe road and the sure road. To compound successfully you need the following: **perseverance** in order to keep you firm on the savings path, and you need **time**—time to allow the power of compounding to work for you. **Time, in fact, is the most powerful element in the process of compounding; nothing comes close to it.**

There is a paragraph in '*The Richest Man in Babylon, The Power of Time*' that explains this perfectly:

"Wealth, like a tree, grows from a tiny seed. The first copper you save is the seed from which your tree of wealth shall grow. The sooner you plant that seed, the sooner shall the tree grow. And the more faithfully you nourish and water that tree with consistent savings, the sooner may you bask in contentment beneath its shade"

— (George S. Clason, 1926).

Study Done by Market Logic

In order to emphasize the importance of time in the power of compounding, I am including this extraordinary study done by *Market Logic*, of Ft. Lauderdale, FL 33306.

In this study we assume that investor B opens an IRA at age 19. For seven consecutive periods, he puts $2,000 in his IRA at an average growth rate of 10% (7% interest plus growth). After seven years, this fellow makes NO MORE contributions—he's finished.

A second investor, A, makes no contributions until age 26 (this is the age when investor B was finished with his contributions). Then A continues faithfully to contribute $2,000 every year till he turns 65 (at the same theoretical 10% rate).

Now study these incredible results: B, who started investing at an earlier age and who made only seven contributions, ends up with MORE money than A, who made 40 contributions but at a LATER TIME. The difference in the two is that *B had seven additional years of compounding than A*; those seven early years were worth more than all of A's 33 supplementary contributions.

I exhort you to introduce this study to your kids. It reiterates the fact that the earlier you start, the richer you will be.

| Age | INVESTOR A | | INVESTOR B | |
	Contribution	Year-End Value	Contribution	Year-End Value
8	0	0	0	0
9	0	0	0	0
10	0	0	0	0
11	0	0	0	0
12	0	0	0	0
13	0	0	0	0
14	0	0	0	0

Age	INVESTOR A		INVESTOR B	
	Contribution	Year-End Value	Contribution	Year-End Value
15	0	0	0	0
16	0	0	0	0
17	0	0	0	0
18	0	0	0	0
19	0	0	2,000	2,200
20	0	0	2,000	4,620
21	0	0	2,000	7,282
22	0	0	2,000	10,210
23	0	0	2,000	13,431
24	0	0	2,000	16,974
25	0	0	2,000	20,872
26	2,000	2,200	0	22,959
27	2,000	4,620	0	25,255
28	2,000	7,282	0	27,780
29	2,000	10,210	0	30,558
30	2,000	13,431	0	33,614
31	2,000	16,974	0	36,976
32	2,000	20,872	0	40,673
33	2,000	25,139	0	44,741
34	2,000	29,875	0	49,215
35	2,000	35,062	0	54,136
36	2,000	40,769	0	59,550
37	2,000	47,045	0	65,505
38	2,000	53,950	0	72,055
39	2,000	61,545	0	79,261
40	2,000	69,899	0	87,187
41	2,000	79,089	0	95,905
42	2,000	89,198	0	105,496
43	2,000	100,318	0	116,045
44	2,000	112,550	0	127,650

	INVESTOR A		INVESTOR B	
Age	Contribution	Year-End Value	Contribution	Year-End Value
45	2,000	126,005	0	140,415
46	2,000	140,805	0	154,456
47	2,000	157,086	0	169,902
48	2,000	174,995	0	186,892
49	2,000	194,694	0	205,581
50	2,000	216,364	0	226,140
51	2,000	240,200	0	248,754
52	2,000	266,420	0	273,629
53	2,000	295,262	0	300,992
54	2,000	326,988	0	331,091
55	2,000	361,887	0	364,200
56	2,000	400,276	0	400,620
57	2,000	442,503	0	440,682
58	2,000	488,953	0	484,750
59	2,000	540,049	0	533,225
60	2,000	596,254	0	586,548
61	2,000	658,079	0	645,203
62	2,000	726,087	0	709,723
63	2,000	800,896	0	780,695
64	2,000	883,185	0	858,765
65	2,000	973,704	0	944,641
	Less Total Invested:	**80,000**		**14,000**
	Equal Net Earnings:	893,704		930,641
	Money Grew:	11-fold		66-fold

Remember that as time passes, the power of compounding accelerates dramatically. If you're a young person, all you need to know is that you must start early to stay ahead in the game of

compounding and wealth creation. The best time to plant a seed was twenty years ago; now is your second opportunity to do the same. Do not waste a day!

Some Fun Math

Let us take an example of Kid A, who gets a supposedly great paying job for a 20-year-old at 45k per annum. He actually survives on the same 15k a year that Kid B, going to med-school, survived on. Now let's assume that the 20-year-old who skipped med-school for that great paying job invested the remaining 30k of his salary in stocks.

Here are the facts:

The med-school student, Kid B, graduates 'on time' at the age of 28; secures a job paying 75k a year and pays all of his debts off by the age of 33—so theoretically, he's 33 before he actually has an effective salary of 75k.

Kid A, who skipped med-school and invested in stocks, earned the historical average of 10.1% annually on his money (10.1% since 1926...but if you skip the Great Depression years the average is actually closer to 13%). So, where is this kid at the age of 33? He has $920,180 dollars in compounding assets. Coupled with his 45k annual salary, he will earn 135k at the age of 33 while the doctor earns 75k.

The doctor cannot mathematically catch up to the scrub (Kid A) who's still at his 45k year salary (maybe more). 13 years hence, he has about 122k to reinvest in the market that year while the doctor will never be able to match that investment; he will always play the catch-up game no matter how much he may earn.

But none of this actually happens, does it? That kid, A doesn't invest, and the doctor stays in debt. The statistics mentioned above are just used as a guide to elucidate a point; it does not mean that the right education doesn't give fruitful results. There are better chances of a financially educated person investing than a college drop out.

What's the point?

The point is that understanding compounding and starting out early makes you wealthy. It's surprising they don't teach real-life economics in school.

The Golden Rule of Accumulation is – START EARLY. Time, without a doubt, is the most important powerful weapon in an investor's arsenal. There is nothing that comes close to it.

> *"When you're young, you have an asset money can't buy: TIME. Start saving now and turn pocket change into riches."*
>
> — (Erin Burt, 2007)

The power of compounding accelerates and creates a snowball of money. At first, your returns may appear unsatisfactory, but if you're patient, eventually, your initial investment will grow enormously.

Effect of a Small Increase in Interest Rate

Another important facet of compounding is that a small change in the rate of return can produce a huge impact over time. For instance, if you gift your newborn son $10,000, and if his portfolio returns 10% annually, then your original gift of $10,000 will grow to $4.5 million by the time he is 65. But if his portfolio returns 8%, then it grows to only $1.4 million. On the other hand, if it returns only 5%, the portfolio will increase to a mere $227,000. In other words, if the rate of return is halved then, the portfolio will be less than 1/20th the size.

This is a very crucial to remember—a minimal percentage change in interest rate can have a huge impact on the final outcome. So, when you are investing or borrowing money for real estate/business, negotiate interest to the second decimal point. Banks and financial institutions understand this because it is their bread and butter. So should you, because if you do not negotiate hard no one will give you an inch. In the game of money, he wins who understands money the best.

A Single Dollar Has the Power to Grow into a Million Dollars

Every dollar bill is a money seed. Like any seed, if it is planted and allowed to grow it becomes a money tree. This tree once grown up will bear fruit year after year. It will also provide with the seeds necessary to plant further trees. If you destroy the seed, it will never grow to be a tree. Now let us see how the one-dollar seed grows into a million-dollar tree.

If you invest one dollar at 5% rate of interest, it would grow into a million-dollar tree in 284 years. If the same dollar is invested at 10% interest rate the time is cut short to 145 years. It will take only 75 years for a dollar to become a million if you invested at 20%. Not planning to live that long? Then plant a few more dollar bills. It is that simple. Let us see what happens if you start planting one dollar every day, i.e. $30 in a month.

A Dollar a Day will make you a Millionaire in your Lifetime

It is easy if you want to become a millionaire in your lifetime then save one dollar a day and invest it sensibly. Please study the following statements carefully:

A dollar a day invested at 5% will take 100 years to become a million.

A dollar a day invested at 10% will take 56 years to become a million.

A dollar a day invested at 20% will make you a millionaire in only 32 years.

Want to be a billionaire? A dollar a day, when compounded at 20% interest, will give you a billionaire in 66 years.

You will say that earning 20% return is not possible. Later in this book, I will show you how you can receive not only 20%, but go as high as 60% to 70% or even a 100% return on your investment.

This magic happens if you plant one dollar bills every day. I am reasonably sure that most of us can do better than $30 a month. We can dramatically cut short the period and become millionaires much faster if we can plant let us say $10 seeds every day.

If you understand this simple mathematics, then that one dollar bill in your hands will never feel the same again. It holds the seed for your financial future and wellbeing. If you lose it or spend it foolishly, then the dollar seed is destroyed forever. If you save it and invest it wisely, it has the potential to make you and your family rich forever. Once it grows into a million-dollar tree— it will bear that fruit for you and your family, year after year.

You will ask if making a million dollars is so simple then why is not everyone a millionaire. The simple answer to that is lack of discipline. Most people lack the discipline and perseverance required over an extended period of time.

Becoming a millionaire can be a very boring and repetitive exercise over a period of time. Most people want excitement and thrill, and in the process, they gamble away their financial future.

There will be sceptics who will say sustained 20% growth is not possible. Well, Warren Buffet, the investment guru, has done it consecutively for the past 40 years for his investors.

Later in this book, you will see strategies that can help you grow at a much faster rate than 20%. You don't need to be a financial genius to achieve this. All you need are a few financial skills and discipline. Justly put, all you need to do is funnel some of your ill-spent dollars into financially sound investments.

Compounding in Reverse - Can Make You Go Broke

The power of compounding works both ways. It can also make you bankrupt. For compounding to work in your favor, you must always spend less than what you earn and invest the difference. When you invest the difference, money starts working for you. It works day and night, twenty-four hours, seven days a week whether you sleep or go on a holiday. As time goes by and as you have more and more money working for you a day comes when you stop working for money.

On the other hand moment, you start spending more than you earn, you are forced to borrow money, and that generally comes at interest. The reverse power of compounding then kicks in. Unfortunately, most people fail to fully understand this reverse power of compound interest. They max out their credit cards. The effective cost of borrowings in most cases is more than 20% and at times over 30%. The result is that they go into a tailspin and go bust.

There is an old adage, *"He who understands interest – earns it. He who doesn't understand interest – pays it."* Be the one who earns interest than the one who pays interest.

How to find Dollars to Invest and Compound?

Saving is the Key to Compounding

You can never build the wealth you desire if you do not spend less than what you earn and learn to invest the difference. In the majority of the cases, the rich are not rich because they earn a lot of money. The rich are rich because they save a lot of money and invest.

Compounding principle is not possible if you spend more than you earn. Even if your salary is a million dollar and you spend million plus one-dollar compounding will simply not work.

The only way you can find dollars to invest is either by increasing your earning power or simplifying your life to reduce your spending.

In the beginning, it is far easier to understand and make changes to your spending habits.

For those living on subsistence level, it may not be possible to change their spending habits by very much because most of their purchases are for necessities of life.

There are however leaks that occur in our spending of which we are sometimes not even aware of. If we can stop the leaks and save a few dollars each day then we can generate funds for investing and be on our way to becoming millionaires. Please find below some suggestions that can generate instant cash flow for investing:

1. Think before you buy – Every time you make a purchase take an extra minute, to think if you really need to buy that item. Rich take that extra one minute and poor don't. Most of the time we buy on impulse and get saddled with unnecessary things that we don't need in our lives. Think also if you can rent an item or borrow it from somewhere if you don't need it for long. These can include renting a DVD or getting a book from the library instead of buying it.

2. Delayed Gratification – This is true for luxury items. Just delay the purchase by a couple of months. If you want to buy a new car, delay it. If you want to purchase a TV, just delay it by a year. This simple act of delaying purchases will add thousands of dollars to your pocket.

3. Increase your Planning Horizon – By only increasing your planning horizon you can save hundreds of dollars. As with airline tickets, the longer the planning horizon, the cheaper the purchase.

4. Ask for a discount – If you don't request a discount, you will never get one. Always ask for one! You will be surprised how many times you will get one. Remember every dollar saved is a potential million-dollar tree.

5. Examine the Receipt for Errors – Always ask for a receipt and examine it for errors. This simple act will save you hundreds of dollars every year for planting seeds for the money tree.

6. File your Receipts – You must file your receipts as soon as you get back home. This serves two purposes. Firstly, you can change or replace an item if it does not work or becomes faulty. Secondly, you can claim a tax rebate if you are self-employed or running a business. Most people throw the receipt, misplace it or dump it into a cardboard box from where it is troublesome to retrieve at the time of filing tax return. If you are in 30% tax bracket- you lose 30% money on each and every receipt you misplace. It may look minor but is a huge loss when you consider it from the point of destroying seeds that would have made you millions of dollars in potential income.

7. Plug in Tax Leaks - What most people do not realize is that the biggest chunk of cash outflow from their pocket is their taxes. These can range anywhere from 20% to 55% of the income. This is huge in terms of dollars. Most people hesitate in employing the services of a competent tax consultant, thinking that it costs money. Nothing can be further from truth. A good tax consultant, through his advice on tax planning, will not only pay for his services but also save you thousands of dollars that can be used for planting money trees. Another suggestion is that even if you are a paid employee, you should think in terms of starting a home business or invest in property to save on tax. Please speak with your local tax consultant before you embark on this course because tax laws are different in each country.

8. Buying Wholesale– Avoid paying retail price for your purchases. Try and buy at wholesale prices or at stores that offer discounts. Use coupons, shop online and compare prices. Make this a habit. It will save you thousands of dollars every year on your primary purchases.

9. Carryout Plastic Surgery – Want to save 20% to 30% in your expenses? Take out all the credit cards from your wallet or purse and cut all the cards except one. Make it a habit to pay off your credit card balance as and when the payment is due. Never pay the minimum balance. It is the costliest loan you will ever borrow. With the use of plastic credit cards we have lost the feel of money. It does not hurt to spend money because we don't see it coming out of our wallet. Buying now and paying later creates a cycle of debt. Instead, we should save now and invest in the future. These simple actions will set you free and save you massively—up to 30 percent in the coming year.

10. Check your Automatic Payments – These days, for the sake of convenience, we set up automatic payments for all our regular expenses. We set payments for our electricity bills, insurance, water bills, rates, hire purchases, mortgage payment, telephone bills, credit card payments, etc. on monthly or weekly basis. If counted this is a massive financial outflow from our pocket. The danger here is that once we set up the automatic payment, we tend to forget about it and fail to regularly audit our cash outflow. We do not analyze our bills. We become complacent and never shop around for new mortgages or insurance even when there are cheaper products available. Regular auditing of your automatic payments is an absolute must if you desire to save dollars for investment seeds.

11. Energy Audit – Energy costs are soaring. They are likely to increase further in the coming years. Our energy bills, whether it is the cost of heating, cooling, lighting, cooking or driving a car will form a fundamental part of our expense basket. It is imperative that we take a hard look at this major source of outflow of our hard-earned money. Most energy companies will carry out an energy audit of your home for free. You must take advantage of these audits and consider technological measures to reduce your long-term energy bills, and make changes to your house, living style and the kind of car you drive—this will not only save you hundreds of dollars every year but also save the environment.

12. Buy Second-Hand – You can save thousands of dollars by buying second-hand. For instance, a new car out of the showroom drops in price by around 20 percent. It is prudent to buy a second-hand car that is one to three-years old, which can be purchased at a discount of 20 percent to 50 percent on the original purchase price. A dollar saved is a dollar earned! — And you are on your way to planting money seeds.

13. Make a Garage Sale – Look around your house and storage. You will find hundreds of items that have outlived their utility for you. Be it a piece of furniture, some book or baby clothes you no longer need. These may be handy items for someone who needs them. Carry out a garage sale or list them on an internet site that specializes in such sales. You will not only clear your house of unnecessary junk but will also generate invaluable dollar seeds that can get you started on the path to become a millionaire.

14. Barter Your Skills – You can save hundreds of dollars by trading your skills; by becoming a member of exchanges that are springing up in most towns and countries. This was the oldest form of business before money was invented and is again gaining popularity. This can be a source of considerable savings in your travel, entertainment and repair bills if you are willing to exchange your skills.

15. Hundreds of Other Creative Ways – There are hundreds of other ways to save money. You are only limited by your imagination. Dine out? Eat in. Use carpool to work. Take the bus instead of a cab. Email instead of using the phone. Go out for a swim in the sea or for a picnic in the park—it is free entertainment. Never buy extra service contracts or extended warranties; manufacturing guarantees are in most cases adequate. Only run a full dish washer. Put on warm clothing instead of room heating. Take a shower instead of a bath. Don't play lottery, casino or go to races— the law of probability insinuates that you will always be a big loser. The list is as big as your imagination. If you take action on even few of the suggestions, you will have more than enough dollar seeds to plant and to become a millionaire.

What is the Right Philosophy?

Many will say, 'why must I plant dollar seeds for the future? Let me live in the present and be merry. Who has seen the future? It is the present that matters.'

The problem with this philosophy is that you will continue to work for money. There will be no respite for you even in your old age, when you want to slow down and be looked after. Your money problems will continue to haunt you. The 'pleasure-now' philosophy is full of ugly potholes.

On the other hand, if you take the trouble of making some changes as suggested in the above paragraphs and start planting dollar seeds then your life will change as soon as the compounding kicks in, and the dollar tree becomes big and powerful. It will also start giving more seeds and as a result, start multiplying further. The money then starts working for you, and you will find financial freedom.

How much to spend? How much to save and invest for the future? Those are profoundly philosophical questions. Each one of us has to find the right balance that is correct our family and us at a particular point in life. But whatever the situation in life, we have to find dollar seeds to plant or our lives will never change for the better.

The Rule of 72

An easy method to calculate compound interest problems in your head is by applying the Rule of 72.

By using this rule, you can find the number of years that are needed to double your money at a given interest rate—you simply divide 72 by the interest rate!

For example, if you wish to find out how long it will take to double your money at 8% interest then divide 72 by 8, and the answer is that it will take 9 years to double your money.

The rule of 72 is very accurate, as long as the rate of interest is less than 20%.

You can also run the problem backwards. If you want to find out at what rate of interest you will double your money in, let us say, 6 years. To get the answer all you need to do is dividing 72 by 6. The answer, in this case, is 12% interest.

Procrastination

You must stop fretting and procrastinating in case you have lost a lot of investing time. There is nothing you can do about it. It is water under the bridge. There is no point in thinking or complaining about the past. Think about the future. You need to start today, right now, this very second! There is no time to waste. You can make a difference to your finances by making an investment today. Twenty years from now, you'll be glad you did.

Procrastination is the natural assassin of opportunity. Every day you delay in investing makes your ultimate goal of financial freedom at risk.

"Every gold piece you save is a slave to work for you. Every copper it earns is its child that also can earn for you. If you would become wealthy, then what you save must earn, and its children must earn, that all may help to give to you the abundance you crave"

— (George Samuel Clason, 1926).

The Cost of Waiting One Year

It's human nature to procrastinate and waste valuable time. Most people do not have a plan for savings. Even if they do have one, they say, "I will start saving next year" or "I'll do it later." Little do they realize that the costs of delaying are enormous? Even one year can make a huge difference.

Let me illustrate this with an example; let us say that Tom makes $5,000 annual contributions to a retirement fund that earns him an 8% return. He'll have $1,932,528.09 saved by retirement. In case he waits, let us say, by five years, his annual contributions would have to increase to nearly $7,500 to save that same amount by age 65.

Five Steps to Harness the Power of Compounding

There are four steps you need to take to harness the power of compound interest to work for you.

- **Spend Less than What You Earn.** This is the starting point. Whatever your income level, at any point in life, you have to spend less than what you earn and invest the difference to apply the power and enjoy the benefits of compounding. If you spend more than you earn, then you will delve into the tailspin of reverse compounding with disastrous financial results.

- **Start Young.** The earlier you start, the more time compounding will have to work in your favor, as illustrated through the examples taken up previously, the wealthier you will become. *The next best thing to starting young is starting now.*

- **Make Regular Investments.** Remember that even a little investment goes a long way. You have to remain disciplined and make saving a priority. Do whatever it takes to maximize your contributions.

- **Be Patient.** Do not touch the money. You will be tempted several times. Resist. Compounding only works with time, provided you allow your investment to grow. The results will seem slow at first but persevere. The magic of compounding returns shows at the very end. You have to be patient for compounding to work its awesome power.

*Interest Rate. Always negotiate the best interest rate. Even a small change in rate of return will work like magic to the final outcome and your financial security.

What about inflation?

Most people will argue that $1 million will not have the same purchasing power in 40 years as it has today. This is absolutely true. This is all the more reason for you to start saving now! Over the years your income will also begin to rise. With each increase in your income, if you will increase your investment, then you will add more fuel to the fire of compounding and be on the path of becoming really rich.

Having a couple of million bucks in 40 years is better than not having any money at all. Start as soon as possible and invest what you can to let the power of compounding work its magic.

Final Thoughts

So, let us recoup: the power of compounding can make any disciplined and prudent man into a millionaire, there is no extra ordinary skill or genius required and any ordinary man or woman can achieve the desired result.

The ability to save and invest is the key to becoming rich. Obviously, a high income helps. The only proven method is to let your investments compound. Higher the return, faster your wealth will grow. Even modest savings will produce a golden nest egg that you can hatch later in life.

Miracle of compounding which wise men refer to as the 'Eighth Wonder' is a sure and slow path to great wealth. It magically turns a small amount of money, invested wisely, into a whole lot of cash.

Always remember that every dollar that you earn or save, is a seed that has the potential to make a million Dollars for you. So, look after each dollar seed and plant them carefully, and make them grow into trees. They will bear fruits for your family, for generations to come and set you on the path of financial freedom.

The only action required is to find dollar seeds and to continue planting them. If you take the initial steps, remain focused and persist whilst facing the 'Tunneling Effect,' then one day, the power of compounding will take over and become self-perpetuating to take you to the destination of untold riches.

You don't need to be a genius to harness the Power of Compounding to grow rich. This is no rocket science. It is the simplest and most B-O-R-I-N-G way of becoming wealthier. The only thing needed to compound your money successfully is a 100% commitment.

Each dollar that you have is a seed that can be planted to earn you hundreds of dollars. These, in turn, can be planted to earn thousands and millions of dollars.

The Power of Compounding is akin to a snowball…roll it down a snowy hill, and it'll build on itself to grow bigger and bigger. Before you know it, there will be an avalanche of money.

GET THE BALL ROLLING! DON'T WASTE A SINGLE MINUTE!

The time it takes to compound is a function of the amount of money (dollar seeds) you invest, and at what interest rate. We have seen that a small change in interest rate can make a huge change to the final outcome. Common sense tells us that a 10 percent growth-rate is achievable, as this is backed by documented data of stock exchanges around the world and of property-price surges recorded in the past 300 years. The next commandment will show you that with little bit of leveraging, you can earn 60% to 70%, or even higher returns.

93

Thou shall Leverage thy Way to Wealth

The power of leverage is perhaps one of the most neglected and misunderstood areas of an average person's knowledge. One fact will become very clear if you are to study the lives of the most successful people around you; these people, without fail, apply the principle of leverage and use it to maximum effect in their life.

Archimedes used to say, *"**Give me a place to stand and with a lever I will move the whole world.**"* This illustrates the awesome power of leverage. Big doors swing on little hinges.

Leverage simply means '**the ability to do more with less**'. Leverage is the power to achieve a lot with little or no effort. Simply put, leverage is the key to building wealth.

To create wealth in large amounts, in little time, one has to understand and master the principle of leverage. Correct application of leverage breaks through the barrier of 10% growth/ yield. With leverage, we can grow at 50% or 60%, and even 100% or more.

Leverage, when combined with the principle of compounding, can create accelerated wealth. No great wealth has ever been created without using either leverage or compounding. Those two, when combined, together can explode your wealth. Let us examine how leverage works in the financial world.

Compounding + Leveraging = Accelerated Wealth

Robert Kiyosaki, in his book, Rich Dad Poor Dad remarks, *'if you want to become rich, you need to work less, and earn more. In order to do that, you employ some form of leverage.'*

He further explains by saying, *'People who only work hard have limited leverage. If you're working hard physically and not getting ahead financially, then you're probably someone else's leverage.'*

'People with leverage have dominance over people with less leverage.' In other words, just as humans gained an advantage over animals by creating leveraged tools, similarly, humans who use these tools of leverage have more power over humans that do not. Saying it more coherently, *'leverage is power'*."

Types of Leverage

There are not one but several types of leverage that can be used to grow rich sooner. I will start with financial leverage, which is the most common one, and subsequently explain the other forms of leverage that help make you very successful.

Financial Leverage

Irrespective of whether you are a businessman or an investor, you need fund to grow. Everyone starts with personal funds, but these run out sooner than later. To create wealth one has to borrow from relatives, friends, banks, financial institutions or public ones. In other words, we have to work with '**Other People's Money**' or **OPM**.

The borrowed funds have to be productively employed to earn a higher return than the interest payable. Banks do this all the time. They borrow money from us at a lower interest rate and then give out loans to businesses and property mortgages at a much higher interest rate. They pocket the difference and create millions of dollars in profit.

If you have money sitting in the bank in your savings account or retirement account, then others are using your money as their leverage'.

To create wealth, you have to think like a bank. You have to use Other People's Money to grow.

To explain this point, let us see how leverage works in real estate. Let us say you buy an investment property for $100,000 at 10% down payment. This means that you make a down payment of $10,000 and borrow $90,000 from the bank. Let us assume that the rent from the property covers the interest and expenses on the property. If the value of that property increases by 7% over the year then the property would be worth $107,000. This would mean that your investment of $10,000 has earned a whopping return of $7000 or 70% yield.

This happens because you get to leverage not only on your investment of $10,000 but also on the borrowed amount of $90,000. There are sophisticated property investors who buy property with 'no money down' or very little of their own money i.e. they work on 100% borrowed funds. In this case, the return on investment will be infinity.

Borrowing money and creating debt is good if the funds are utilized intelligently to create wealth through business and investment. The profits need to exceed the cost of borrowing. A debt created for consumption purposes: for buying luxury items such as cars, television, etc. is bad debt. Such debts take money out of our pockets and have to be treated with great caution.

Good debts make us rich. Poor debts make us go broke. The power of leverage in finance, when applied correctly, can make us grow rich exponentially.

Leverage of Knowledge

Perhaps the leverage of knowledge is the greatest lever that a person can apply. Your wealth creating ability depends on what lies between the two ears. One has to develop financial muscles in the brain. Intellectual leverage is the most powerful leverage. **I have seen entrepreneurs amass massive wealth with nothing more than an idea.**

"Thinking is hard work. When you are forced to think, you expand your mental capacity. When you expand your mental capacity, your wealth increases."

— Robert Kiyosaki

The fastest method to achieve intellectual leverage is to use '**Other People's Experience**' or **OPE**. It takes too long to learn on your own—become an apprentice and find a mentor. Learn from the experiences of those who have travelled the path.

Secondly, knowledge has become so complex that no lone individual can acquire all the knowledge one needs to grow rich. Wealth is created through knowledge or ideas of other people. One has to learn the art of using '**Other People's Ideas**' or knowledge. This may require collaboration or buying the right expertise to cover any grey areas that exist in our knowledge construction.

What is needed by a wealth creator is the judgment—as to what knowledge is needed for a particular project and from where it can be imbibed at the cheapest price. Our world is full of specialists who do not know how to apply their knowledge to create wealth. It is wealth creators who leverage the knowledge of the specialist to amass great wealth.

You have to develop a keen eye for talent and look out for skillful people, because these are the kind of people who will make you rich. You have to leverage and harness the intellectual strength and talent of these people. Intellectuals consist of professionals such as accountants, legal advisors, tax consultants, etc. They fill the gaps in your knowledge. Their intellectual strength helps you grow rich.

Microsoft Corporations grew mainly due to its ability to harness the intellectual strength of young computer whiz-kids on its pay roll. If Microsoft can do it, why can't you?

Leverage Other People's Time and Effort

All of us are born with different talents and proclivities. Some have a higher IQ, others are taller or better looking. But all of us have one thing which is universal, and that is time. All of us, without any exceptions, have only 24 hours in a day. It goes without saying that to be successful we have to leverage our time.

Most people look for job security rather than opportunity. They will sell their time, effort, resources and connections for a very low price. Wealth creators leverage the time and effort of others to generate wealth for themselves. This is the simplest form of leverage in labor intensive industries.

In fact, most businesses in today's world are founded on other people's time and effort.

> *"People without leverage work for those with leverage."*
>
> — Robert Kiyosaki

If you are an employee, your company is leveraging your time and effort to increase their profits. It may sound cruel but it is the truth. This has been happening since the dawn of civilization. It is high time you started thinking of breaking out of this cycle and empowering yourself by using other people's time and effort to build your wealth.

You have to become a master at offloading routine jobs; to free up your time to concentrate on areas that are more creative and will help you create wealth faster. I am amused by people who are so self-efficient that they will not trust another human being even with the most mundane jobs, because they do not trust their competence. This is the sure route to stagnate.

To succeed and progress in life, you have to find people to replace your management and skillset in the shortest possible time frame.

You have to use the effort and energy of others to grow rich. This might be as simple as hiring someone to clean your house, mow your lawn, dry clean and press your shirt or hiring technical people to do your routine jobs at work. You should first write down and offload your bottom 10 routine activities (you don't enjoy doing,) that take up your time and energy from productive work, which in turn, can generate revenue for you.

You have only 24 hours in a day. No matter how talented or efficient you are, you can earn only a limited amount of money if you are paid by the hour. With a 40-hour work-week you can, at best, work for only 2000 hours in a year (assuming you take a 2-week vacation time and work 50 weeks).

If you employ, let us say, 100 people in your business, your work output will be 200,000 man-hours and your income that much higher

---

"I would rather earn 1% off 100 people's efforts than 100% of my own efforts."

— John Paul Getty

You can also benefit from a percentage of other people's efforts and dramatically increase your income and freedom by learning to leverage your time.

"He who stands on the giants' shoulders; sees farther than the giant"

— Puissant

To apply this technique, great human and management skills are needed. If you lack management skills; a more practical and pragmatic approach is to outsource jobs that need co-ordination of human skills. In this way, you avoid the hassle of managing people.

Leveraging Technology

Technology allows us to do things with greater precision, more efficiently and faster than ever before. Today, computers can process data and calculate results that needed hundred and thousands of man-hours. Similarly, the internet can provide access to information that would have taken hundreds of hours to research and collate.

Emails, modern telecommunications and internet have revolutionized communication. These technologies, when mastered, give leverage in terms of quality and speed of decision making— and they help save time and effort, thus resulting in huge cost savings. They are also impacting how we network, socially interact and conduct our businesses. To create wealth in today's world, one has to master leveraging these new technological advances.

To use this leverage, you have to be open to technology and buy the best of what your pocket allows.

I was privileged to be able to hear Bill Gates lecture at a conference in the early nineties. He emphasized on the importance of computers in our lives, especially that little extra technological edge that our children receive in this competitive world. At the time I had a computer at work, but not one at home. I was planning to buy one, but the high cost prohibited me from doing so back in those days. I was continuously delaying my decision to buy—the prices were regressing with every passing month and I was waiting for the appropriate moment to buy.

After attending that Bill Gates lecture, I went straight to a computer store and bought a PC for our home use—it was the best decision I ever made in my life! That PC not only helped me leverage my time and knowledge, but also gave my children an opportunity to grow up with the technological edge.

Since then, I have developed a habit of upgrading technology at home and at work: computers, mobile devices, communication systems, access to fast speed networks, etc. Access to information and sharing it with your customers provides the best possible leverage, in terms of customer relationship, sales and profits.

I have given an example of information technology for the ease of understanding, as it affects our day to day life; there are many other machines that replace human functions more efficiently and at a much cheaper cost. For instance, robots are able to assemble cars with more precision and in much lesser time than human beings. The fastest growing companies on our planet are those that are making technological breakthroughs on a regular basis in their respective fields. *Apple* is one such company.

Technology leverages work only when applied productively. There are people who waste time surfing the net endlessly, playing video games, socializing or using it only as source of entertainment. Nothing wrong indulging in such activities because we all need to keep informed and entertained – the problem is when lose we lose focus and become obsessed with it and spend endless hours socializing.

To create wealth you have to apply leverage of technology to your advantage rather than get lost in technology indulgence.

Social Media Leveraging

Social media platforms like Facebook, Twitter, YouTube and LinkedIn are the latest technological breakthroughs that are changing the way we do businesses and leverage ourselves. Viral marketing has taken up a new connotation due to the leverage provided by social media.

Unknown talents are discovered each day and made famous by the power of these viral information sharing platforms. These platforms are creating instant millionaires of those who know how to harness this new technological wave.

To apply maximum leverage, you have to use and market technologies that are most efficient and cutting edge.

Leveraging of Networks

"It's not what you know but who you know that makes the difference"

— Anonymous

A key contact can 'make it happen'. If you know the right person, things happen. The key contact is crucial to your success. He is the leverage that will work wonders for you. The value of a large network is that the chances of finding the right contact increase exponentially.

To succeed, you need the power of a large network. There are people who control large networks. You have to know who these people are in order to gain access to their networks. For example, if you are marketing a product, it is far easier to find one contact who controls a large network and market your product through him rather than selling your product independently to thousands of unconnected buyers.

The trick is to know either how to build a network or have some access to people who control networks. Understanding the power of networking is a very important leveraging tool.

If you wish to create wealth fast, then you have to master the art of networking. By forming a network of nurtured relationships, you get support, information, referrals, advice and access to resources.

It is your contacts who make you rich. If you know the industry leaders, you receive important information before anyone else—if you know the bankers, you get access to finance…if you are friends with your boss, you get promoted. The list is endless.

Cavett Robert, the dean of American speakers, rightly put it: *"you have to make contacts to get contracts"*. Your net worth will be equal to the size of your network.

You don't create a network by simply capturing names, telephone numbers and email addresses into your address book or database; you create a network by building a meaningful relationship over a period of time with the people who can trust you. The way to do this is to help everyone within your sphere of influence to the best of your ability. If you go an extra mile, you will put the Universe in your debt that will be repaid to you a hundred times over.

The best relationships are formed when you participate in someone's growth with the attitude of making them strong and independent. If you help people with the aim of getting something in return, to make them dependent on you financially or emotionally, then that relationship will not last for long. A plant can never grow under the shadow of a big tree.

You have to give something away for free that is of value to your network, to build relationships. This act of giving will foster trust and bring attention to you. Do not expect reciprocity in return or the value of your gift is lost.

The return you get for your free gift is trust and recognition. This will result in strengthening the foundation of your network and give it the longevity it needs.

The golden rule of networking is:

"Be very quick to build connections and extremely slow to break them"

— Robert G Allen

Your network will collapse if more people are leaving it as compared to those who are joining. To sustain your network, you have to keep adding value.

How to build a large Network quickly

To build a huge network, it is not a necessary condition for you to know thousands of people, to begin with. You initially have to start building a network by adding one person at a time. This is a very slow process at the beginning, but as you add value to your network, more people will gravitate towards it through word-of-mouth advertising or referrals. Sooner than later, key contacts who have large networks of their own will start taking note of your network.

And before you know it, you will find a key contact that controls a large network of people. To build a large network, you don't have to find just one key contact but several key contacts. The value of your network is the square of the number of people in it.

To find your key contact you will need to network with a large number of people; this will increase the possibility of finding the one key contact that will not only increase the size, but also the value of your network hundred-fold. The only way to build a large network is through consistency.

Examine your list of contacts critically and focus on those who have large networks and yield the maximum influence—make a special effort to build relationships with them and spend your time maintaining them. If they endorse your product or service to their database, your profits will multiply.

"Position yourself as the center of influence - the one who knows the movers and shakers. People will respond to that, and you'll soon become what you project."

The two aspects that increase the size of your network quickly are: what value you provide to your network and how many key contacts you can bring to your network.

You don't have to look too far; just look at the phenomenal growth of Google and Facebook! They provide invaluable services to their clients for free and as a result, have millions of subscribers joining them every month. This results in billions of dollars in revenue to these companies. If we can replicate even a little bit of their strategy in building our networks, we can become rich very quickly.

Weak Ties Network

Most people believe that it is important to have people whom they already know and have strong ties with, which will make their network stable and help it grow but nothing can be further from truth. It is your weak ties, or the people whom you don't know so well, that bring growth and new impetus to your network.

The reason for this is simple—the people who are close to you have much in common with you. They share the same value system, experiences and similar view points. The information they possess is already known to you and is of very little value to you. Your weak ties, on the other hand, bring fresh perspective and new ideas. It is imperative to keep in mind that it is your weak ties that add value to your network.

In addition to that, your weak ties will bring in a new circle of influence with their own set of friends and relatives to your network. In all likelihood, your inner circle of friends will not contribute towards the growth of your network to the same extent due to the limited number of new members they can add to your network.

The most influential people who will increase the size of your network are the 'connectors,' who are masters of those weak ties. These connectors have the energy, the self-confidence and the social attributes to connect with a large number of people—their special gifts create large networks of weak ties.

Either you must master connecting with the weak ties or with the connectors, who will bring weak ties to your network.

Networking the Networks

Another way of growing your network fast is by 'Networking the Networks.' There is a high number of existing networks in related fields that you can interact with to work towards a mutual advantage. Once you have built a network of considerable size, you can collaborate with other networks. This works in a similar way as the 'weak ties network.'

To give an example, if you have a network of real estate investor clients, it may be worth your while to collaborate with a mortgage broker who has a network of clients who borrow money to fund their real estate. You can also collaborate with accountants and attorneys who have a database of real estate investor clients—by giving cross referrals, all the key players can increase the size of their networks.

These days, it is relatively easy to find related networks by doing a search on the internet and building a relationship with the key players in those networks. The people who operate large networks understand the importance of increasing the size of their network by collaborating with other networks. So, don't be shy in approaching these people.

Metcalf's Law

"The value of a network grows in proportion to the square of the number of users"

An average person will know around, at least, 200 people. Each of those 200 people will have their own sphere of influence and will also know 200 people. So, if you build a network of 200 people, you will have access to over 200x200 (40,000 people.)

If you take this one step further, those 40,000 people will have their own spheres of influence of 200 people each—the possibilities are endless!

It is therefore critical that you start building your network with integrity as you sit at the center of your sphere of influence. If you try and fake your network, you will not succeed. Keep adding value to your network without any expectations of return, and watch your network grow.

Centre of Influence

Always remember that you are the center of influence in your network. Even if you have a great dream-team, you remain the leader of your team that will exert the key influence in creating your network.

You have to develop the traits that help influence your network: you have to make yourself immensely likable and radiate positive energy, and your personality and eye contact should radiate warmth and friendliness. Develop a personality that is always looking to help others grow in whatever their endeavor or goal may be in life, and always be willing to give and add value without any hope of reciprocity—that will make your influence grow.

Integrity, integrity, integrity. There is no substitute for integrity. Never promote an idea, service or goods to your network that you are not using or have doubts about. You cannot fake and build a network. Be yourself and act honestly. You will attract the right kind of people into your network, which will help you grow in leaps and bounds with their support.

Ethical leverage is essential in networking. You have to use your contacts wisely. If you try and use your contacts without thought of return on everyone's time and effort, then you may succeed in lifting your load, but your strategy, in the long run, will fail. Your network will collapse.

I get hundreds of emails every month from internet marketers trying to promote affiliate products. It is very easy to find out a fake promotion coming from a person who has never used a product or has very little knowledge about it. I immediately unsubscribe from the list of those who try and promote such products. On the other hand, I continue to be on the list of those who email me information that is of value to me and, at times, buy products on their recommendation.

- The power of leverage comes from using your networking skills wisely. There are two fundamental rules to networking:

- Pay It Forward- Assist 3 people to succeed and in return of what you do for them, request them to help 3 others. This is leverage.

- Share the Rewards – Share the rewards of your success and prosperity with all those who are involved in your network.

If you are honest, genuine and helpful your sphere of influence and network will grow. Your network, if built correctly, will, without a doubt, make you rich.

Leveraging Systems

The ultimate aim of any income stream is to make it work on autopilot or with minimal supervision from you. This can only be achieved by putting proper systems in place so that it can function without your intervention. This is the ultimate leverage that will free up your time and effort to devote to other important things in life such as family, travel, leisure, creativity or other ventures that will create new sources of wealth for you.

When I was in the Navy, we had a saying that it was a system designed by a genius to be run by fools. All the procedures were laid out for us to the last detail. We knew what action to take in an emergency, what logs and forms to fill up, how to demand stores, etc. When an order was given to 'dive' or 'surface,' every crew member who was on-board the submarine knew exactly what action to take. Nothing was left to chance.

A well-run income stream or business should be run in a similar manner. The problem is that most of us know how to work within a system designed by others but are clueless when it comes to designing a system for our own work or business.

The answer to this problem is to buy into a system that is very closely related to your work and adapt them to your requirement. An alternate solution is to work with an expert who has the skills to design and set up systems.

To leverage our time and effort, we have to be on a constant lookout for setting up systems to free our effort and time. These can be very straightforward things like: setting up automatic online payments for our bills or more sophisticated automated systems to put our business in auto pilot. There may be some cost and effort involved to initially set up the systems, but once they are in place, they free up your energy to do more creative work. The aim of any good system is to take care of the routine work thereby leveraging time and effort for creative work.

To become rich, you need to have proper systems in place–QED. Without SYTEMS, you are doomed to failure. Research has shown that 94% of the failures are not due to the assumption that people don't do a good job, but because either they are using the wrong business systems or have no systems in place to start with.

For the ease of understanding, the right acronym for systems is:

Save **Y**our **S**elf **T**ime **E**nergy **M**oney

If you want to make money, then search and find a money-making vehicle that has successful systems. You will save time, energy and money if you have systems in place before you embark on money-making ventures. If you don't have the skills to set up systems, then buy into business/ investment ventures that have systems in place. Every enlightened wealth creator knows this simple truth. They buy into time-tested predictable systems that will do the job for them. That is why when initially starting your own business; it may be wiser to buy into a franchisee that has strong systems rather than building your own from scratch. Chances of failure will thus be reduced. As you gain experience, you can develop your own system.

Once you have systems in place, the system will churn out money for you. All the work is done upfront to set up the system. You will only need to fine-tune it, once in operation, to make it work optimally.

Characteristics of an Ideal Money-Making System

Zero Time

This means that once you have a project up and running, it should run more or less on autopilot and require minimum time intervention from you.

I am a property investor and I treat each property as a separate money-making stream of income. My process is very simple; I buy family homes with surplus land to build a second house on it. I focus on properties that are being sold at a price that is, at least, 15-20% below market value and aim towards a long-term settlement.

Delayed settlement gives me time to get all the clearances from the City Council for building plans and renovations. At times, I also get capital appreciation even before I have settled.

I then try and make renovations to the older house so as to increase its rent. I also contract reputed builders to build a second house on the additional land—thereby increasing the cash flow further. These two actions along-with delayed settlement increase the value of the property by 20-30% and give me cash flow in excess of 10%.

Once the project is completed, I hand over the property to a competent property manager. I never manage a property myself. I make sure that my investment-properties have adequate cash flow to pay the mortgage, expenses and the property management costs. This frees up my time to do the next project.

There have been times when I do not exchange a single phone-call with my property manager for a whole year. Once a project is completed, properties bring in money on autopilot without my interventions. I then move on to my next project and repeat the whole process. The increase in equity from buying low and adding value gives me money to use as down payment for the next property.

This method of investing in property is only an example. You can buy into proven franchises or self-perpetuating viral programs on the internet that take very little of your time, once they are set up correctly. The goal is to build a massive amount of passive income with little or no investment of your time.

Zero Out Of Pocket Money

Columbus borrowed money for his expedition from the royal family of Spain. Discovery of Americas brought huge returns for Columbus regarding recognition and finances.

You will need money to fund your investment or business. You have to find systems to get the funding from outside and use little or no money of your own.

In real estate, you must have heard of 'Nothing Down' deals. It is fairly common for sophisticated investors to buy properties with no money of their own. Even if they have to put money into a deal, they try and take out their investment at the first opportunity available.

Zero Risk

Once you learn to do investments and business without putting your personal money into a deal, then your risk is virtually zero.

Many will argue that 'No Money Deals' increase the amount of leverage and the risk of bankruptcy. Sophisticated investors set up corporations and other legal entities to protect themselves from any adverse fallout and limit their liability if something untoward happens.

The more sophisticated you become as an investor your risk management skills to put right systems in place to avoid/ minimize risks will improve.

Zero Management

You have to be constantly on the lookout to find systems and technology to replace yourself. To go to the next, higher level of income, you have to keep finding competent people and systems to replace you.

You have to master the art of outsourcing and delegation. You have to find businesses and investments with systems in place that take up the least of your time and effort. Most people forget to take into account the cost of management time and base their business and investment decisions purely on ROI (rate of return). This can have disastrous results in the long run as it will not only impede your financial growth, but also have adverse effects on your health, family time and relationships.

Robert Allen, in his book One Minute Millionaire, justly states, *"**You have to learn to ZERO OUT your life**"* in order to succeed.

Caution about Leveraging

Leveraging is a great way of creating accelerated wealth but it comes with a warning: if leveraging is applied incorrectly it can destroy your wealth equally fast.

The higher the leverage, the greater is the risk to your investment and business. At the same time, there is greater potential for profits. Leverage works both ways; it is a double-edged sword.

Before applying leverage, you have to understand some basic truths about leveraging or things could go dramatically wrong and you can get yourself hurt and go bankrupt.

State of Knowledge

The financial crisis of 2008 was caused when excessive greed led people to use leverage without proper understanding of risks involved. The most important factor for using leverage correctly is your state of knowledge.

For instance, if you lack knowledge about finances or the business/ investment you wish to start, there is no point in rushing to get 100% finance in order to try making a no-money-down deal. Similarly, if you lack the knowledge of systems and how to set them up, there is no point in rushing to fully automate your operations. Same is true for any form of leveraging.

You should make a correct assessment of your financial, emotional and spiritual knowledge in any given situation before applying leverage as an instrument for accelerated wealth creation. Greed is the product of a lacking emotional and spiritual intelligence. Leverage driven by greed is the worst enemy of wealth creation.

Leverage is like a power tool that can make your job of wealth creation very easy but its improper use, without adequate knowledge or precautions, can cause you tremendous hurt.

There is a saying that, '*It is never the investment that is wrong. It is always the investor who is wrong*'. So, take the time and trouble to learn about the business or investment before jumping onto the bandwagon of leveraging for quick gains.

Market Conditions

In uncertain market conditions, when the outcome is not known or when the market is moving downwards, the amount of leverage should be reduced.

You could increase the leverage as you gain confidence, and when the market forces are moving in a positive direction.

For example, in property investment, it is extremely easy to do 'no money down deals' if you have the right knowledge and the market is moving up. This is because even if you make a mistake, the rise in price of the property will cover your error. On the other hand, doing a low equity deal when the property cycle is moving southward then even a small error in your judgment will wipe out your equity.

If you are using leverage for accelerated financial returns, then you have to be very alert towards changing market conditions. If the market conditions deteriorate, then you have to take measures to reduce your leverage in time. People go bankrupt when they hesitate to act or foresee a developing situation. Reducing your leverage by selling some of your assets is no shame. You can always buy assets and increase your leverage when favorable market conditions return.

Age Factor

The amount of leverage to apply is also dependent your age. When you are young, you can risk applying high levels of leverage. This is because even if things go wrong, you have the time to recover and start all over again. Once you age time is not on your side and if things go wrong there is no time to recover and restart.

As you grow older, it is wise to reduce leverage even if you have become more proficient at applying leverage with experience. The last remark will, no doubt, be debated because there are many elderly people who are still young at heart and ready to take all kinds of risks in life. I, unfortunately, speak for the majority.

Risk Appetite

Before applying leverage, you have to access your risk appetite. This is because if things go wrong, then people with less risk appetite will start to panic and make incorrect decisions that can set them back by years in their financial growth and planning.

Greed

Greed is the biggest enemy of leverage. It is greed which makes us blind to applying leverage without appropriate knowledge, skills and timing. Before applying leverage, one has to develop checks and balances provided by spiritual, financial and emotional intelligence.

How to Maximize Leverage

Acquire a Mentor

You can avoid making mistakes on the learning curve by finding a mentor who can guide you through the whole process. Your mentor has climbed the mountain—he knows the terrain and knows what works and what does not work. You can learn from the process and avoid making mistakes.

In addition, your mentor has systems. The most efficient facet of leverage is to transfer your mentor's systems to your use. Learn from those systems and apply those systems to your business, real estate, stock market and internet.

Acquire a Team

Nature made us incomplete—we have incomplete knowledge and experience; we have to collaborate and build dream-teams to fill gaps in our knowledge and competence to succeed. Our teams can fill up our blind spots.

If you want accelerated leverage then find a competent team to help you. Your team will help you go faster. A 4X100 meter relay team runs much faster than an individual runner.

Your team can consist of people with expert knowledge in their respective fields. They don't have to be your employees but should be available for advice. For instance, if you are a real estate investor your team will consist of your accountant, solicitor, and real estate agents who bring you deals, mortgage broker and your builder/ handyman. If these people are property investors, they will be able to give you better quality advice.

Before you start building your network, find your core groups that will help you build your network. When likeminded, joyful and success-oriented people work together, enormous energy is released. Try and avoid people with negative energy around them—they will drag you down.

Your core group or dream-team will provide the synergy to create an invisible force that will attract people to your network. 1 + 1 is, not 2, but 11. The sum of the parts is far greater than the whole. This is what your core group can help you achieve.

Jesus selected a core group of 12 men, and the world was never the same again. Their network and influence has lasted over centuries and continues to expand even today.

Bill Gates and Paul Allen collaborated to found Microsoft and became the richest men of all times. Larry Page and Sergey Brin founded Google that is used by millions of users and is presently expanding incessantly.

Facebook, which is the biggest networking platform of all times, was created by a team of four Harvard University students: Mark Zuckerberg, Dustin Moskovitz, Eduardo Saverin and Chris Huges. The examples that history provide are endless.

A core group constituted of an aligning team (that is not pulling in different directions) will always out-perform an individual. So, don't try to do it alone. Build a core group first and then your network.

Loverage

Mike Littman coined the term 'Loverage'. If you love what you are doing and are spiritually and emotionally connected with it, then success will come much easily. When your thoughts, mind, body, emotions and spiritual self are congruent you achieve unassailable heights.

Ask any sportsperson about their greatest sporting moments, and you'll find them acknowledge that at the height of their achievement, their mind, body and spirit dissolve into a singular force. Do what you love doing and you will apply the 'Loverage' even without knowing.

Final Thoughts on Leverage

There is no such thing as a hundred percent leverage. It is a myth perpetuated by certain vested individuals who want to market their books and products. There will always be some financial, time, and effort commitment in the beginning. In due course, as the business or investment progresses, finance and time involvement can be reduced, and leverage increased.

The above arguments should not dissuade you from using leverage with prudence and intelligence. Leverage, without doubt, is the most important and powerful tool in the armory of wealth creators. However, it is of paramount importance to understand its correct usage before applying it in a fit of excitement. Initially, start applying small forms of leverage and as your confidence grows, you can increase the amount of leverage to one that you are comfortable with.

Even if you start applying a little bit of leverage in your life, you will be amazed at the results. Leverage is power, strength and intelligence.

Mark Victor Hansen and Robert Allen, in their book 'One Minute Millionaire,' provided a formula:

Leverage = Speed = Goals

This, in my view, sums up how you can use leverage to reach your financial goals within the shortest period of time. You can increase your returns from 5-10% offered by banks and financial institutions to over 60-70%, or even higher through leveraging.

Remember, without applying some kind of leverage, there is no possibility of creating accelerated wealth.

Multiple Streams of Income

Once you learn the use of systems to run your businesses/ investments you will be able to create multiple streams of income with ease. This is because none of businesses require your time or physical intervention.

You develop one income stream, put it on auto, free up your time and look for another opportunity to build another source of passive income.

Keep repeating the process—this will provide you with safety and stability. It will also reduce your risk. In case, one income source dries up, you have several others working for you. Never become content nor rely on one source of income.

The next commandment will elucidate how that is done.

SIXTH COMMANDMENT

Thou shalt Create Multiple Streams of Passive Income

> *"Wealth is when small efforts produce big results,*
> *Poverty is when big efforts produce small results"*
>
> — George David

One of the fundamentals of wealth creation is to know that not all income streams are created equal. When you work and are paid only once then your income is linear.

In the case of passive income, you work hard once and it unleashes a steady flow of income for years and maybe even a lifetime or beyond. It is often said that the lower and middle-class work for money whereas the rich make their money work for them; the key to wealth creation lies in this simple statement.

Royalties from Elvis Presley's songs and movies earn an income more than $40.0 million every year even though he has been dead for over three decades. Although everyone cannot be an Elvis Presley, it is definitely possible to focus on work that will create a residual income rather than spend a lifetime in working for linear income.

Doctors, dentists, sales persons and attorneys may appear to have impressive incomes but they are linear in nature. Their incomes are capped depending upon the number of hours they work. If they don't show up for work due to any reason, their income comes to a grinding halt. They trade hours of work for income.

This kind of an income comes with potential risks. In case of ill health or an accident, their income dries up immediately. This has dire consequences for the financial wellbeing of the individual and their families. Even if one is insured, the money runs out ultimately and there is a need to downgrade—changing lifestyles and making adjustments that can be very painful.

The true definition of wealth is the time period in which you can sustain your lifestyle in case you stop working today. If you can sustain your lifestyle for only a few months then it is a cause for serious concern but if you can do it for a couple of years, you are better off. On the other hand, if you can sustain your lifestyle indefinitely without work then you can be termed as wealthy. Once you reach this stage, you can retire.

It must be remembered that, contrary to what many think, you need more money after retiring because now you have all the time in the world to holiday and spend money, and also to pay off those medical bills. If you are banking on social security or pension as your only residual income source, you are in for serious disappointment.

Almost all of us, with the exception of a few very rich people, start with a linear income. The smart ones are those who start shifting their incomes from linear to residual from a very young age.

Every day when you wake up, you must ask yourself the question: "What percentage of my income is residual?" Also ask yourself, "How many hours am I going to devote today towards creating a residual income." If you don't ask these questions, you will remain where you are.

You are in big trouble if you devote zero hours towards creating passive income. Remember: true wealth is created by focusing on work that creates an income for a lifetime. For every hour of work that you put in, you should be paid again and again and not only once as in the case of linear income. Therein lies the secret of wealth creation.

"How many times do you get paid for every hour of work you put in?" The answer to this question will tell you if your income is linear or passive—if you are paid only once for your work then your income is linear. If you don't show up for work, you don't get paid. You work from paycheck to paycheck. When the source of your income is residual, you get paid for your effort again and again.

One of the main reasons why people find it difficult to leap from linear or earned income to residual income is that the entire education system is designed to prepare people to get jobs that can pay them salaries. This helps the big businesses to get trained labor for their industries and also works well for the government in collecting tax dollars because paid workers pay the highest amount of tax.

"When a Man tells you that he got rich through hard work, ask him "Whose?"

— Don Marquis

You have to create a shift in your thinking before you can start generating residual income. You have to free yourself from the shackles of the unfortunate education system that has gripped your psychology.

This commandment will educate you not only on the importance of residual income but also how you can shift gradually from earned income to residual income and find financial freedom for life.

The Myth of Job Security

"A job is really a short-term solution to a long term problem."

People with jobs believe that their 'income' is representative of their wealth. The questions they ask are, "who you work for, how much do you earn?" or "which car you drive?"

These people fall into the category of "looking good, going nowhere." They buy stuff to look and feel rich. To sustain their lifestyle, they continually work harder, longer hours and constantly educate themselves to become even more specialized.

A paycheck, no matter how big, cannot be defined as wealth or riches. Most people think that getting a bigger pay check or salary is making them richer. Nothing can be further from truth. In fact 95% of people spend every dollar they earn. By the way, job could be considered as an acronym for "Just Over Broke."

We need cash flow to pay our bills, put food on the table, send our kids to school and sustain any kind of lifestyle. But if your cash flow is solely reliant on your pay check, you are at grave risk. You can fall ill, have an accident or lose your job! Ask the millions who have lost their jobs in the financial downturn.

"Job security is a myth…it is also risky for self-employed people in my opinion. If they get sick, injured,

or die, their income is directly impacted."

— Robert Kiyosaki

Having a job severely restricts your cash flow capabilities. You can work for only X hours in a day. Your pay check will be limited to the number of hours worked multiplied by your hourly rate.

Your first step to creating wealth comes when your cash flow starts coming from passive income rather than your regular paychecks. In other words, your investments and businesses pay you money whether you get out of bed or not.

The next step forward is to create long-term passive income cash flow backed by a solid asset base. Wealth is all about owning assets. However, an asset must have both capital growth and income. You must first concentrate on generating a rather large passive income. Cash flow not only complements your lifestyle but also has the ability to get loans to help buy income producing assets.

Passive cash flow is generated from investments (paper assets or properties that are fully paid for), businesses that have systems in place and do not require your day to day presence, or your income is generated because of royalties from intellectual property rights that you have created. To grow rich, you have to make either money or people work for you even when you are sleeping.

The quickest way to become rich is to generate a massive cash flow through a business that has proven, working systems in place. You then have to buy assets that give you not only a passive income but also capital appreciation. If you do not have a huge capital to start a business, join a good network marketing company; it is a good passive income generator, you will receive personalized coaching in business, marketing and leadership skills from those who have stakes in your business.

Every night before you go to sleep: calculate the number of hours you have spent in creating passive income for yourself as against the number of hours you have spent in generating linear income that has helped others get rich because of your effort.

You must set a target each day to add more and more hours towards generating passive income. If you do this simple exercise on a regular basis, you will make a giant leap towards attaining financial freedom.

To understand the difference between residual and linear income is critical to your financial wellbeing. Most people do not understand this distinction and stay stuck to a job profile their entire lives or run a 'mom-and-pop' business that requires their attention and presence seven days a week. So, whenever you are looking at a business or an investment opportunity, look at the residual aspect. If it is not there then give it a miss. Never ever forget the commandment if you want to become truly rich: ***Thou shalt work once and be paid for a lifetime.***

What is the Problem with Linear Income?

The main problem with linear or earned income is that you are trading your time and skills for money. Your earning power will be limited by the time and skills you personally have which is a very inefficient and arduous way of earning wealth. You have only X number of hours in a day and there is a limit to the skills you can acquire—these limiting factors will put a cap on your income.

As soon as you stop working and your skills become outdated, your income will stop. You can take time out to upgrade your skills but during that period, your income level will either drop or stop altogether.

When it comes to linear income, you are the golden goose. As you grow older, your physical and mental capacities regress. This will reflect directly on your earned income. In case of an adversity, your income will drop to a virtual zero.

Another major issue with earned income is that in virtually every country, it is taxed more heavily when compared to investments or residual income. The biggest financial outflow in your life is the taxes. You pay virtually 40–70% of your earnings to the government in the form of direct and indirect taxes. These include: income tax, GST, customs and excise duty, capital gains tax, estate duty, stamp duty, service tax, VAT, property taxes, regional council taxes etc. Some of the indirect taxes are invisible and you don't even come to know about them.

Linear or earned income has a limited number of loopholes to save on the taxes. If you are in working as an employee, you have to start investing or start a part-time business to save on the taxes that will provide you with additional funds to build residual income for you and your family. This may seem unfair but it is true. Most governments want you to invest your money so that capital formulation creates more jobs. This is why they give huge tax breaks to investors and business owners. You should take advantage of these tax breaks to create residual income for yourself.

If earned income have so many drawbacks, why most people seek jobs? The reasons are unequivocal: jobs do not require a start-up capital, nor does it come with a risk. Most people when starting out in life do not have capital and are risk-averse. The fault also lies in our education system which was designed during the industrial age to train people for jobs that the industries run by capitalists required. Things have changed dramatically with the advent of the information age; it is now possible to earn residual income with very little or virtually no start-up capital and risks.

There is no harm in starting out with a job because of economic circumstances. A job may also be essential for some people because it can instill discipline and teach skills that are required to succeed in life. The trick is to convert your linear income into residual income within the shortest period of time.

Can you become wealthy from earned income? It depends on your definition of wealth. Some professionals like doctors, investment bankers, lawyers and engineers are highly paid. But are they really rich or simply appearing to be rich? Do their jobs provide long-term financial security? Can they sustain their lifestyles if they lose their jobs for any reason?

According to me, the true secret of wealth is not that you have more money but that you have more freedom of time—you do not have to trade your time for earning money! You will be rich when you not only sustain your lifestyle without working, but also improve on it. In that case, you have sufficient residual income to not only sustain your lifestyle but also make your wealth grow by further investments into generating passive income.

When you are trading time for money, you do not have time-freedom. You can definitely become wealthier if you invest a part of your earned income into creating residual income, which in due course of time can surpass your earned income.

Why is Residual Income Important?

Residual income is important because every dollar you earn from this source is not dependent on your time or effort. Residual income gradually frees up your time to enhance creativity and improve quality of your life. It gives you financial security and strengthens your relationship with your family members as you rid yourself of time and financial constraints in your life.

Residual income frees up your time and also gives you tax breaks to give you even more dollars to create residual income. When you understand the residual game and implement it methodically, your income will spiral upwards along with freeing up your time.

You can never become rich on earned income because you are trading time for money. To become truly rich, you have to separate your time from the money you earn. Creating wealth does not have to be about extracting every last ounce of your energy. If you take a conscious decision, you can gradually shift from linear income to generating residual income that will remain with you for generations to come.

The primary benefit to multiple streams of income is the consistency and security of your income coming from non-related sources.

- Benefits of Generating Residual Income

- Freedom to choose when and where you wish to work

- Residual income is generated 24 hours 7 days a week

- Freedom to create an unlimited amount of income

- Have time to spend with your family and friends or go on a vacation

- Retire young

- Financial security for your family in case of illness or ill health

- Ability to give to charitable causes dear to your heart

Residual/ Passive Income Misnomer

Before we discuss residual income, let me clarify the misunderstanding that has been created by the term 'passive income.' The terms 'residual income' and 'passive income' have become interchangeable but there is a subtle difference. From a marketing point of view, the term passive income is very seductive as it equates to "No work", "No brainer", "Easy", "Just sit back and relax and money will come rolling in." People get excited and join a business opportunity thinking that there is no work involved. They get disillusioned when they find that income is not passive after all.

Nothing can be further from truth. To create residual income, there can be a huge amount of time and effort required. It may take an author months or years to write a book. There is no income upfront. But once the book is published, royalties from it can flow for years to come giving passive income.

Residual implies that some work must be done before you can reap the rewards for years.

There is no such thing as "100% passive income." Every income stream you create will require some effort initially and also some maintenance to sustain it as passive income. You must keep these two work factors in mind before embarking on creating a residual income stream. So you have to roll up your sleeves and get to work to start a residual income stream.

The good part is that once you have created your residual income stream, it will create a fulltime income for you with very few hours of work each week. There was a point in my life when I took a decision: I will not devote a single hour of my time in generating linear income to make someone else rich. This is the best decision I ever took in my life. Someone rightly said, ***"Wealth is not a material gain, but a state of mind."*** It took me several years of financial education to gain the state of mind that prompted me to stay away from the pitfall of linear income and focus only on creating passive income.

You will need some involvement in management of your assets, although it may not require day-to-day direct involvement. The trick is to put systems into place to minimize your time involvement even if it comes at a slight price. Your free time is the most precious commodity that will not only improve the quality of your life but also help create additional income streams.

Why Creating Residual Income is the Holy Grail of Investing?

Simply put, residual income is an income that is not dependent on your time or effort. It is dependent on an asset and management of that asset. You have to leverage other people's time and money to create residual income and manage your assets.

Businesses can be a source of passive income only if you can replace yourself. If you are directly involved in your business on a day-to-day basis, then it cannot be termed as passive income. To turn your business into a residual income source, you have to put the right kind of people and systems into place so that it operates without your presence and interference. Most entrepreneurs start businesses to generate millions but instead land up shackling themselves to their business and can't even afford to take a holiday in years.

The best kind of residual investments are those where you – as the owner of the asset – can exercise active control even when you are not involved in regular operation. You must have adequate control over your assets so as to positively impact the level of generated income.

Using other people's money and resources is the key ingredient of creating residual income. It buys you time and effort. Once you start creating residual income, you will start attracting more and more of other people's money to grow even richer. If done correctly, you will get caught in an upward spiral of residual wealth creation.

Residual income, without a doubt, is the holy grail of investing and the key to long-term wealth. This is a critical step on your road to wealth creation. The earlier you begin this journey, more success you will achieve. You can create a tidal wave in your financial security and prosperity if you do not waste a day. It is simple and easy. You just have to begin and there is no better time than today.

Why Create Multiple Streams of Residual Income?

If you have only one source of income then it is like standing on one leg and you are extremely unstable and vulnerable. You will be financial stable if you have multiple sources of income. If one income source dries up then it will not matter because you will have other sources of income to support you and your family.

Rich people do not depend on only one source of income but grow orchards of money trees.

The famous Nile is the longest river on planet earth; if you look down from a spacecraft orbiting the earth, you will be able see it and its two main tributaries quite clearly—it is that voluminous! But what you can't see from outer space is all of the thousands of little streams and rivers that run into the Nile: it is all that water from thousands of small streams that pour into the Nile, making it so large and invincible.

If you examine the rich you will find that their income is like the river Nile. They have several streams of income pouring in from different sources to create a huge cash flow of residual wealth.

"Prosperous people have always known...If one stream dries up, they have many more to tap into for support. So-called ordinary people are much more vulnerable. If they lose one of their streams, it wipes them out...In the future, you will need a portfolio of income streams – not one or two, but many streams from completely different and diversified sources – so that if one stream empties, you'll barely notice. You'll be stable. You will have time to adjust. You will be safe."

Multiple Residual Income Generators

Now let us examine some passive income generating opportunities. You may use one or a combination of the methods to generate passive income.

- Investors
- Real Estate investors get cash flow from rent in addition to capital gain
- Saving Account owners earn interest
- Investors in shares get dividends and appreciation
- Discount mortgagers earn interest
- Tax lien certificate holders earn interest penalties
- Debenture holders earn interest
- Businesses

- Entrepreneurs who auto pilot their businesses earn passive profits

- Franchisors get a percentage of gross revenue or profits

- Partners get share of profits

- Venture partners get percentage of profits

- Royalties

- Authors get royalties from their books and tapes

- Musicians and song writers get royalties from their work

- Visual artists get royalties from paintings

- Inventors get royalties

- Game designers get royalties

- Actors get a percentage of the profits

- Miscellaneous

- Company Pension Plans offer income flow

- Retired persons get pensions

- Network marketers build residual income through leverage

- Corporate managers get stock options

- Insurance agents get residual income from their sales

- Securities agents get residual sales

- Celebrity endorsers get a gross percentage of profits

- Mailing list owners get rental fees

The above list is not exhaustive. It is possible to automate virtually any business by putting in systems and delegating authority. It is also possible to franchise businesses for passive income or sell shares to create wealth. There are always some costs involved, but the effort is worth it because what you will create is something more powerful: you will create income streams that do not need your presence.

The trick is to let your money work for you and not you working for money. Once you start generating passive income, your money will be working for you night and day even when you sleep.

Categories of Residual Income

- For a clearer understanding, we can divide residual income into two broad categories:

- Residual Income sources that require start-up capital or additional fund to maintain and grow

- Residual income sources that require little or no start-up capital or maintenance money

The first category will need initial capital from your earned income, family money, funds from investors or borrowed funds from banks to purchase assets that will generate passive income for you. When you borrow money, you create debt, which provides you leverage to create accelerated wealth but it also comes with associated risks that can destroy your wealth.

Examples of this type of residual income will be: investing in stocks & other paper assets, real estate investments or buying businesses that have systems in place that need very little of your personal time to run the company. Another example would be that of a good franchise business like the McDonalds – It has systems in place and will need very little intervention on your part.

The second category of residual income requires very little financial out lay and is generated through assets that you create by writing a book, song, software, patent or trade mark. The internet has provided a new medium to generate residual wealth through creation of Virtual Real Estate.

Virtual Real Estate is the new gold rush and without doubt, it is the new frontier that you have to master to create residual income. The internet is creating new millionaires every minute even as you read this book. What is virtual real estate? These are the assets you create on the internet. These include your websites, domain names, email lists, online businesses, Facebook, Twitter and other social media accounts. Once you create these assets you can generate residual income from them for years.

We will discuss this at greater length.

- You can further categorize residual income into:
- Offline Residual Income
- Online Residual Income

Offline residual income generally requires more capital. You can take advantage of a variety of financial advisers and products to start investing in residual income investment schemes like paper assets and real estate. You can also get bank funding for buying these assets and hence can leverage your time and money.

On the other hand, online residual income or creation of Virtual Real Estate requires very little, and in some cases, no start-up capital. There are many online gurus but no financial advisers. Banks will not fund it because the risks are too high; it is a new frontier of wealth creation that is still in progression. It is still Wild West out there. You have to make the effort to increase your knowledge to create wealth in this new environment. There are many scam artists who will make you part with your hard-earned money on the internet. You have to be extremely careful before pulling credit card out of your wallet. There are risks but very high rewards as well. Opportunities are endless! If you make the effort of mastering the new environment, you can create large amounts of residual income with very little effort in the shortest possible time frame.

Creating residual income on the internet does not give you financial leverage but technological leverage; financial leverage creates debt with associated risks. Technological leverage, on the other hand, is debt free and faster.

The best instrument to be used to create residual income will depend upon your financial situation, time availability and state of knowledge at a given point. If you have plenty of capital and cash flow from your job or business but no time, then it will be better for you to employ services of a professional financial adviser to invest in offline assets such as real estate, stocks, bonds, CDs, commodities like gold, silver etc.

Alternatively, if you are internet savvy with little or no capital then creating a Virtual Real Estate to generate residual income may be the right choice for you. You have to also take into account your risk appetite for a particular type of investment. Your assessment of your situation is the key to making a successful choice.

Investment in Residual Income

You will need to make a significant initial investment to create a passive income, which can be in terms of money or investment in time.

Investing Time

Most time investing, passive incomes comprise of ideas that will need energy inputs as well. Generally, you will be turning your spare time into some sort of product that will provide a steady stream of income over time.

Everyone has some unique knowledge or skill that can be converted into electronic books and sold on the internet to create passive income. The beauty of life is that each one of us has a unique experience that can be shared with others in form of blogs and books. I have written a few books. These books are working for me as passive income generators. I am simply sharing my experience with others and creating value in their lives; each book that I write is a new source of passive income for me.

Publishing books was a problem earlier on as only few big authors were accepted by publishing houses, which is no longer the case. You can now self-publish a book with Kindle, Barnes and Noble, Nook etc. The options for self-publishing are getting better and better with each passing day.

You can also create blogs with the information you wish to share with others and monetize them. Once the blog is in place you will be required to spend some time developing links to it so that Google can find it. After that, your blog or website will keep generating a steady trickle of advertisement and referral revenue.

Investing Money

- If you have money to invest then you can simply invest that money into generating passive income for you. You can consider some of the following paper assets to generate passive income:

- Dividend-bearing stocks If you buy, let us say, $20,000 worth of Coca-Cola shares then you will be entitled to receive regular dividend payments that will give you passive income. Over a period, your stock will multiply and gain in value increasing your dividend payments. You should choose a very stable company that pays out a very steady dividend, this type of approach can earn a very reliable income for you. You might also want to invest in mutual funds that are indexed to spread out your investments over a large number of stocks (less risk.) I will cover more of this strategy later in the book.

- Treasury inflation-protected securities (TIPS,) are bonds that you can purchase from the government whose face value adjusts according to the rate of interest, so that when the TIPS mature, you will be able to sell it for more than the initial purchase price. TIPS return is at a very low rate but they have the advantage of being rock-solid investments that will match inflation growth when you sell them.

- Savings accounts and CDs are similar rock-solid investments. They are also very liquid (meaning you can cash out your money whenever you need it). The interest rates are generally on the lower side. There are, however, times when a savings account or CD is very solid.

- Annuities are investments you can purchase from an insurance company that will pay you a certain amount of residual income every year for the rest of your life. The younger you are, the smaller will be your contribution. Let's say, for example, that you purchase a $30,000 annuity, one that the insurance house quotes at 4%. It would mean that you would receive $1200 each year for the rest of your life from that company. The risk you have here is that the insurance company may eventually become insolvent, leaving you with nothing at all. You must therefore seek out an insurance company with a long history of stability and good bond rating. You must also diversify across multiple insurance houses.

Steps to Create Residual Income

In most cases, people start out in jobs as their primary source of income. You have to start using a part of your actively earned income into generating passive income on a regular basis. You will be surprised at how fast your residual income will grow if you start out early. Your investments will multiply if you apply the power of compounding properly. A dollar a day if invested correctly will make you a millionaire before you retire.

If you are new to the stocks and mutual funds, then I advise you to go for investing in indexed funds using Dollar Cost Averaging. This strategy gives highest returns with minimum amount of risk. Let me explain:

Indexed funds

Indexed funds are a type of mutual funds with a portfolio constructed to match or track the components of a market index, such as the Standard & Poor's 500 Index (S&P 500). An index mutual fund provides broad market exposure and low operating expenses as no fund manager is involved. The lack of active management generally gives the advantage of lower fees and lower taxes in taxable accounts. This increases your returns as an investor. It has been found that indexed funds outperform funds managed by fund managers as there is no human intervention and mistakes.

Dollar Cost Averaging

This technique involves buying a fixed dollar amount of a particular investment on a regular schedule, regardless of the share price. More shares are purchased when prices are low, and fewer shares are bought when prices are high. Eventually, the average cost per share of the security will become smaller and smaller. Dollar-cost averaging lessens the risk of investing a large amount in a single investment at the wrong time. No financial expert has been able to predict the behavior of stock market accurately.

Dollar cost averaging will reduce your risk considerably. In dollar cost averaging, you will need to decide on three parameters: the fixed amount of money invested each time, the investment frequency, and the time horizon over which all of the investments are made. The longer the time horizons, the better are the results—the minimum recommended period is 12 months.

The best way to start building residual income is to combine investing in indexed mutual funds using dollar cost averaging strategy. This way you will get the highest returns with minimum risk. Many fund managers will advise you against this strategy because they do not benefit from it. Take the human element out of investing – let the market magic work. It has shown time and again that index funds beat the performance of most fund managers. The exception to the rule is Warren Buffet! If you can find a fund manager backed with 20 years track record of beating the market then go for it … I am yet to find one.

Great Passive Income Ideas

There are hundreds of ways in which you can create passive income. Let us first look at some offline business ideas that are easy to implement.

Start a Bulk Candy Vending Business

You must have seen vending machines in cinema halls or lobby of hotels and restaurants. Have you wondered who owns these machines? Most of these machines are owned by independent business entrepreneurs who have negotiated to place the machines with the parent business owner either by paying a fixed rent or giving them share of the profits.

Vending machines business needs small initial investment; it has a very low maintenance cost and provides excellent return on investment and its success depends upon finding good secure locations.

This is an excellent way to start building your residual income if you do not have large capital or do not qualify for a loan to start buying real estate. The difficult part of this business is to find good locations and you may have to knock on several doors before you secure your first location. Once you are in business and have built a good profile, it will become relatively easy to find and secure new locations.

Network Marketing

Network marketing is perhaps the most misunderstood and the most controversial concept of passive wealth creation. It generates strong emotions. Most of us were invited to a fancy presentation and got excited with the prospect of working from home, firing our boss, no office politics or commuting to work. There was also no cap on the income potential.

The prospect of generating great amount passive income excited us as it would give us time with our families, travel the world and pursue our other fantasies. It was better than any retirement plan or job security. It could be started part-time with minimal start-up costs. There were dreams in our eyes of a better future. But then what happened? Reality broke through: we suffered rejection from our friends and families. Our recruiting drive never took off. We never saw those fancy checks coming into our bank accounts.

On the other hand, there are people generating great amounts of passive income through their efforts in network marketing. Network marketing is an industry that is experiencing an exponential growth with a turnover of billions of dollars and over 55 million distributors worldwide. It is being taught as a subject in many business schools around the globe. People like Warren Buffet and Donald Trump, who are not only some of the richest people on the planet but also have the most astute business minds, own direct selling companies.

Richard Bronson, who owns over 300 companies worldwide, is involved in network marketing. Robert Kiyosaki, the author of 'Rich Dad Poor Dad' book series and one of the greatest financial educators recommends network marketing as the 'Perfect Business' to achieve financial freedom and security. Why are these business leaders staking their name and fame to promote a business model that has generated so much debate and negativity? They believe network marketing is the wave of the future.

Many highly respected companies such as AT&T, Direct TV, Gap, Google, Macy's, Nordstrom, Travelocity, and tons more have started to borrow from the concepts of network marketing. These companies have realized that the impact of their multi-million-dollar advertising budget pales in comparison to the power of word-of-mouth advertising.

What most people do not realize is that how much the network marketing industry has evolved. Network marketing is a relationship building and mentoring business. To succeed, you have to build a network of strong relationships and train your distributors to replicate the business model. The internet has made these tasks easier as you no longer have to drive long distances to meet people and can use 'skype' or send webinar recordings to give product demonstration.

There is big residual income to be made in network marketing—make no mistakes about it, it is a low investment business model that gives huge returns if you do it properly and sustain your effort.

Set up an automated eBay Business

If you can source a reliable wholesale product, then you will have over 50 million customers on eBay to whom you will be able to market your product. You can fall into the trap of making your eBay business into a full-time day job. To create residual income, you have to automate the whole process. There are hundreds of software programs available to automate the eBay auctions.

The software will automatically start a new auction as soon as an item sells – it will do everything for you except ship the product. Even shipping of products can be outsourced to make it a complete hands-off business that generates residual income for you.

The key to success and profit from eBay business is to source the right product to sell. You can buy these products at a huge discount from eBay itself from the "Wholesale Lots" section. You can then turn around and sell them one at a time for a profit.

Online Residual Income

The internet is the new gold rush and without a doubt, it is the new frontier that you have to master in order to create residual income with minimum amount of investment of time and money. This is a revolution happening right before your eyes—new millionaires being born even as you read this book. It is just the beginning of the new wave of wealth creation. Such unique opportunity happens only once or twice in your lifetime. You will have to grab this opportunity with both hands or you will regret for rest of your life.

Why Build Residual Income on the Internet?

- The reason why you must start building residual income using the internet is because it is revolutionizing the way we think, work and shop.

- It is the most Powerful Media much bigger than television

- It is the Biggest Market Place

- It is the Most Profitable Business

- It is Getting Bigger Every Day

- Internet Business Never Stops 24 hours 365 days

- Requires Very Little Investment and hence No Risk

- It has created more Millionaires and Billionaires than any other opportunity

- It is for everyone

- You can automate your business very easily to create residual income

There was over $4000,000,000,000 generated through sales over the internet last year – this figure is growing exponentially each and every year. Even if you are able to capture 1/1,000,000 part of this business, your earnings will be $400,000 per year. How many shares are you prepared to capture?

Once you build your internet income, it will provide you with passive income and freedom of time to travel the world in style, meet people and share your ideas.

Steps to Create an Online Residual Income

Find a Way to Make Money

There are hundreds of ways to make money on the Internet. Your aim is to find a business that can be automated easily.

Some of the methods you can use are:

Affiliate Marketing

This is passive income derived from setting up a niche blog or website that presells a company's products; you provide reviews and information that drives traffic to your affiliate link and you get paid by the company if someone buys the product from your affiliate link. The trick is to find products that are not only popular but pay good recurring commissions. This will create a monthly residual income for you once a sale is made. One such example is: selling a monthly subscription to a membership site. You could also find products that pay multitier commissions and get paid if your affiliate makes a sale.

You must also look at the sales page of the product you are promoting. If the sales page of the product you are promoting is not a good one, then your conversion rate will be poor. This means that if you refer 1000 visitors to a sales page through preselling on your website and only a handful convert, then your effort will be in vain. If a sales page converts well then you will make more money for the same amount of effort.

Information Products

People search the internet to find information or solution to their problems. They may be looking for information on weather, health issues, travel information, holiday destinations, cheap tickets, relationship problems, how to make money or how to fix a problem. Human appetite for information is insatiable. They also come on the internet for socializing, fun and recreation. You can create information products to satisfy these needs. You can create a software, report or a book to help them solve their problems and sell it on the internet.

- What are the Benefits of Creating an e-Book?

- Low cost – The cost of creating an e-Book is extremely low. Once you set up the website with a good sales page, you can make sales 24 hours, 7 days a week for years to come. You can also take advantage of Clickbank or self-publishing platforms like Amazon to market your books.

- Books are Easy to Create – All you need is an e-Book creation software. You can create a short report or a book in a few days. A large book may take a few months or years to write. It is better to create short e-Books of 30–40 pages with no fluff. You must write a book to the point and on subjects that people are searching on the internet.

- Add an Affiliate Program – It is easy to add an affiliate program to increase sales of your book by sharing the sales revenue with people who promote your book. This will greatly increase your residual income.

- Promote Affiliate Links - You can promote affiliate links of related products from within the book to increase your residual income even further. In this book, I have added links to some of my website and other books that are not only relevant but will also provide value addition the reader of the book.

- Resale Rights – You can charge a fee for allowing resale rights to people. Once they buy the resale rights, they will be able to sell the book and keep 100% of the profits. The advantage to you in this arrangement is that you get to keep the affiliate links inside the books and if a sale takes place then you get to keep the profits.

- Free E-Books – Anything free on the internet gets downloaded very fast and goes viral. Writing a free e-Book with affiliate links inside the book is a great way of creating residual income. It is so convenient that you will not be able to stop your residual income even if you want to stop it once your e-Book goes viral.

Note – Writing books establishes you as a knowledgeable leader in your field. There are spinoffs such as speaking assignments, consulting and TV shows. As your fandom shoots up, you can recommend related products and earn affiliate income by sending emails to your client base.

You can also convert your eBooks into printed books, audios & videos for additional income.

By being smart, work done once can result in multiple streams of income.

Creating Software Products/ Applications

You don't have to be a software engineer to create a software product. All you need is a great idea of what people want to do faster and easier.

The best example is Bill Gates who created the Windows Operating System. Everyone who has a PC needs it—you could do the same on a smaller scale.

Once you have an idea, you can go to a software developer to develop that product for you. If you don't know any software engineer to execute the job, then you can go to elance.com or guru.com and post your requirement. Software developers will give their quotes and you can hire one of them after determining their credentials.

You get paid to solve problems. The bigger the problem your software can solve, more you can charge people. Start by solving small problems and then graduate to developing software for more complex problems.

There are plenty of problems in this world that need solving. I am a real estate investor and I use software for analyzing properties, accounting for my properties, calculating depreciation rates, making presentations to the bank for getting loans, analyzing cost of mortgage, managing tenants & checking if rents are paid. I pay for the software which someone has developed. I need this software for saving time.

Some of the software I use does not have the functions that I need. Here is an opportunity for me to create new software with enhanced functions that will help other property investors who are facing similar problems.

If you look into your daily life you will be able to analyze what functions you need to automate to reduce your workload. You can develop software to automate those functions and market it. But before you start developing software, check in the market place if such software with the functions you need is available otherwise you will be reinventing the wheel.

Creating software will not give you a residual income – you will have to learn the skill to market the software. Clickbank is a great place to start because it is a market place where you can recruit hundreds if not thousands of affiliates to promote your software product on profit sharing basis.

Advertising Income from Websites/ Blogs

You can generate residual advertising income from your website once you have organic traffic coming from search engines. You can offer advertising or banner space to various advertisers for a fee or revenue sharing. Some great programs on the internet are : Google AdSense, Info link, Chitika, etc. You can earn decent income from your videos by posting them on YouTube on revenue sharing from advertisements.

Create a niche website with great content and build backlinks so that search engines not only find your website but also rank you high in the search engines, which will drive traffic to your website. Your residual income will increase in direct proportion of the traffic to your website.

You can also generate advertising income by allowing placement of ads in your Newsletters or E-zines and e-Books.

You can use material from your blog to create eBooks and videos. The trick is to create original, unique content that provides value to your visitors. If your content is not original or does not provide quality information to help solve problems, then this will not work. You don't have to be a great writer – just write from your heart. There so many fake people on the internet and they fail because they are not genuine. Creating residual income takes effort and time in the beginning but it is worth your effort. You have to master the medium and that takes a bit of time.

Create Membership Site

You can create a membership site and charge a monthly membership fee for accessing information on your website if you are an expert in a field. People will pay for your knowledge, resources you offer and the support you provide. The more members you gain the more residual income you make. You can increase membership of your site by offering an affiliate program wherein you share your monthly revenue with people who bring in new members to your site.

Because you are an expert in your field, you can also recommend other affiliate products and services to your members, from which you earn commissions.

There are excellent software programs on the internet that will help you create a membership site in days.

Pay Per Click Campaigns

You can earn a good passive income by setting up a Pay per Click campaign using Facebook, Google AdWords, YouTube or Instagram for some high paying popular affiliate products that are in demand. Once you set up a campaign successfully, you can generate excellent passive income from it. I will not recommend this program for a newbie on the internet who does not have good knowledge of marketing using paid advertising. You can lose a lot of money if the campaign is not set up correctly or you don't have the understanding of analytics of monitoring your return on investment.

Before jumping into PPC AdWords, you should take the trouble of educating yourself on how to set up a successful campaign. There are several great books and training videos on the subject. Take the trouble of educating yourself before spending your hard-earned money. When starting out, you should experiment with a small budget. Once a campaign is successful and starts generating profits, you can scale up to increase your budget and your profits. Once you set up the campaign properly, it can generate residual income for you with very little monitoring. You scale your budget and increase your profits progressively.

I have covered only a few strategies of generating residual income on the internet. These are not exhaustive and will change as the internet evolves. Email marketing can be a source of passive income once you have created a large email subscriber list. There is very little investment required to generate residual income on the internet and hence, there is very little risk. It also gives you time and movement flexibility. You can operate and monitor your business from anywhere in the world where there is an internet connection. In addition, the whole world is your market place. You can sell your product anywhere around the globe.

It takes time and effort to master this medium but once you get it right, there is minimum amount of effort involved in generating passive income of your dreams. Most people fail because they tend to lose focus and jump from one opportunity to another. When it comes to the internet, one can get distracted easily because it has so much to offer in terms of information, entertainment and social interaction.

Action Steps to Create Passive Income Online

I have discussed various residual income opportunities but nothing will come of them if you don't take action. You have to do independent research based on your knowledge and passion. Find a business that is best suited for your temperament and situation. You can convert your knowledge and passion into dollars. Don't fake it, be real. Each one of us is born with some unique talent and we experience life in a manner that is unique to us – we have to share this unique experience with others to earn money on the internet.

Next, you must find a business model to share your unique knowledge, talent and experience. Focus on a business opportunity that can be automated. Buy the best product that teaches you the technique, then simply focus and don't stop till the money starts to flow in.

The Dreaded Product Life Cycle (PLC)

- Every product or business has what's known as a "Product Life Cycle." Each and every product or business goes through the following four phases:

- Market introduction stage

- Growth stage

- Maturity stage

- Saturation and decline stage

What effect this has on your effort to create residual income? Your residual income source is either growing or dying. Some residual income steams will last through your lifetime but some may dry up prematurely – it is great to enjoy the benefits of a residual income stream for the period it lasts. But eventually outside factors will decrease the profits. Eventually, every residual income stream that you create will go away forever. Nothing lasts forever: it is the law of life.

I am a great believer in the power of residual income—but one has to be a realist. Eventually, the residual income flow you create will disappear, which is why it is important to create multiple sources of residual income. If you create large number of income streams they will be in different phases of growth, maturity and saturation stage. All your income streams will not dry out at once. Your cash flow will continue uninterrupted.

Even as you are enjoying the benefits of one residual income stream, you should be in search of new residual income streams. These are known as "**growth activities**." Once you create a residual income stream, its maintenance will take very little of your time. You have to use your time creatively by engaging in growth activities to multiply your residual income streams.

"The key to wealth and happiness in today's world is to create multiple streams of income using diverse models and combination of passive and active income in areas where your passions and talents can be most thoroughly engaged."

Problems in Creating Multiple Streams of Income

The concept of creating financial security through multiple streams of residual income is very appealing; you diversify your investment and business risk. However, when people jump into trying to build multiple streams of income without adequate preparation or thought, reality hits their face. The idea may be great but the problem lies in its successful implementation. Instead of creating a relaxed lifestyle, they get sucked into a situation where they have to become hyperactive in trying to control and maintain their residual income sources.

The reality is that we live in a highly competitive and fast changing world. To succeed in any business – you need highly specialized knowledge. It is extremely difficult to compete in widely varying fields without adequate skilled knowledge.

"It is better to have a permanent income than to be fascinating"

— Oscar Wilde

We are also limited by time to be able to implement different business strategies. There is a pressing need to balance our family, health, relationships, recreation and spiritual needs. Happiness lies in balancing our needs correctly rather than focusing only on one aspect of life. Financial security is extremely important but it must not be allowed to dominate every aspect of our lives.

Financial success comes from focused attention on one specific outcome. The effort in creating multiple streams of income diffuses your focus and creates extraordinary demands on your limited time. It can cause undue strain and stress on your life; your chances of failure increase in proportion to your defused focus. In order to succeed in creating multiple streams of residual income, you have to learn to reconcile two seemingly contradictory realities: how to focus and how to create multiple streams of income at the same time.

Most people find it extremely difficult to build one stream of residual income successfully during their lifetime. How can they be expected to create multiple streams of income? Let us examine this idea a bit further.

Is Creating Multiple Streams of Income the Right Strategy for You?

- Creating multiple streams of income is not suitable for everyone. You must ask yourself the following questions to check if the strategy is right for you:

- Do you have the right knowledge and experience?

- Do you know the principles of time and technology leverage?

- Do you have any previous business or investing experience?

- Do you have a team of experts who can advise and assist you to create multiple streams of income?

- How important are multiple streams of income to you? Are you ready to commit your time and energy to creating multiple streams of residual income?

Remember that each income stream you create will need its own set of skills, expertise and experience. It will make demands on your time, energy and resources. You will need to pay a price in creating each multiple income stream…are you willing to pay the price?

The Wrong Way to Create Multiple Streams of Residual Income

The wrong way to create multiple streams of income is to get all fired up and start buying stocks, investing in real estate or jumping into internet businesses without any knowledge or preparation. This is a sure way to failure because you will spread your resources thin and cause undue strain on your system.

You have to learn to walk first and then run or you will fall flat on your face. When you are in the game of money, you can destroy your wealth quickly because in each field of wealth creation, you will be competing against experts. These people live and breathe in the space they have created. You will need to become an expert before you can compete successfully.

It is fairly simple to create multiple streams of income if you go about it systematically. It is a tough game but it can be made simple if you take the trouble of learning the ropes.

It is not a smart strategy to take undue risk. You can eliminate risk only through acquisition of the right skills and knowledge, and if you don't have that knowledge, then you should either be willing to pay for that knowledge or team-up with people who have the expertise.

The Right Way to Create Multiple Streams of Residual Income

You can maximize your chances of success by taking the following steps:

Step 1: Become an Expert in One Stream

Select your first income stream with great care; it should be based in a field that you have knowledge in and are passionate about. Broad categories such as: real estate, business, paper assets or internet income are present for taking, however, it will be difficult for you to master a broad category. Within each category, there are sub-categories. For instance, in real estate, you can become an expert in - apartment flats or buildings, single family homes, foreclosure properties, retail shops, industrial properties, office flats or buildings, motels, hotels, buying rundown buildings and making improvements, flipping properties, etc.—the list is endless. Each subcategory requires its own skills. Apart from sub-categories, you have to become an expert in one city or locality.

Step 2: Systemize the First Income Stream

Once you have created your first income stream, you must automate your income stream so that it does not require intervention on day-to-day basis. There will be some maintenance required but if you put proper systems into place, then the time required for maintenance can be minimized.

There is a saying that goes, "you must find a jockey first, before buying a business."

You will need either good managers or technology to automate your business operations to create residual income for you. You have to find the right managers, business systems and also invest in right technology to back them up.

You have to master the skills of systemizing your business and investments in order to generate income streams that do not require your presence.

Step 3: Leverage Your First Income to Create Additional Streams of Residual Income

Remember: your first income stream is the most important one because you are going to leverage your knowledge and resources from this stream to build other income streams.

Once you have systemized your first income stream, you will free up your time to create a second residual income stream. The second residual income stream you create has to be intelligently leveraged out of knowledge, skills and experience gained out of the first income stream. Do not try and create a totally new income stream.

The second income stream may just be a repeat process of the first income stream. You can now make improvements based on your experience in creating the first income stream. You will also need lesser time, effort and money because of your experience. The returns from your second income stream will normally be much higher than your first venture.

Repeat the process again and again till market conditions do not change. Once you hit on a successful residual income formula, just keep refining and repeating it. Creating residual income can at times be a very boring process however; the money part is certainly very exciting. Be warned: the human mind seeks excitement! It will ask you to try out new ventures and divert your resources from the project that is creating new multiple streams of income. You have to resist this temptation and remain focused on repeating and maximizing your success formula.

A stage will come when you will need to branch out and create new streams of residual income because you can't risk putting your entire income source in one basket. This should be done without changing your field of expertise.

Robert Kiyosaki, bestselling author of "Rich Dad Poor Dad", got out of the rat race through real estate before adding paper assets and leveraging the financial knowledge he gained from his investment business experience into a successful information publishing business.

Robert G Allen got out of the rat race through paper assets before leveraging his investing knowledge into real estate, and then re-leveraging that same skillset into information publishing business.

There is a pattern to creating multiple streams of residual income from the successful examples I have quoted above. You have to learn the base skills in one stream and leverage those skills later to create additional streams. You have to learn to walk with one stream before running with multiple streams of residual income. You have to leverage your existing resources. This concept, in the corporate merger world, is known as 'operating efficiencies.' It takes less effort to operate each additional stream of income because they are all built upon the same foundational resources.

If you attempt to create multiple income streams by taking on different fields of activity, you will be creating mayhem instead of leveraging your resources; it is the sure route to failure. If you follow a step-by-step process as outlined in this book, you will maximize your odds of success.

- Practical Steps to Creating Multiple Streams of Residual Income

- Make a Schedule. Take some time out each day to create residual income. You have to shift from the linear income trap to creating a residual income that will someday grow more than your job income. You will not be able to achieve this in a single day – it will take time. Make small changes to your daily schedule to incorporate time for creating some residual income. Devote more time each day towards creating residual income, as your residual income increases and dependence on linear income goes down. You can only succeed if you target achievable goals, make a schedule and remain focused.

- Know the Difference between Maintenance Work and Growth Work. There is no such thing as a totally passive income. Every passive income will have some maintenance work. It may not require your day-to-day involvement but monitoring of work will be needed. Even as you carry out maintenance work, you should be on the lookout for new growth opportunities. Growth work creates multiple income streams.

- Engage in Only One Growth Activity at a Time. There is no point dissipating your energy on several growth opportunities simultaneously—you will inch slowly towards these opportunities. It is better to focus on one growth opportunity at a time; creating a successful residual income from it before moving on to another growth activity.

- You will make money more efficiently by following this simple strategy without overwhelming yourself: let us say, you have 4 growth projects that will take one week each to execute. If you start all of them simultaneously, it will take you four weeks to complete the projects. If you follow this strategy, you will have residual income coming from your projects after 4 weeks. Now let us say that you decide to take one project at a time. On completion of the first week, you will have one income stream bringing in residual income. At the end of the second week, another stream of income will go online and so forth. This is a far superior strategy as you will start generating residual income much quicker without stressing or overwhelming yourself. This is a very simplistic example because it takes much more than a week to start creating a residual income stream.

- The More the Merrier. The more residual income streams you create more financial security you will have. Small trickles will result into a stream and small streams will result into a river someday. Don't discount the little ones. A website may pay you $50 in a year, which is fine as long as it does not take your precious time in maintenance. Your passive income sources can be shares, government bonds, mutual funds, interest earned from bank accounts, blogs, affiliate sales, email marketing, royalties from book sales, etc. Each of these can create a small residual income stream for you.

- Not all Passive Income Streams are Worthwhile. Not all remaining income streams are equal. Some may require more maintenance effort than others. You may need selling some of your income streams if they become irksome. I sell my properties that are difficult to manage or have very little cash flow. By selling, I create time for myself and redeploy the capital into something that can generate better residual income for me.

- Don't Burn Bridges. You might push aside certain income stream to generate higher efficiency—it does not mean that you should turn off the tap altogether. Keep monitoring an income stream by visiting it periodically. If the circumstances and economic conditions change then, you should be in a position to take advantage of that income stream.

- Quickest Method of Creating Residual Income is Buying Paper Assets. If you have some capital sitting idle, then buy paper assets that generate the highest rate of return – it is the Warren Buffet formula. You buy an asset for cash flow. The capital gain will happen if the asset you have purchased has proper management behind it.

- Generate Multiple Streams of Income Online. The Internet is the fastest and easiest way to generate multiple streams of residual income with the least amount of investment and risk; it is effortless to automate your online business. Why most people fail to generate income online is because it is relatively easier to create a website but challenging to drive traffic to it. Without traffic, there are no sales – traffic is the life blood of online residual income. You have to master traffic techniques before you can create a successful online business. So spend some time, effort and money in learning how to generate traffic. Once you master traffic skills, then creating multiple streams of income on the internet will become relatively more straightforward.

Final Thoughts

I cannot over emphasize the importance of making a shift from linear income – where you trade your hours for money – towards creating a residual income where money and systems work for you day in and day out regardless of your presence; it is perhaps the most important secret of wealth creation. If you carry one message from this book, it is that creating residual income is the most important step towards gaining financial freedom.

Creating multiple streams of residual income is a step further and a very desirable objective, provided you implement the strategy properly. With little effort, you can leverage your existing resources and knowledge to create additional revenue streams. There will be challenges along the way as you will need to shift your thinking and acquire new skills. You will radiate with joy and confidence when you see small streams of income joining to become a full flow of residual cash, which will bring prosperity to your family and loved ones for generations to come.

Real Estate as Basis of Residual Income

Once you have built some capital through the strategies mentioned in this commandment, you must start investing in real estate. Why must you invest in property? This is because real estate investment has produced more self-made millionaires in history than any other instrument of investment. We shall discuss this in depth in the next commandment because this is the mother of all residual incomes, but so few understand it completely.

Thou Shalt Invest in Property

"Ninety percent of all millionaires become so through owning real estate."

— Andrew Carnegie

Why Invest in Real Estate?

To understand the power of real estate investing, you have to first understand the 'Why' of real estate. It is the 'Why' that will provide you the motivation and the energy to invest in real estate. Once you are convinced that real estate is one of the best vehicles of wealth creation, understanding the 'How' becomes easy.

"Real estate is an imperishable asset, ever increasing in value. It is the most solid security that human ingenuity has devised. It is the basis of all security and about the only indestructible security."

— Russell Sage

Most people who lack an understanding of real estate will tell you that investing in shares gives you better returns than those that come from real estate. There are others who say that renting is cheaper than buying your own house. You have to understand how real estate compares with other investment avenues such as savings account, shares/stocks, commodities and businesses.

Rate of Return

Return on investment (ROI) is definitely one of the most important criteria you should consider whilst making an investment decision. However, simplistic calculations based on yields can be very misleading.

Yield, by definition, is the ratio of annual income generated by the investment divided by the dollar amount of investment.

Rate of return should be considered after taking into account the risk involved: is the investment is inflation adjusted? Is there any capital growth on the principal invested? Does the investment provide tax benefits and is it possible to leverage your money to get higher returns?

Real estate investments – as compared to bank deposits – are definitely superior in terms of yield and capital appreciation. Savings in banks do not provide hedge against inflation and your money depreciates in value over a period of time.

Shares and stocks are perceived to have higher returns than property and provide hedge against inflation, but they are pale in comparison to real estate when you take into account the leveraging power of real estate investing and tax advantages of property. It is possible to buy properties by using Other People's Money (OPM) with returns that are 20–100 percent, or more per annum.

Financial Leverage

No one has ever become rich without applying the power of leverage—as stated in an earlier commandment.

Financial leverage in the investment world comes from the use of OPM or Other People's Money. In real estate investing, we buy property on a 10% down payment and yet we control 100% of real estate.

For example, let us say we buy a property of $100,000 on $10,000 down payment. Let us assume that the rent from the property covers the mortgage payments and the outgoings. If the price of property moves up by 10% over the year, the market value will increase to $110,000. This means that we would have made a profit of $10,000 on our investment of $10,000, which is a 100% return on investment and was made possible only because of the power of leverage.

Our return on investment would have been infinite had we bought the property with no down payment. This kind of financial leverage is only possible if you invest in real estate. But before you rush to buy your property with no money down, you must understand how leverage works. There is no greater leverage in life than the leverage of knowledge.

It is extremely difficult to finance other types of investments such as stock and businesses because funding is always an issue. Banks love property because of the low risk and capital appreciation associated with real estate.

Leverage can be used for quick wealth creation. If you know how to use leverage, you do not need large amounts of initial capital to start your real estate investment portfolio.

Buy Below Market Value

You must have heard the saying: ***"you make money when you buy,"*** and not at the time of selling. Is it possible to buy stocks or diamonds, commodity or gold below value? When you buy $100,000 worth of stock, you pay $100,000 in cash.

Investing in real estate after gaining a bit of knowledge, you can buy properties that are 10 or 20 percent, or even more below market value. There are many reasons why people sell their properties below value. You can amass great wealth by simply buying property below market value.

Increase Value of Investment

Can you increase the value of your stock or bank deposit by tinkering with it? There is simply no mechanism by which you can increase the value of your stock or any other investment because you do not control them. However, you can greatly increase the market value of your investment property by spending a small amount of money on making cosmetic changes or applying for a change in the use of property or zoning.

Investment Risk

Banks are perceived to have the least risk when compared to other investments but of late this confidence has been shattered due to the high rate of failure of banks.

Stocks carry a much higher risk because their values fluctuate on a minute to minute basis. Stocks also do not go up in value, and business disasters – like Enron – can have a nasty effect on your stock market wealth plan.

Investing in businesses can be very profitable if you know what you are doing. The failure rate of new start-up businesses is around 80%. In business, you invest in people and ideas which are usually not as solid as bricks and mortars.

Property, on the other hand, goes up in value slowly and steadily. This is proven by the record of past 300 hundred years when property values have consistently doubled every 8 to 12 years. In the market crash of 2008-2009, when the stocks nosedived to 50–80% of their value and wiped out the fortunes of millions of people—real estate prices went down by 5-30% of their value.

If you wish to understand risks, then just check what banks are willing to lend their money for – are they willing to loan money to buy paintings, antiques, diamonds, mutual funds, CDs, commodities, stocks & businesses? If so, what level of funding is available? For properties, banks will easily lend to 70-90% and in some cases, even 100% of the value. Banks are the most risk adverse institutions and if they are willing to invest in real estate up to 100% of value, then they consider the investment risk to be extremely low when compared to other investments. You should take your cue from banks.

Control over Investment

When you invest in stocks, you have no control over your investment until and unless you have the controlling shares in a company. You can hand over your money to a fund manager but you still do not have any control, and are at mercy of the competence or incompetence of the fund manager.

Shakespeare rightly said, "***Fool and his money are soon parted.***" There are many Madoffs in this world waiting to rip you off your hard earned money.

Invest in real estate and you have full control over your assets. You are not at someone else's mercy—you control the shots and have peace of mind.

Real Estate Investing is forgiving to Mistakes

In every investment decision you make, there are chances of making mistakes. No one has a crystal ball that can predict the future. When compared to other vehicles of investment, real estate is very forgiving to mistakes. Property prices tend to increase relatively smoothly and consistently. The rise in property price will cover any mistake you make. Real estate investment is the simplest, most reliable and most consistent vehicle of wealth creation. You can convert even a little bit of financial IQ into lot of cold hard cash. And above all, you have total control over your investment and assets. There are no Madoffs who can run away with your hard earned money.

Real Estate Offers Exceptional Tax Advantages

The biggest expense in your lifetime is the taxes you pay to the government: I must repeat once again! You will find that you pay more than 50% of your earnings to the government in the form of taxes. Most people are not even aware of how much they pay because some taxes are indirect taxes.

The rich are rich because they pay little or no taxes. If you are smart, you can do the same and fund your lifestyle and investments by saving on the taxes.

Real estate tax laws differ from one country to another. However, universally applied tax principles throughout the world hugely favor those who invest in properties. As opposed to other investments, you can run your property investment as a business and claim back depreciation, interest payments and other expenses as a part of your business.

It is sufficient to say that tax refunds from real estate investments provide you with additional cash flow to buy more investment properties and create residual income.

In case of stocks and shares, you have very little or no tax benefits and have to pay tax on interest and dividends received. Governments at times give incentives when you invest in certain types of infrastructure bonds or mutual funds. These normally offer very low returns and many times do not justify investing in these instruments even after taking tax breaks on offer; this unique advantage makes investing in real estate very attractive when compared to other investment opportunities.

Monitoring Your Investment

Unlike other investments, you do not have to monitor your real estate investment from moment to moment like a hawk—there is peace of mind.

The whole point of investing is to create multiple streams of residual income that can fund your lifestyle. There is no fun if you have to monitor your investment on an hourly or daily basis, which is the case with investments in stocks, foreign currency or commodities, the values of which change constantly. You have to watch these investments like a hawk if you have to succeed.

Property prices tend to move very slowly, smoothly and constantly with minimum amount of fluctuations. This makes it very easy to monitor your real estate investment.

Invest in real estate and you will have the most passive and hands-free of all available investments opportunities.

Fluctuations to National Average

The price of each stock fluctuates on its own merit and there are numerous imponderable variables that dictate the price of a stock. It is therefore very difficult to monitor every stock in your portfolio because each one is very different from the other. It requires a genius of Warren Buffet's caliber to beat the market averages consistently. Even expert fund managers struggle to keep up with market averages.

In the case of real estate, fluctuations of any one property relative to the national average are very low. It requires very little expertise to beat the national average for property and increase your return on investment.

Real Estate is without doubt the safest way to create long-term residual income.

Cash Flow from Property Investment

Many people buy property with the hope of creating passive cash flow in hopes of retiring peacefully. Sometimes, they get disappointed because their properties do not generate adequate cash flow to retire even after they have bought 5 to 10 properties. The problem arises because they buy negatively geared properties that are highly leveraged. In order to create residual income, you have to buy cash flow properties and reduce your mortgage over a period of time.

Properties take time to create residual income. As time goes by the prices and rents go up: these two factors will increase your equity and cash flow. You can also convert equity into cash flow to create residual income.

Also do not confuse property flipping, forex, commodity or share trading as instruments for creating residual income. These are nothing but full-time jobs with little or no chance of building an asset or generating residual cash flow. These activities are nothing but skill-based jobs in which you have to work full-time to make money. They may be great strategies for generating cash flow but cannot be termed as investments for creating residual income.

I hope you are convinced by now that real estate is the perhaps the best vehicle to generate long-term passive income – it is solid and time tested. We shall now examine some of the fundamental principles of real estate investing.

Real Estate Investing - Basic Principles

The most common mistake while investing in property is that people buy with their emotions. They buy in the wrong place for all the wrong reasons.

They buy property based on:

- Opinion of people who have no knowledge of investing

- In a place they were born

- They love to buy in places they like to holiday

- Buy in a place where they may like to retire

Does this sound familiar to you?

Although local knowledge is an important factor when buying real estate, this should not limit your options and restrict you to areas that you are familiar with.

You must never buy a property based on emotional reasons! If you wish to succeed with investing in property, you need to make logical decisions based on sound principles of real estate investing.

You can use different strategies in real estate to grow your portfolio. These include investing in rental apartments, single family homes, industrial property, retail real estate, office space, hospitality or overseas properties. You can also gain expertise in lease options, investing in off plan property or buying at foreclosure sale. But these can never replace the fundamental principles of real estate investing.

There can be various strategies but the principles of real estate investing are eternal.

There are many experienced investors who become overconfident and violate these principles—they invariably suffer grave consequences. So please take time to study the following fundamental principles of real estate investing with care.

'Buy and Hold' will Make You Rich

Always remember that you buy property for capital appreciation. Real estate first and foremost is a capital business. Rent and cash flow are important to help you own the property for long term.

"Don't wait to buy real estate, buy real estate and wait."

— Will Rogers (1935)

Investing means owning real estate for long term. Flipping properties and lease options strategies are used to generate cash to fund your long-term investments and should not be confused with the long-term goal of creating wealth through capital appreciation.

Real Estate is not a get-rich-quick scheme; capital appreciation happens over a period of time. You have to have patience, perseverance and persistence. For this, you have to understand the compounding power of real estate investing.

How many times investors have sold their property for peanuts only to realize a few years later that they would have made a fortune had they had the patience and wisdom to hold it a bit longer.

Please remember the times you have cursed your ancestors for selling a piece of real estate that would have changed your financial future and of the generations to come.

If you can help, never ever sell your property: this is one fundamental principle of real estate investing you should never forget.

'Cash flow' Funds Your Real Estate Business and Gives You Peace of Mind

When I started out in real estate, there were no books or real estate investment seminars. My mentor was a rustic real estate agent who gave me one great piece advice that has stuck in my mind for the past three decades. His advice was very straightforward: "***Only buy***

Cows that give milk." This one advice has kept me out of trouble in downturns in the property cycle and made me a successful investor.

It is cash flow that funds your lifestyle and gives you peace of mind. The happiest times of my life have been those when I was flush with money to pay my bills, take holidays and meet all my financial commitments. My worst nightmares came when I was low on cash flow to meet my mortgage requirements even when I owned millions of dollars' worth of real estate in my portfolio.

The main reasons why people get into trouble, have foreclosure sales and become bankrupt are that they fail to understand and monitor their cash flow.

You should subscribe to Warren Buffet's philosophy of investing for cash flow: whether you buy real estate or stocks … buy only for cash flow. Capital gain will happen over a period of time with any good investment and cash flow, in the meantime, will help you fund your life style and keep you and your banks happy.

Never buy 'negatively geared' properties. A negatively geared property is a property wherein rent received from the tenant does not cover expenses related to the property such as mortgage payments, maintenance charges, rates, insurance, property management costs etc. There is no fun in buying properties that you will need to fund from your pocket on a monthly basis. There are many property gurus who will teach you to buy 'negatively geared' properties to avail tax refunds. This is plain and simple stupid—keeps away from such gurus.

How many properties can you buy if you have to keep supporting them from your hard earned money? What will happen if the interest rates go up, you lose your job or fall ill? Will you be able to continue supporting these properties? Always buy 'positively geared' properties that put cash into your pocket after paying all the expenses including mortgage payments.

Buy land only if you have adequate cash flow from other sources. Otherwise, stay away from land investments as they have little or no cash flow. Most people who got into trouble during the crash of 2008 - 2009 were investors with large land holdings or with negatively geared properties in their portfolios. When the market went down, they could not sell their properties even at a discount, resulting in mortgagee sales and bankruptcies. Stick with rental property investments that are cash cows and you will never go wrong.

Remember the good old saying, ***"Buy cows that give milk***." This is the secret mantra to success in real estate and will keep you out of trouble when things go wrong.

Do the Math

Real estate investing has nothing to do with emotions. It is only numbers that matter. When you buy a house to live in, there are emotions involved: you have to have the comfort level, practicality and pride of ownership. Your house reflects your personality and provides security and warmth to your family.

Real estate investing is all about getting your numbers right. It is about yields on purchase price or market value and capitalization rates. You have to understand terms such as Market Value, Cash on Cash Return, Internal Rate of Return and Deposit Re-cycling Time. I have explained these terms at the end of the book (Refer Appendix 2). They may sound difficult at first, but are relatively easier to understand once you start applying them.

You have to take into account mortgage financing costs, out goings or cash deductions to work out pre-tax cash flows. And finally, you have to take into account the depreciation and other tax refunds to work out the after tax cash flow.

It is not humanly possible for anyone to work out these figures manually when you are comparing, let us say, five prospective properties to buy one. Fortunately, we have real estate investing software's and investment property calculators to help us in getting all the figures we need to make an invest decision.

If you concentrate on the numbers, it will be easier for you to **keep your emotions out** when buying an investment property.

To do the math is very important but you have to temper the mathematical outcome with subjective analysis and human judgment with regard to quality of construction, location, quality of the tenant and lease terms. You should never get carried away by numbers alone but subject them to your common sense judgment.

Location Location Location

If the location of your property is right you will never have problems in finding tenants. There is no point in buying a property that shows a great rate of return on paper but has high vacancy rates. Many investors fall prey to not taking into account the vacancy factor and get carried away in purchasing properties that show high yields.

The property you buy should be in the right demographic area where employment and population are on the rise. Once you have found the right geographic area focus further on neighborhoods that are close to places of employment, shopping centers, schools and transportation centers.

If the location is right, you will have capital growth because of demand.

People often question me, "If the location is so great, then the price of the property will increase because of a high demand and will pull down the rate of return, which will inevitably have an adverse impact on the cash flow from the property, won't it? Although there is some merit in this argument, astute investors will find ways and means to add value and increase cash flow by making improvements to the property.

Always Buy From a Motivated Seller

You make money in real estate when you buy. Even if you master the best skills, it is virtually impossible to sell a property above market value until and unless you find a really stupid buyer, which is rare. To make instant money in real estate, you have to buy below the market value, which can only be done through buying a property from a motivated seller. If a person has no motivation to sell then you will never be able to negotiate a great bargain price.

It is not unethical to buy property below its actual value. Selling at a low price becomes desirable when people wish to dispose of their property because of various reasons, which could be due to some urgent financial need. Property is an excellent investment but, at times, difficult to liquidate. You solve the vendor's problem by coming to their aid with immediate cash. If cash problems are not solved, banks can take over the property and they may lose everything.

There can be many reasons why vendors want urgent settlement and cash. Some of the reasons can be vendor going overseas on a lucrative assignment, divorce with couples wanting to separate move on with their lives, illness or death in a family requiring funds, business needs that require urgent injection of capital. While investing in real estate, you have to understand the vendor's problems and try and solve them in a way that it can work to the parties' advantage.

You can accumulate great wealth quickly by simply learning the art of finding motivated sellers and purchasing below market value. Supposing you buy a million dollar property for $900,000 – which is 10% below market value – if you are able to achieve that then you have created an instant wealth of $100,000.

Use Other People's Money (OPM) to Fund Your Real Estate

No one has ever become rich by using their personal money. Sooner than later, individuals and companies run out of money to fund their growth. You have to learn how to use Other People's Money or OPM to grow your net worth.

The business of banks is to use other people's money to make profits. They borrow from you and loan it to businesses at a higher interest rate to make money. You should think like a bank and borrow at reasonable cost of finance to fund your real estate business for much higher profits.

Real estate provides you with a great opportunity to use financial leverage to grow your wealth. Banks and other financial institutions love to finance real estate. The only way you can accelerate your growth is by using OPM and using financial leverage sensibly.

You have to insure that returns from the real estate investment are greater than the cost of borrowed funds.

Make Use of the Property Cycle

> *"Be fearful when others are greedy and be greedy only when others are fearful."*
>
> — Warren Buffett

Property Cycle, unlike stock prices, is very slow moving and comparatively easier to understand.

The easiest option for you is to buy real estate at the bottom of the cycle—but in real life, things are not so simple else everyone would be rich. The bottom of the property market is difficult to predict.

> *"Buy when everyone else is selling and hold until everyone else is buying. This is not merely a catchy slogan. It's the very essence of successful investment."*
>
> — J. Paul Getty (1976)

If you will wait for the property cycle to bottom out (which is hard to predict,) then you will be able to buy properties only once in seven to ten years and you will miss out on all the other opportunities that happen in other parts of the property cycle.

In real estate, you make money either through Cash flow, Capital Growth or Equity. These are known as the three corners of the property triangle. You will rarely be able to achieve all three at a particular stage in the property cycle. For instance, when the property prices are regressing, you cannot buy real estate for capital growth but it is an opportune time to buy properties below market value and create instant equity—which is better than waiting for capital growth. At the bottom of the cycle, you will be able to buy properties that give high cash flow as the prices are down and return on investment much better.

The beauty of property cycle is that it is very slow moving; you will get ample warning signs on things to come if you are not blinded by greed and emotions.

Negotiate Everything

If you are to be successful in real estate, you have to negotiate everything whether it is the price of the property, rent and lease terms with your tenants, mortgage rates with the banks, property management contracts or repairs, and upgradation costs with the traders.

Every time you negotiate, you save money and improve your chances of success. For example: by negotiating a 0.2% lower interest rate on a 30 year mortgage loan with your bank, you can save hundreds of thousands of dollars over the lifetime of the loan.

Everything in business is negotiable. If someone tells you otherwise, the person is a fool. Please stay away from him! Real estate negotiation is one skill that you have to master to become successful.

Learn to Walk Away from a Deal

Do not get emotionally attached to a deal. Learn to walk away if the numbers are not correct. The deal of a life time comes along every single day if you are on a constant lookout.

"The single most powerful tool for winning a negotiation is the ability to get up and walk away from the table without a deal."

Knowledge of Real Estate Investing is the Key to Success

Knowledge of real estate investing is the biggest leverage you can apply to succeed in real estate. Whether you are a newbie or an experienced property investor, you have to continuously upgrade your knowledge.

A brilliant investment property is never seen with the eyes but always with the mind. Thousands of people will pass a property and will see no any value in it. It takes an educated mind to understand what is the real value and potential of a property. At times, even vendors do not understand the full potential of their properties. Like everything in life, education is the key.

You have to constantly view deals, visit properties, read books, watch videos, attend seminars and, join property investor's forums regularly for fresh information; you have to acquire knowledge to an extent that it becomes your second nature. When you reach this stage, you will be able to spot a great real estate investing opportunity when you browse the internet, see an inconsequential advertisement in the newspaper or during your morning walk.

Buildings Depreciate, Land Appreciate

This is an extremely important principle to understand. Land appreciates over a period of time whereas buildings depreciate. The value of a property consists of land and improvements. Land generates very little or no cash flow; it is mostly the improvements or buildings on the property that generate cash flow.

Buy properties that have large land element whilst keeping an eye on cash flow.

Generally speaking, city apartments have higher rentals but little or no land element. Over a period of time, apartment buildings become old and dilapidated—they lose in value. Single family homes, on the other hand, have lesser cash flow due to the land element. The trick is to buy discounted properties from motivated sellers and increase the rental returns through improvements such as adding additional rooms or building an additional home on the vacant land if permitted by the council.

Even as buildings depreciate in value, the underlying increase in value of land will make you rich.

"Buy on the fringe and wait. Buy land near a growing city! Buy real estate when other people want to sell. Hold what you buy!"

— John Jacob Astor (1848)

Take Action

Taking action is the key to your success. There is no point in having all the knowledge and not applying towards your success.

It is fear that keeps people away from buying real estate. Knowledge – to some extent – abates this fear. However, no one can reach a state of complete knowledge to overcome fear. You have to act in good faith and intelligence; inaction will keep you tied to poverty. Once you start taking action, your experience and confidence in real estate investing will increase.

Action is always superior to inaction. When I started out, I had no knowledge of real estate investing. My mentor was a very rustic real estate agent. He pushed me hard into buying my first property probably because he wanted to make a commission. The only sensible thing I did was to take the leap of faith and get pushed into buying my first investment property. I have never looked back since. For the first few years, I was a 'street smart' real estate investor ... I was learning by taking action.

I never learnt anything new at a property seminar that was not in a book. What helped me was the synergy of like-minded people: it helped me overcome my fear of investing. If so many people could do it successfully, so could I. The best way to overcome fear and taking action is to find a mentor and join a group of successful real estate investors.

Take action even if you have limited knowledge about real estate investing. Think big but start small. A few small steps will change the outcome of your life.

Finance

Finance is the life blood of real estate. To be successful in real estate, you have to understand how to fund your property purchases with the least cost and risk involved. It is important to understand how the power of leverage works: proper leveraging can make your wealth grow exponentially and its improper use can make you bankrupt within a very short period of time.

It is also important to understand property tax laws and how a property investor, you can take advantage of those laws to fund your real estate purchases. The biggest expense in your lifetime is the taxes you pay to the government. If you are smart, you don't have to pay those taxes. Real estate investment gives you an opportunity to save on those taxes legally and fund your lifestyle from those savings. There are ways and means to structure your real estate investments not only to save on taxes but also to provide protection to your assets.

Understanding and applying these basic principles is the key to success in real estate investing.

Real Estate Investment Strategies

There are many exciting real estate strategies you can use to create massive wealth through real estate; you do not have to use all the strategies but master only a few. The investment strategy that is most suited to you will depend upon your investment plan.

Investment Plan

It is extremely important to have an investment plan!

A person who is starting out in real estate will have a totally different strategy as opposed to those who have experience and substantial funds to invest. For instance, if you are with no money and bad credit rating you, will need to improve your credit rating first, become a property finder for other investors, do quick deals to generate cash flow and build equity. Once you have some money, it is advisable to start with residential homes as they are easy to understand and rent.

On the other hand, if you are an investor with high income and tax problems you may look to buy to buy properties with high capital growth potential even though they have slightly lower cash flow. A high net worth investor will look at buying commercial buildings, shopping malls or overseas investment properties.

Your plan will be defined by the starting point of your journey and the final outcome you wish to achieve. If you do not know the starting and the final destination points, you will not be able define the investment strategy you need to follow.

Your starting point will be defined by your knowledge of real estate investing, the amount of capital and cash flow that you have. It will also depend on your risk taking profile and your age. If you are young, you will be able to take more risks but if you are older, you need to be more conservative.

The destination point will be defined by the scale of your ambition. Real estate strategy you use will also depend upon how fast or how slow you wish to reach your destination and what kind of time and effort you are willing to devote.

Investment Strategies

Some of the real estate investment strategies that you can use are enumerated below:

Property Assignment - In this investment strategy you negotiate and find a property deal. Get the property under contract and then pass it on to a real estate investor for a fee.

Contemporaneous Settlements - This is a property transaction in which you buy and sell property on the same day. If this investment strategy is applied correctly you can make a fantastic profit without having the need to settle or raise a mortgage.

Buy off the Plans - By using this investment strategy you benefit from the developers and buy property at a discount off the plans.

Generally by the time property is constructed there will be some capital appreciation.

Delayed Settlement - By putting a property under contract and delaying settlement you get the advantage of capital growth when the market is moving up. Alternately you can use the time to make improvement to the property and increase its value.

Use Credit Cards to Purchase and Renovate Properties - This is a good investment strategy wherein you use zero interest money from credit cards to make the down payment and increase the value of your property through renovations. You then refinance the property to pay of the credit card debt before it becomes due.

Use Non Traditional Lenders - By raising capital from second tier lenders, private investors, equity partnerships, bridging finance you can pump up your profits dramatically.

Vendor Finance - By using this investment strategy you can buy No Money Down properties.

Negative Gearing - When this investment strategy is used correctly, it is like getting interest free loans from the Government in form of tax refunds. Negative gearing is advisable only for individuals who have very high cash flow and taxable incomes. I personally do not subscribe to this strategy, but it's important that I state it explicitly because as an investor, you will come across this terminology when developers are trying to sell overpriced properties.

Equity Release - This is another great investment strategy to use your equity to either buy more real estate or fund your life style. Better still the money is tax free cash.

Lease to Buy Options - There is a saying in real estate: ***"it is not how much property you own that matters but how much property you control."*** By using 'lease option investment strategy,' you can control a very large amount of real estate without actually buying it.

In a lease option, you lease a property with option to buy at a later date when you have the money. By putting lease to buy option in your agreement, you control the property and capital appreciation will accrue to you when you buy.

Foreclosures - Many investors become experts at buying properties at foreclosures or mortgagee sales. By applying this investment strategy alone, you can become a very successful real estate investor.

This list is not comprehensive but only indicative.

Each real estate investment strategy has its place and can be used effectively to meet your stated goal in life. Which strategy you use at a particular point in time will depend upon your plans based on personal circumstances and the position of the property cycle. But whatever strategy you use, you should do it with a very clear objective; you should always have an exit strategy in place in case things don't go as per your plans.

You will need to define your investment goal clearly before embarking on a particular strategy.

Retirement Planning

There are various investment strategies aimed towards retirement planning. Many people buy property to generate passive income so that they can go into early retirement and live life of leisure.

Most people in order to supplement their income during retirement either do reverse mortgage or take out a fresh loan against their equity in the property. The problem with this strategy is that they increase their leverage on the property at a time when they should be reducing their leverage. During retirement most people do not have cash flow from income to support additional mortgage payments.

It is wiser for retirees to readjust their property portfolio for cash flow before retirement. I will discuss this at length with an example.

Example of Retirement Planning

Raj Babar migrated to New Zealand at the age of 50 years in April 2003 with $150,000. His plan was to retire with a passive income of $150,000 per annum through property investment at the age of 65 years.

He attended several property seminars (free & paid) to understand the property market in New Zealand – to get better grasp of the real estate environment he became a real estate consultant as he felt knowledge was the key to growing rich.

Raj debated whether to buy an investment property or a residential house for his family. Although his investment knowledge and instincts told him to buy an investment property first, he decided to buy a house for his family to provide emotional stability to his wife and children in a new country.

Finance was easy during the period and after purchasing the house with 20% deposit he was left with enough money to pay deposit for an investment property.

The first property he purchased was a brand-new leasehold flat in the heart of Auckland CBD that had a ground rent holiday for 7 years. Although he knew capital appreciation on the property will be low as compared to a freehold property, he bought the property for 12% net return ROI. He improved the cash flow to 14% by furnishing the flat with furniture, television, refrigerator and kitchen utensils – he did this in order to improve his position with the banks for future borrowing.

Raj's strategy was very simple: his aim was to buy freehold property with a minimum of 10% return … such properties did not exist in

Auckland. The rate of return on investment (ROI) for a freehold single family home in Auckland, New Zealand at the time was 5–6%. This was well below his stated goal. So he focused on single family homes that had additional land to construct a second house.

Raj would scout hundreds of property to find a motivated seller who was willing to sell his property at least 10–20% below market value for immediate settlement, which would give an initial return of around 7% on his investment and also give him instant equity. To increase his rate of return, he made cosmetic improvements to the first house and construct a second house on the property without sub-dividing the property. This was because sub-division costs were around $60,000 and this expense would not add to his rate of return. The aim was not to sell the second house but to increase his return on investment.

The rent after construction of second house on the property normally increased his return to over 10%. The act of constructing the second house and improvements to the first house increased the valuation of the property by 20%. The fact that he bought the property below market valuation worked in his favor, and subsequent improvements increased his equity in the property by over 30%. He then used the additional equity to pay deposit to buy another investment property. Banks were happy to loan because cash flow from the existing properties added to Raj's income.

It took Raj around 6 months to complete one project. He repeated the process again and again as it was a winning formula.

Once a project was completed, he handed over management of the property to a competent property manager. From then on, it became a hands-off operation with residual cash flowing from it. His only work was to check receipt of rents every month and once in a while give decision on a major maintenance issue. There were times when he did not speak with his property manager for months or even a year. By increasing the return on investment to over 10%, he ensured that the property became not only self-supporting (pay for the all its expenses, mortgage and management costs,) but also gave him a small residual cash flow every week.

There are people who try and manage properties themselves and then cry foul about the headache of managing tenants. This is not residual or retirement income; Raj paid his property managers 6% of the gross rental but this is an expense. In effect he paid them only 4% because of tax rebate. His vacancy rates were much lower as compared to when he was managing his properties. He calculated that if his property manager could reduce vacancy by one week in a year, then there was zero cost of management. By appointing competent property managers several properties owned by Raj have not had one day of vacancy in over 7 years.

Finding a good property manager made Raj's income stream residual. Every property manager is not equal but with some experience, proper research and interviewing you can find property managers who will take all the headaches of property management from you—which is true for any business!

As a result of his property investment, Raj did not pay a single dollar tax on his income for the first 12 years. In later years, he was getting tax rebates to the tune of $35,000 per year. He used this money to fund additional property purchases.

Raj treats each property as a separate business center and an independent source of residual income stream. He repeated this simple formula several times over.

After years of successfully following this strategy, Raj had to change tack because of increase in Council fees and construction prices; nothing lasts forever. But for as long as it lasted, he managed to buy several properties that gave him residual income.

Raj then worked on a new strategy of finding large houses in key locations that could be converted into room by room rentals for young professionals. This provided him with even larger cash flows.

Using strategies outlined above, Raj bought $8.0 million worth of residential properties and built equity of $3.0m. He had built substantial residual income but it did not match up to his goal of $150,000 p.a. to retire. This was because of his liabilities of monthly mortgage payments and outgoings.

As part of his final strategy to retire, Raj sold all his residential investment properties and used the proceeds to buy unencumbered commercial properties worth $3.0 million giving 8% net return. The advantage of investing in commercial properties is that tenant pays all outgoings such as rates, insurance, body corporate fees and even the property management fees: he now has no borrowings and can enjoy his retirement in peace.

The story that I narrate is not work of fiction but based on true life story.

Residential Vs Commercial Real Estate Investing

It is important to understand differences between residential property investments as compared to investing in commercial real estate. They are completely different kettle of fish.

Complexity

Residential real estate investment, as the name suggests, is investing in property that people use primarily for residential accommodation. These include apartments, town houses, free-standing homes, duplexes, condominiums and apartment buildings.

Residential real estate investment is comparatively less daunting than commercial real estate when starting out your journey because everyone knows what constitutes a home that some could live in.

You will straight away notice absence of a bathroom and a kitchen or if the property suffered from poor ventilation.

Commercial properties include offices, industrial sheds, free standing retail shop, bulk retail, block of shop, medical centers, service stations, motels, hotels, back packers, health clubs, churches, funeral parlors, child care centers, car yards, convenience stores, shopping malls, to name just a few. Each type of commercial real estate investment has its own peculiarities, strengths, problems, rewards and risks.

In addition, you have to deal with contracts and leases that can affect the price of the property.

Commercial real estate investment is the natural progression from residential property investment. Experienced property investors tend to move into commercial real estate sooner than later – and for very good reasons.

Once your portfolio grows, it is very difficult to manage your investments if a large portion of them is tied in residential properties. Imagine you have $15 million worth of residential properties – that would be lot of homes and tenants to take care of.

On the other hand, $15 million will buy only a very small number of commercial properties, which will be comparatively easier to manage with much lesser overheads.

Tenants

In residential real estate investment, you are essentially dealing with people. Unfortunately, people create problems. Your tenant will ring you up at all odd times with even the smallest of complaints: at times the rent is not paid in time, the lawns are not mowed or they will not keep the property clean and in worst cases, they damage your property.

Residential tenants have little or no interest in maintaining your property.

> *"The working components of a rental home (heating, cooling, electrical, plumbing, dishwasher, garbage disposal, doorbell and refrigerator) will break down 90% faster on the rental than the working components of your own home."*

If the tenant is not complaining, then you will find the neighbor complaining about the tenant for making too much noise or their children running into the neighbor's property. So, you need people skills to manage your property or you will need to employ a property manager.

> *"The sweet little girl with the baby you rented your house to will always have an abusive boyfriend, and their loud, passionate lovemaking at night, nasty quarrels and scream fests will be the talk of the neighborhood."*

If you have ever worked as a landlord—this reason will be very clear to you: residential tenants complain about everything on earth and mostly in the middle of the night or when you are watching a good game of football.

Commercial property on the other hand, is a space for doing business. It is a place from where a tenant sells his products and services. The success of his business depends on the presentation of the property and number of visitors they receive each day.

The tenant bases his monthly rent on a commercial property on a certain percentage of the profit the business makes each month.

When a businessman approaches you to rent a property, they do so because the location is suitable to them.

The tenants know the value of a good location and they will pay to be in the right place.

Most commercial property tenants will fix problems and carry out minor repairs on their own without calling the landlord. This is because they realize that problems need to be taken care of immediately or they will interfere with their business. Residential tenants on the other hand, will always look for help from the landlord to take care of repairs—they will never spend a dime on the property.

Commercial property tenants can spend substantial money to upgrade the property for their business requirement. These improvements stay with the property long after the tenant has moved on.

Most commercial tenants need to put in networking and cable wires, sound systems, and electrical outlets – all of which increase the market value and marketability of your commercial property.

In commercial property, you tend to deal with contracts where as in residential real estate investment you tend to deal with people.

Vacancy Rate

The biggest advantage of residential real estate investment is that it is fairly easy to find a new tenant once your property becomes vacant, which reduces the vacancy rate and there is always cash flow coming from your investment.

There is only one reason for your property to remain vacant for too long: your rents are too high for that location at the particular time. If you drop the rent by 5–10%, you will normally find a tenant, which is because people have to live somewhere at affordable costs.

In commercial real estate, properties are far more specialized and in case of a vacancy, you may not find a tenant for months or even a few years: this is a huge risk for a new investor who is not familiar with real estate investment and requires deeper pockets in case of vacancy.

Rate of Return

The return on investment in commercial real estate is much higher than residential property: the income is net and not gross because the tenant pays all the outgoing expenses and is also more stable because of the long leases.

The rate of return on residential real estate investment is much lower because in residential property, the owner has to pay all the outgoing expenses such as property rates, insurance, body corporate fees and maintenance costs. In commercial real estate, it is the responsibility of the tenant to pay these costs thereby increasing net returns.

It is typical to have returns of around 7–10% net for a commercial real estate investment and anywhere from 5–7% net return for a prime property.

The net return from residential property tends to be from 2–6% and can be a bit higher in less desirable neighborhoods and apartment buildings.

Value of Property

The value of a property is determined by its location, land size and improvements. This is true for both residential and commercial property.

What is peculiar to commercial real estate is that its value is also greatly determined by the quality of the lease. In general, the value is determined by taking net contractual rental being paid and use of a capitalization rate to arrive at a value. The value is also determined by the quality of the tenant and length of the lease.

There is a saying in commercial real estate: *"More leases you read in bed the richer you will become."*

The value of a commercial property can drop substantially if it becomes vacant. Often commercial properties are sold at 10–50% of their value if they are difficult to lease.

The value of residential real estate on the other hand, is determined to a large extent by location of the property. If the house is in a desirable area, it will command a better price.

Property leases

Residential property leases tend to be very short when compared to commercial leases that can run for several years. As discussed earlier, it is much easier to find a tenant for vacant residential property.

Finance

The funding for commercial real estate investments is harder to get as banks look at the quality of tenants, length and terms of lease.

In general, commercial properties are more expensive than residential properties. Banks will lend up to 90 % or more on residential properties and only up to 50% to 70% on commercial property. You will therefore need more equity to buy. This reduces your leveraging power to buy more property

The lending rates are also marginally higher, which reflects the risk that banks associate with commercial real estate investment.

You will require much lesser seed capital to start with residential real estate investment and will be able to leverage your money better with residential property.

Government Laws

Government laws with respect to residential property are far more stringent and can override anything that you may have written in the rental agreement with the tenant. Politicians and bureaucrats put these protections in place so that residential tenants are not exploited.

In some countries and states the laws are so much in favor of the tenant that you cannot evict them even in case they are behind on their rents.

Real estate law is more flexible towards commercial lease contracts. You can insert any clauses in the sale or lease agreement that is agreeable to the contracted parties without any interference from the governing agencies.

It is common to charge penalty interest on the outstanding rent or lock the premises on continued default of rent.

Property Management Costs

Residential real estate investment management takes time and effort because you deal with people. Once you have several residential investments, it can become a full-time job.

Residential property managers' charge anywhere from 6–8% of the rent collected towards the management fee.

Commercial properties on the other hand, do not require much of your time in managing them. Commercial tenants usually stay in the property for many years and it is in their best interest to maintain and make improvements to the property.

Commercial property management is also much simpler because tenants have a strong vested interest to maintain the property to a high standard: they usually derive their income from the property. They have to keep the property looking good and maintain functionality to impress their clients.

Commercial tenants spend hundreds of thousands of dollars to make improvements to the property. Most of these improvements stay with the property long after the tenant has left the property.

Commercial property management fees reflect the reduced work involved and charges range from 2–6% of the rent collected. The best part is that you can charge the management cost to tenant as a part of the out goings. In case you choose to manage the property then the management charges become payable to you thereby increasing the return from the property.

Risks and Rewards

So far, the biggest risk in commercial real estate investment is finding a new tenant in case of a vacancy. In commercial real estate, the requirement of each tenant in terms of size, location, use and rent payment capacity is so different that it is very difficult to get the right tenant for the right property.

For the reasons mentioned above, it is also difficult to sell or lease a commercial real estate investment. Generally speaking higher the value of property will result in lesser number of investors to buy the property.

A commercial real estate investment is less liquid than other investments because there are very few players in the market. For a residential house, there will be hundreds of potential buyers, which is not the case with commercial properties.

Commercial real estate investments are generally sold on capitalization rates and rarely on replacement value. It is therefore possible to purchase a poorly rented commercial property well below its market value. You can also increase the value of your commercial real estate simply by leasing the property or raising the rents during rent reviews or renegotiating the lease terms when it come up for renewal.

Commercial real estate investment provides professional investors higher returns and ease of managing them. For these investors, commercial property is their 'bread and butter' and they drive their speculative income by trading in residential properties.

Some commercial investors focus their attention to improve and add value to their commercial portfolio. Whilst others use their rental returns to fund development projects that show much higher returns, they need different and more advanced skill sets.

Commercial real estate investing is very rewarding but requires more knowledge, experience and capital out lay. It is not advisable to jump into commercial real estate from the very out set until and unless you have very deep pockets and risk-taking ability. It is advisable to start with residential real estate investment to build your equity and cash flow.

You should buy at least 8–10 residential property investments before venturing into the world of commercial real estate investment that is far more complex.

For a new investor, it is much easier and less risky to get started with residential real estate investing because of the easy in understanding residential property, getting the finances, leveraging money and managing vacancies.

Real Estate Finance

Understanding real estate finance is the key to your success. As stated earlier, finance is the life blood of real estate: without finance there is no real estate.

"Empty pockets never held anyone back. Only empty heads and empty hearts can do that."

— Dr. Norman Vincent Peale

It is critical for you to understand how to finance investment property if you are to be successful with your real estate investment business.

A generation ago, the only viable option for most people was to get a loan from a bank. Today, you can get mortgage finance from myriads of banks, financial institutions, lawyers' client funds, real estate companies, building societies, insurance companies, credit unions, contributory mortgage companies or even the vendors.

Contrary to what people might have told you, banks want to loan you money. It is their business to loan money to make money. It is also equally important for an investor to use Other People's Money to leverage.

Banks and financial institutions that provide real estate finance look at your cash flow, equity position, credit rating and soundness of your real estate or property that you wish to buy.

Banks can be conservative with their money because the bank's risk is greater than yours as they loan you anywhere from 50–100% on the market value of the property. They don't even have direct control over the asset once the loan is given; they try to protect themselves with various clauses in the mortgage document. You have to understand these clauses in the loan agreement before you sign it.

You have to be sensitive to banks advice and concerns—they are your partners in business. You have to prepare to meet their lending criteria rather than attempting to fool them by hiding or furnishing wrong information. You will damage your long-term interest if you try and take short cuts. No bank will provide you with real estate finance if your credit rating or the reputation in the market suffers.

You have to organize your personal finances, improve your credit rating, prepare your financial information and that of the property that you wish to buy before approaching the bank for real estate finance. If you do not do your homework, lack confidence and don't present yourself properly then, no bank or financial institution will give a loan.

It is important to understand that the lending criterion of banks change from time to time. They may reject your application for a loan even if your finances are in great shape – this is because the lending criteria for a particular type of property you wish to buy may not match the lending criteria of the bank for that property. In such a situation, it is wiser to approach another bank for a loan. It is better to utilize the services of a competent mortgage broker who is well informed regarding the lending policies of various banks and will guide you to the most suitable lender.

You should shop around for the best interest rates. Believe it or not, interest rates are negotiable! It is a good idea to compare the interest rates of various lenders so you can negotiate with a lender of your choice. At times, interest rates can differ between different branches of the same bank. You can save from tens to hundreds of thousands of dollars during the life time of a loan by simply doing some research and negotiating hard.

Your profits and success will increase when you get a better grasp of various real estate finance strategies such as: revolving credit, vendor finance option, credit cards, private investor funding, using second mortgages, partnerships and joint ventures, refinancing and recycling your deposit.

You have to also understand the various types of mortgages available in the market to make use of them to your advantage. These include fixed and floating rates, interest only loans, capital repayment loans, reverse mortgages, split loans to name a few.

Understanding real estate finance is the key to your success. You have to understand how to get high on OPM. The secret is to find the best and cheapest source of funding of your property with least strings attached.

Strategy to Buy Outstanding Investment properties

Once you have your finance approved, the next crucial question is how to buy investment property. If you are newbie, start with residential investment property because it is less risky and easy to understand.

The first property you buy is the most crucial—you cannot afford to make a mistake with your first buy. Once you have cash flow from several investment properties then a mistake in purchasing a wrong investment can be covered up. If something goes wrong with your first investment, it will set you back by several years before you can recover. It may also dent your confidence.

Some of the important criterion for selecting the right investment property is:

Area to Buy

Your first step involves buying an existing property in an area you understand (in your neighborhood) at or below market value. Buying below value will require some education and experience – this should not deter you because you have to start somewhere. So, this is the right time to start.

The property should be close to the area you live in. There is no point in buying properties that are 6 to 7 hours' drive away. You will waste your energy in commuting rather than renovating your property and increasing its value.

Try and buy property in a high capital growth area if possible. As investors, we make money through capital gain. However, cash flow is the key. Cash flow from property should support your investment purchases so that you can pay for all the outgoings without any stress. Also keep in mind interest rates as they may change in the future – check how they will impact your investment.

If you look around, you will find great investment opportunities in your neighborhood. The numbers have to stack up. Take all expenses into account. Amateurs at times over look certain expenses when carrying out calculations due to their optimism and excitement.

Once you start viewing and analyzing large number of deals, your mind will open to some of the finer points of investing.

Buying and Renovating

Buy a property that is structurally sound but in need of minor cosmetic repairs. You will be amazed how much value you can add to a property by doing some simple and inexpensive cosmetic changes. These can involve trimming the over grown garden, mowing the lawn, replace some light fittings, polishing the floorboards or changing the carpets, painting the walls or by simply removing the rubbish you can increase the value of the property by thousands of dollars.

Adding Value to a Property

You can add value to any property by making improvements but it should make financial sense. Each dollar you spend on improvements must add value by two to five times otherwise your effort is a waste of your resources.

Be very cautious of over capitalizing. If houses in a street are selling for, let us say $500,000 then even if you spend an exorbitant amount of money in renovations, you will never be able to increase its value over half a million. On the contrary, it makes sense to buy over capitalized properties even at market price especially when you wish to reside in them. Most people forget how much money they have sent over long periods in improving their properties.

You necessarily do not have to spend huge amounts of money in improvements to add value to a property – never ever buy a property that has structural problems! You can spend tens of thousands of dollars in corrections but they will not add a cent to value of your property. The only time you buy a property with structural issues is if it is being sold for a massive discount and you have the exact numbers on what it will cost you to get the repairs done. Once you open the Pandora's Box, you will be astonished by what you will find.

Some other strategies include:

- **Change of Zoning** –Purchasing property in an area where zoning is likely to change can enhance its value without spending a dime: change in number of units permitted on size of land, improving height restrictions, and conversion of land usage from farm to residential or residential to commercial all play a part.

- **Change of Use** – You can apply to Council for change of use of property. One such example is conversion of residential property to a boarding house. Recently, one of my clients purchased an old Church and converted it into a childcare center and soon after the conversion; he sold the property at thrice the purchase price.

- **Sub-Division** – You can buy a large piece of land then sub-divide it into small parcels and sell them at a huge profit.

- **Unit Titles** – You can buy multiple flats or units on a single certificate of title and then apply to council for individually unit titling them will greatly enhance the value.

- **Development in the area** – Buying properties in area with knowledge of future developments can greatly add value to your purchases. These can include roads, trains, schools, new factories that will generate employment, shopping malls, golf courses, clubs etc.

- **Buying a vacant commercial building and leasing it will increase its value**

- **Renegotiating lease terms and increasing rents** – You can buy under rented properties and then negotiate with tenants to increase rents to market will greatly improve your cash flow and increase value of the property.

Adding value means having knowledge that not many people have garnered. Most real estate agents – who are basically sales people – will not be able to guide you. This is something you, as an investor, have to develop through reading, investigation and awareness in the market place.

Someone right said: *"The best property you have to invest in is that What Is In Between your two ears."*

It is specialized knowledge that separates winners from losers or men from boys. Once you attain sensitivity towards property, you will be able to visualize value that an untrained mind cannot see.

Renting

> *"Landlords grow rich in their sleep"*
>
> — John Stewart Mill

The basic principle of investing is that your tenants must pay your mortgage. You have to get your numbers right when buying an investment property; the rent must cover not only your mortgage but also the out goings such as rates, body corporate, insurance and maintenance. In some high capital growth areas rents may not cover the expenses. In such cases, you will need to cover the short fall from your salary or cash flow from business.

You must check the rents and vacancy rates in the area before buying a property. The property must be in an area close to schools, markets, communication centers, job centers, where there is large demand by tenants. There is no point in buying a property showing a very high return on investment but in an isolated area that is difficult to rent. Vacancy will reduce your return on investment.

Repeat the Process

The quickest process to grow your portfolio quickly is to learn the art of buying property below value. Then add value to the property by carrying out cosmetic renovations. For every dollar you spend on the property the value must go up by at least three to five times. You must then get your property revalued. The extra equity that you create can be used as deposit for your next purchase.

The faster you repeat this process; faster will your net worth grow. This is called the 'Deposit Recycling Time' which means how fast you can get your initial deposit out of your investment property and use it as deposit to buy another property. Do not get lured into projects that show huge profit but will take very long time to complete or are risky in nature. Keep it simple and quick. Sorter your deposit recycling time the richer you will become.

Cash flow

A word of caution: you must always keep a tab on your cash flow. Most people do not comprehend the importance of cash flow and get into trouble. Most mortgagee sales and foreclosure take place because people under estimate the importance of cash flow.

When you're starting out, buy only cash flow positive properties – do not buy negatively geared properties (that take money out of your pocket.) Banks will lend you if you have both cash flow and equity;

you will need to balance both these aspects if you are to become a successful property investor.

How to Find Good Investment Properties

The next obvious question is: how to find the perfect property?

Which is the best place to start? Without doubt, your search should start with the internet. The internet will save you hours and hours of your time and effort.

The old theory on how to buy investment property will tell you to visit 100 properties, short list 30, make offer on 10 of them, get vendor response on three of them and finally buy one does not work in this fast-paced world. You will lose interest after viewing 5 properties because of the leg work involved.

The internet has changed how you find good investment properties. There is so much data available on the internet, not only regarding properties for sale in your area of interest but also recent sales, council rates, rental rates, vacancy rates, mortgage rates etc. that you can check the numbers on your investment if they meet your buying criteria before rushing to view the property.

You must sign up for a popular internet real estate site in your area; most sites will give you an option to search by price range, location, number of bedrooms and key search terms.

In your preferred area and price range (depending upon your finance approval) look for properties that have maximum number of bedrooms and land area. Number of bedrooms will decide how much rent you will get from the property. A four-bedroom house will normally command a better rent than a three-bedroom house. So, in your budget, try and buy a house that has maximum number of bedrooms. A large land area will give you options for the future. Always remember buildings depreciate whereas land appreciates in value.

By entering words like 'motivated vendor', 'diseased estate', 'mortgagee sale', 'urgent sale' etc. in the search criteria, you can short list properties that are likely to be sold below value.

Once you have short listed the properties, don't rush to view them – save fuel! It is very expensive and you will also save the environment. You must now speak with the real estate agents of the short-listed properties on phone to find out about the condition of the house, construction materials, likely rent, vacancy rates in the area, government and market valuation, location of the house in relationship to the land, proximity to schools, public transport, other amenities and as to why is the vendor selling the property.

Try and collect all the facts and financial figures like land rates, body corporate expenses, insurance rates etc. You must feed these figures into a property investment software (you can choose from many software's available in the market depending upon your budget) to arrive at gross return, net return after tax, IRR and cash flow. Buying an investment calculator is a small investment that is absolutely necessary and will help you compare various options available to you.

Only once you are satisfied with the quality of property, numbers and financial returns should you fix up a time to view the property.

The above process should not lull you into becoming an armchair investor. There is no better way to get the feel of an area without viewing several properties. Attend as many open homes you can and talk to various people like your accountant, lawyer, real estate agents and other property investors. This is especially more important when you are starting out.

Another important fact you must remember is that most good investment properties sell before they are advertised in the newspaper or come on the internet. You have to befriend few real estate agents in the area where you wish to buy the property and tell them of your requirements. Other sources of information can be lawyers, mortgage brokers, accountants and bank managers.

Real estate agents love to work with professional real estate investors because they get repeat sales. It is very important that you give them due respect and not waste their time. A good real estate agent will inform you regarding properties that are not even listed and are likely to come to the market shortly. You can do your due diligence on these properties and react before anyone else does with cash offers.

Remember that there is no perfect investment property—it is always a trade-off. If it is high cash flow, the capital-gain prospect may be low. If there is more land for future development, then the initial cash flow may not be as per your expectation. If the price is low, there may be additional costs involved in doing up the property before it can be leased. The property you buy will depend upon your situation and long-term plan.

Buying investment property can be a very simple and an enjoyable process if you follow the fundamentals correctly.

Conclusion

I will conclude this commandment with the great words of wisdom written by an unknown writer on land. I hope and pray that they leave a deep imprint on your mind.

Who Am I?

I am the basis of all wealth, the heritage of the wise, the thrifty and prudent.

I am the poor person's joy and comfort, the rich person's prize, the right hand of capital,

The silent partner of thousands of successful people.

I am the solace of the widow, the comfort of old age, the cornerstone of security against misfortune and want.

I am handed down through generations, as a possession of great value.

I am the choicest fruit of labor, the safest collateral and yet I am humble.

I stand before every person bidding them to know me for what I am and asking them to possess me.

I am quietly growing in value through countless days.

Though, I might seem dormant, my worth increases, never failing, never ceasing.

Time is my aid and the ever-increasing population adds to my gain. I defy fire and the elements, for they cannot destroy me.

My possessors learn to believe in me and invariable they become envied by those that have passed me by.

While all other things wither and decay, I alone survive.

The centuries find me younger, always increasing in strength.

All oil and minerals come from me.

I am the producer of food, building materials and the home to every living thing.

I serve as the foundation for homes, factories, banks and stores.

I have not been produced for millions of years, yet, I am so common that thousands,

Unthinking and unknowingly, pass me by.

Who am I? "I AM Land."

My only addition to the wonderful thoughts of this writer is: buy land with improvements on it so that there is adequate cash flow.

In the next commandment we will learn how to generate massive cash flow to buy property and other paper assets that will create multiple streams of passive income. We will discuss why standing on two or more strong financial legs is very important to your financial health.

Thou shalt become a Sophisticated Investor

Have you tried balancing on one leg? It will be extremely hurtful and, in all probability, you will fall after some time. It is not only stressful but highly risky to stand on one leg – the same holds true in your financial life. If you stand on one leg, you will definitely fall and hurt yourself, yet so many people keep standing on one leg financially all their lives.

To be financially stable you have to stand on minimum two legs:

- Employee + Investment

- Self Employed + Investment

- Business + Investment

Investing is the key to your financial stability whether you are an employee, self-employed or in business. There is a view that only people in jobs who do not invest are financially vulnerable. You will be surprised to learn that even very smart businessmen do not invest and their financial empire collapses because of this reason. Nothing can be further from truth. There are smart guys who build a great business and sell it for a profit of millions of dollars. They then want to repeat the process and start a new venture only to lose their entire capital.

Businesses, as they grow, demand more and more capital. In some cases, businessmen continue pouring money in expansion of their business rather than investing a part of their profits outside their business to gain financial stability.

Even a most profitable business standing on one financial leg is unstable. Smart businessmen, however, choose to do otherwise: Bill Gates sells his shares of Microsoft every year and invests in other areas to continue growing rich. His current holding in Microsoft is only 4%. Yet he continues to one of the richest men on earth.

The strongest financial legs are: business + investor, because you generate excessive cash flow from a well-run business to invest in passive income investments. Employees and self-employed people are limited in their capacity to create huge cash flow because they do not have tax advantage, leveraging power or time freedom for wealth creation. They can become wealthy if they invest intelligently but will find it extremely difficult to create accelerated wealth.

Let us examine in detail on how you can systematically graduate from your current situation to create not only financial stability but sustainable wealth that can last for generations.

In this commandment, we will focus on how you can create sustainable wealth by standing on two or more financial legs.

Sustainable Wealth

What is sustainable wealth? The answer to this question is in this statement by Robert Kiyosaki: ***"The rich have lots of money but the wealthy don't worry about money."***

It is important to understand the difference between being rich and wealthy. A rich person can have a lot of money and possessions but a wealthy person has adequate passive cash flow to fund his or her lifestyle whether they work or not. You will be surprised to know that there are very rich people in high paying jobs who will not be able to sustain even a very basic lifestyle if they were to lose their job for some reason.

You will also be surprised to learn that a very large percentage of high income earners such as sportspersons, movie stars, doctors, engineers etc. who buy expensive cars, boats, houses, clothes, jewelry and even fancy planes to impress people; do not believe in investing and lead financially unsustainable lifestyle. They often appear to be rich but are going nowhere – they spend their money recklessly, their expenses keep them worried at night.

Have you heard about Mel B of the Spice Girls fame? She earned over $50 million and blew it all up on fancy cars, private jet holidays, clothes and shoes. It is claimed that she never wore a dress twice. Her financial miss-management highlight was a gift of an island to her beloved husband who later divorced her and sued her for even more money – Mel is the perfect example of being rich and not wealthy.

Wealth means number of days/ months/ years you and your family can survive without physically working and still maintain a standard of living you are used to. If you can survive only for a few days or months, then you are not doing well. If you can sustain your lifestyle indefinitely without working, you are wealthy. You are super wealthy if you not only sustain but constantly keep increasing your wealth each year without working.

Your aim should be to create sustainable wealth. This is only possible by standing on two strong financial legs—one of which is investing. If you wish to be wealthy, you have to continually buy assets that give you passive cash flow. As you buy more and more assets, your cash flow will grow and make you wealthy. As a matter of principle, you have to keep your expenses less than the cash flow your assets are generating and with the surplus cash, you need to continuously buy income producing assets –this will not only keep you ahead of inflation but also compound your wealth.

Your first step to financial freedom should be to become wealthy. Your next step should be to become rich and wealthy. We will examine this in some depth and how it can be achieved.

Active and Passive Cash flow

'The most important word in the world of money is cash flow'

— Robert Kiyosaki

Cash flow is not only important for buying assets that create passive income but also to pay your bills and fund your lifestyle. If you dispassionately look at the most stressed period in your life, more often than not, it will be a time when you did not have enough money to meet your financial commitments.

Managing cash flow is important to the happiness of your family and loved ones; most individual and business bankruptcies occur when people lose sight of cash flow. Perhaps, the three most dreaded words in English language are 'negative cash flow.'

Active cash flow is from sources where you have to physically be present and work for money. Passive cash flow is when funds flow into your pocket without any physical effort on your part. Passive cash flow is far superior to active cash flow. When money works for you day and night without you having to lift a finger … that is a state you should aspire to be in. I am not saying that you should stop working or being creative—it is important to lead a productive and fulfilling life. Passive cash flow from diverse sources will give you financial stability that you and your loved ones so richly deserve. It will put an end to your financial worries so that you can lead life of your dreams.

Let us examine some passive wealth generators.

Passive Wealth Generators

For most people, passive income is generated from investment in real estate, stocks or bonds that pay rent, dividends or interest. Investment in commodities like gold, silver, antiques, art work or oil do not qualify as income generators as they do not provide any cash flow. If an asset value is based on what a future buyer may pay then it is pure speculation and not an investment. If your aim is to create passive income then stay away from such types of investments.

Real Estate is, without doubt, one of the best passive income generators for reasons explained in the last commandment. However, only few properties fit the criteria of cash flow investments and you must be conscious of this fact before buying an investment property. Properties also require substantial amount of deposit to buy. T build deposit to buy your first investment property you should invest in stocks, mutual funds and bonds under a Systematic Payment Plan (SIP).

The other source of passive income generation is big businesses that operate without day-to-day monitoring or interference from the owner of the business. Small businesses do not qualify as passive income sources as they require considerable time and effort involvement of the business owner. We will later study this in depth.

You can also generate passive income from royalties if you are a talented writer or musician. Only very few people can earn this kind of passive income as it needs special talent. If you possess talent then by all means, use it to generate wealth but make sure that you don't sell rights of your books or music to other entity as the Beatles did when they were young.

Steps to Creating Sustainable Wealth

The best part is that you don't have to be super rich to create sustainable wealth: anyone can do it with some knowledge, self-discipline and perseverance! The process involves conversion of earned income into passive income as efficiently as possible.

It is important to understand the mindset required to succeed in each stage of financial growth. If you wish to graduate to a higher stage of financial success, your mindset has to evolve and change or you are doomed to fail. Eighty percent of new start-up businesses or investments fail primarily because they are started by people who have the mindset of an employee. If you wish to become a millionaire then you have to develop the mindset of a millionaire. To become a billionaire, you need to develop mindset of a billionaire.

Reality Check if you are an Employee

If you are an employee and want to start investing then you will need to accumulate funds to buy assets. In the majority of the cases people find themselves in 'job trap.' They barely make enough to make their ends meet with little or nothing left for investing.

There is nothing to despair because almost everyone starts at this point. There are only very few lucky ones who start with a silver spoon in their mouths. If you are not one of the lucky ones, then you must seriously analyze what a job entails and how it holds you back.

As an employee, your cash flow comes from trading hours for money; you are a one-man army. This imposes huge restrictions on your cash flow growth prospect. You can only work X number of hours in a day. It is also highly risky. If something happens to your health or you get fired from your job, your cash flow ceases. What happens to your loved ones who depend on you? This is an extremely unhappy situation.

The worst part of being an employee is that you get taxed before you get paid. There are hardly any tax incentives. These are mainly reserved for those in business, which reduces your limited cash flow even further.

Gone are the days of job security but unfortunately, people still hold on that idea. In this knowledge based, rapidly changing economy, jobs become redundant faster than you learn a skill. For instance, there are no jobs today for COBOL and Pascal programmers that were high in demand merely a few years back. In the current economy, companies make more profit by laying workers off than hiring them.

Advances in automation are shrinking workforce and the middle-class. In the next two decades, robotics and artificial intelligence will further create pressure on jobs and redundancies will be on a rise at a pace never seen in the history of mankind. Taxi, bus and truck drivers are likely to become jobless in the next decade or so as driverless cars hit the road. Industries will opt for part-time workers and consultants as compared to offering full-time employment. Most people will be engaging in several part-time jobs just to make their ends meet.

This is the reality of our times and no amount of government intervention, closing borders or trying to bring back jobs by introducing isolationist economic policies will reverse this trend. It is only through re-educating and adapting that one can survive in this ever-changing and technological, accelerating world.

Job security is the relic of the industrial era; when a person joined a company and remained there for life. The company also looked after you in your retirement. The faster you realize and start making adjustments, better it will be for your financial future.

There is nothing riskier than a job. Relying on a job to fund your cash flow is stupidity in today's world – don't be fooled by a few high paying jobs at the top of the corporate ladder. Wages, in real terms for the mid-level jobs, have been declining since peaking in mid-seventies. Only the top one percent of the one percent in the highest pay bracket will have adequate cash flow to invest from their salaries for comfortable retirement. Don't envy them because they are brilliant and have sacrificed a lot to reach pinnacle of success. Path of an employee to wealth creation is very thorny and a difficult one. There are better and easier ways to become wealthy.

Jobs in most cases provide a false sense of security till the axe falls. The most problematic part is the mindset it produces: it kills the risk-taking ability of an individual. To survive, most people keep their heads down and avoid rocking the boat that may endanger their livelihood. They will suck up to unreasonable demands of their bosses and keep their creative ideas locked within. After a few years, this becomes a habit resulting in a total lack of initiative. Employees will nurture dreams and talk big about breaking free from the stifling environment but in most cases, they lack the courage to start afresh.

Most employee conversations go like this: "Who do you work for?", "How much do you earn?", "where do you live", and "What car do you drive?" … Lest I sound rude, I call this "Looking good, going nowhere."

Employee time is structured by the needs of the corporation leaving no freedom or initiative to the individual. Most jobs are so draining that it leaves no time or energy for an individual to explore new ideas, explore and analyze new investments and wealth creation opportunities.

The problem for most employees is that they make decisions based on fear of what can go wrong rather on vision; trust and what can go right.

The most important aspect of wealth creation is to get rid of the employee mindset that holds most people back; it is this mentality that keeps a person trapped in a job. They find it difficult to break free. You can be working a job but you have to get rid of the mindset that holds you back. There has to be a fundamental change in your thought process from fear to that of trust.

Every great endeavor in life requires a leap of faith – greatness lies in taking a step into the unknown. It takes courage and self-belief that things will turn out right. It also cannot happen till the time you take an action.

The best way to foster a new mindset is to found a small part-time business in your spare time. It can be something small like network marketing or internet-based business: these require very little capital outlay and have time flexibility. Running a small business will teach you about leadership qualities, communication skills, marketing, accounting and importance of networking.

The most important skill you will learn is sales. No money is ever made in business without a sale. You will learn how to overcome objections and rejection. Most people hate selling because of the fear of rejection. To become truly successful, you have to overcome rejection and gain the self-confidence that these small business ventures will provide.

The best part about running a part-time home business is that it will give you tax breaks that will provide you with extra cash flow to start investing. The biggest companies in the world today like Microsoft, Apple and Amazon were founded in garages.

The only two reasons to be an employee are: accumulation of some capital and acquisition of skills to get to the next level. Of the two, gaining knowledge is more important than accumulating capital. Learn from other people's mistakes. Get a job under someone who is a great mentor. Work in a field that will give you the experience to launch your own business.

It must be remembered: income does not equal to wealth but it is what you do with your income that determines your wealth. As an employee, you may have limited spare cash but you have to tighten your belt and take first tiny steps to start investing. Don't buy unnecessary stuff that you don't need and invest instead. I keep repeating this......a march of thousand miles starts with the first step.

"Someone's sitting in the shade today because someone planted a tree a long time ago."

— Warren Buffet

The first important financial challenge you should take in your life is to create adequate passive income to cover your monthly expenses so that you can quit your job. It will allow you to feel secure and give time freedom to explore new creative ideas. This will lay the foundation to become truly wealthy and financially secure.

If you are really smart, you will be able to reach this stage by your mid-thirties. In most cases, couples reach this stage sometime in their forties so that one person in the family can quit their job and start their business. Real cash flow begins only once you successfully launch a business—all businesses are not equal. There are various stages to growth in business and each stage requires a different mind shift and skill set.

Self Employed/ Small Business – The Stepping Stone Financial Freedom

Being self-employed or starting a small business is the first step on the entrepreneur ladder. Most people get excited and fired up when starting out on their own. They want to be their own boss.

The emotional trigger of an employee is security. For a small business owner/ self-employed person, the main driving force is to control their own destiny. In most cases, people start out with just one employee: themselves.

In the majority of cases, the impulse to start their own business comes when people are unemployed or between jobs. They get a flash idea that they can do a much better job than their boss. Without much preparation or thought, they start their own business. Their mindset is still that of an employee. They feel they are the experts in their field. This is the first major mistake. They start a business on what they can make rather than starting a business on based on what product they can sell.

This is the starting point of self-employment trap.

They don't have a vison or know how to grow the business. Their business is centered on their particular skill. A TV technician will start a TV repair shop and will be satisfied if he has enough work to keep him busy. In most cases, small business owners are worse off than those employed because they find it difficult to even go on a holiday. They are still trading time for money but without the perks of an employee. Their attitude towards money is same as an employee. They have to "make money" in their business which is the same thing as "earn money".

Most people have little or no knowledge about cash flow. They think advertising is a waste of money. They lack the skills to put systems into their business so that it can operate without them. Their entire business is centered on them, and they do not trust or delegate authority.

This is also true for self-employed professionals like lawyers, accountants, and medical practitioners etc. who try and set up their businesses.

Most small business entrepreneurs become frustrated sooner than later and give up at this stage, which is why 80% start-ups fail within two years of their launch.

Being an entrepreneur is like walking through fire, whereas being self-employed or owner of a small business is the most robust stage of financial growth. When starting out, you are a one-man army and don't have funds to hire best people to advise or support your business. Unfortunately, there is no way to bypass this stage and climb the next step on the financial ladder to freedom.

There are some solid reasons for you to succeed as a self-employed:

- **No Hourly Rate** - You learn the art of selling. If you become good at marketing and selling there is no hourly rate. You can determine the level of your income through your determination and hard work.

- **Company Structure** – you will learn about company structure such as holding company and trading company.

- **Accounting** – This is the lifeblood of any business. You will learn about cash flows and balance sheets. Cost reduction is a critical aspect of running a business that you will learn.

- **Work Ethics** – As you are central to your business you will learn values of hard work and discipline.

- **Communication skills** – To succeed in your business, you will not only have to improve your communication skills but also learn to develop networks.

- **Taxation** – To improve the bottom line of your business, you will be forced to learn about tax and legal aspects.

- **Time Structuring** – Compared to an employee, a self-employed person has control over his time. In order to run an efficient business, a person improves his time management skill.

- **Cash flow Management** – To succeed at this stage, you have to learn cash flow management.

Running a small business or being self-employed is a steep learning curve that pays rich dividends at next stage of financial growth.

Self-Employee Trap - A self-employed person is an extremely busy person. Firstly, they have to chase work i.e. find new clients through sales and marketing. Then they have to work to complete the job and deliver on schedule. They are always buried in work and tend to lose the vision for which they started the business in the first place.

Moving Up from Self-Employed – To move up from being self-employed, you have to first broaden the vision for your company. You have set higher goals for your company. Next, you have to chalk out a plan for growth of your company. You have to draw out an organization chart for your employees and assign specific jobs.

Most importantly, you have to stop thinking yourself as a worker but as a business owner. If you are an electrician, then do not think yourself as an electrician but the owner of an electrical business.

The next step to wealth creation is to graduate to being a business owner.

Business Owner – Time to Relax?

A business owner has huge rewards but problems as well.

A business owner, in all probability, will be making more money but it will not be enough. One of the byproducts of growth is the shortage of cash. To grow, you will need more and more cash. Cash management becomes crucial to your success. You will also need organizational changes, build systems and leadership within your organization.

As your business grows, you will hire more employees. There is a saying, *"employees cause more headaches than machines."* You will be let down time and again if you do not hire a properly qualified manpower and train them for their tasks. Unfortunately, instead of relaxing, your problems will grow exponentially and you will find yourself working harder and longer hours.

At times, the situation becomes so stressful that an owner wants to hire a manager as you have money to do so and run away from all the problematic issues. If this is done pre-maturely, it can cause a company to collapse. You will need to place systems, checks and balances in place before you can think of handing over your business to someone else and retire.

On the other hand, there are owners who find it extremely difficult to hand over managerial control of a company they have worked so hard to build—it is their baby, after all! They think that no one can do a better job than them.

To succeed at this level, you have to first find someone who is perhaps as smart as or better than you to run your business. Once you have found such a person, you have to develop the mindset to let go – it may sound simple but is very difficult as you have been the hands-on person all your life. You have to trust the person you have appointed to run your business and refrain from interfering on a daily basis in running of the business. You are now an owner/ leader and no longer the hands-on person … it is time for you to now relax and work towards a strategic view of your business and growth.

Your focus now should be on finding new investments and increasing the profitability of your business. Maintaining a healthy cash flow is the responsibility of your manager. Although you are not involved in running your business on day-to-day basis, you have to keep a tab on your business from monthly/ quarterly or through annual reports. You have to intervene only when things are not progressing as planned.

Once you reach this stage, you no longer have to perform any physical activity in running your business. Your income from the business becomes passive—this is where the fun begins. You will be devoid of any daily pressures of running a business. This will give you time freedom to read, meet people, grow your business network and prepare yourself to next step of financial growth and challenges.

At this stage, your focus should be on building capital to invest in other businesses. This is important if you wish to become rich and wealthy. After this stage, you simply become an investor. You buy assets that will give you even more passive cash flow.

Investor

Investment basically means, *'Make money with money to become wealthy.'* As an investor, you are interested in Return on Investment (ROI).

> You can either be an employee, self-employed or a business owner to be an investor. They all may be investors but they operate at different levels of cash flow and knowledge. For example: an employee invests money that grows with time.

This is because the principle of compounding works with time. On the other hand, a business owner –when he buys a new business – is basically leveraging another person's time to grow rich. We will look into this in more detail later.

There are basically two types of investors:

- **Passive Investor** – A passive investor is the one who is either an extremely busy person or a person who lacks the knowledge to make investments. These people either trust their money to fund managers or buy mutual funds to diversify the investment risk. This generally results in very slow growth of investment portfolio. In the majority of the cases, these investors only make money if the market is moving up. Their investment loses value if the market value of the investment goes down.

- **Active Investors** – These are investors who take the effort of learning about investing. Most active investors take time to analyze and find deals that are below market value and therefore give higher returns. They actively follow the market trends and carry out both technical and fundamental analysis of their investment before buying. They make money irrespective of market dynamics, whereas passive investors are satisfied with a 10% growth in their investment each year an active investor looks for 20–50% or more. They understand risk and take steps to contain than risk.

Types of Investments

There are basically three types of investments:

- **Real Estate** – This is simple, robust and most forgiving to mistakes. Property prices move very slowly and therefore do not require constant monitoring. Real estate investment also provides financial leverage that investing in stocks and businesses do not provide. It, however, requires a deposit and cash flow income for banks to approve your loan.

- **Stock Market** – Investing in stocks requires knowledge to get started or you may land up losing your principal amount. You also have to monitor your investment regularly as stock prices fluctuate constantly. You have to buy stocks at market value - they can never be purchased at a discount. There is very little financial leverage as banks hesitate to give loans against shares. To make serious money out of stock market, you have to become sophisticated and accredited investor. For this, you need assets worth $ 1 million and an annual income of over $200,000 in USA. This amount can differ in other countries. Once you are an accredited investor, you will be able to invest in securities that give higher returns but also carry higher risk. If you have limited knowledge or no time then stick to buying mutual funds. Buy index funds that track markets such S&P 500 funds, BSE, ASX etc. These funds operate without interference from fund managers and carry no management load and therefore give higher returns. It may seem strange but statistics show that very few fund managers beat market on regular basis.

- **Businesses** – This gives the highest returns if you can buy low performing businesses for cents to a dollar and turn them around for profit. However, you need to have experience as a business builder to turn around companies in your area of expertise. For inexperienced operators and first-time buyers, it is advisable to either buy a reputable franchise business that have all the systems in place or a well-run business. After you have gained experience in operating a business for couple of years and gained some confidence, you can look to buy businesses below their value and increase profitability by increasing the turn over and reducing costs through better management.

Skills of a Knowledgeable Active Investor

Many active investors make huge loses because they lack financial skills or do not have adequate control over their investments. To become a sophisticated investor, you have to master the following skills:

- **Knowledge of Taxes** – Taxes can make or break an investment. An otherwise attractive investment opportunity may have a huge downside after taking account its tax implications. It can erode the bottom-line. You have to have knowledge or seek advice on the tax implications of an investment. This will differ from person to person depending upon the financial situation. A knowledgeable investor can gain higher returns with low risk after studying the implications of tax law, corporate law, securities law, capital gains tax, stamp duty etc.

- **Management of Investment** – When making an investment you have to take into account on how you will manage the investment. Some investments are messy and very difficult to manage even though they may promise very high returns. For instance, it may be very attractive to buy a property or business overseas as it shows excellent cash flow and growth prospects. Your financial analysis may be right but before making such investments, you have to take into account travel and administrative costs to manage the investment. You will need to create legal entities in a foreign country, hire a tax accountant and managers to look after your asset. You have to understand time and management cost of an investment before rushing to make a decision.

- **Brokerage** – High brokerage fee can sometime make an otherwise good investment into an average one. There are many investments that have re-occurring brokerage fees.

Many times, it is only the broker who makes a profit and not you. An example of this is when you buy a property in an area that does not have stable tenancies. Re-leasing cost will dramatically reduce the net return from your investment.

- **Control Over Income and Expense** – A good investment is when you can exercise control over income and expense of your investment. Investing in hotel units on profit share basis may sound very attractive especially when you can live in them for 2 to 4 weeks each year. Unfortunately, in such investments you neither have control over the income or expense. In most cases, returns from such investments are extremely poor.

- **Information** – Information is the key to making sound investment decision. If you do not have adequate or transparent information about an investment, refrain from buying it. Always cross check the information provided to you for its authenticity. Don't get duped by slick salesmen who appeal to your greed and put you under time pressure into making decisions with incomplete facts about an investment. Warren Buffet says that secret to his success is that he spends 80% of his time reading financial reports.

- **Terms and Condition of Agreements** – It can be tedious reading through fine print in most agreements. This is especially true for agreements drafted by crafty lawyers of big corporations to be signed by small-time unsuspecting investors. Most novice investors sign agreements without knowledge of the implications of certain clauses in the agreement. These can come to haunt you when you least expect. Ask anyone who has gone through an insurance claim. If you are not sure about a clause, seek legal advice. It may cost you a little in the beginning but save you considerable amount of distress at a later date. Best situation is if you have the control of setting your own terms and condition of an agreement.

- **Buying and Selling** – You should have control over buying and selling an investment. There are investments that have long lock in periods. It is best to avoid them. By having control over buying and selling, exiting an investment if things go wrong becomes possible. It can also give you much needed liquidity in times of distress or if you wish to invest in a better opportunity. Remember there will always be a time when you will need to sell a long-term investment to maximize your profit.

- **Management Control** – This may not be possible for small-time investors but when you make major investments then always endeavor to have some management control. This will give you inside information regarding your investment. As you're starting out, you may not be able to gain control in large corporations. It may be better for you to investment in small and medium size companies depending upon your budget. Better still, start your own company that gives you a total control over your investment.

- **Business Entity** – A knowledgeable investor creates entities not only to take advantage of taxes but also to protect the asset. These include forming Corporations, Limited Liability Companies, Trading Trusts and Family Trusts. It is best to seek legal advice as this will depend upon your situation, country you live in or location of your investment as laws differ for each country and sometimes states.

Fundamental & Technical Investing

With the advent of online trading many investors have become 'day traders' operating from the comfort of their home office: they buy and sell shares by using various types of software available in the market. Most of these people are engaged in technical investing. Though 'day trading' strictly cannot be termed as investing, if the aim is to create passive income, it is good for generating cash flow if done properly.

A truly knowledgeable and sophisticated investor takes investment decisions after doing both fundamental and technical analysis of an asset.

Fundamental Analysis – This involves careful analysis of the following:

- Financials and future earning potential of a company

- Economic outlook as a whole with especial focus on country and state where the company is located

- Economic outlook of the specific industry in which the company is involved

- Direction of interest rate movement

Technical Analysis – These days, markets fluctuate wildly because news travels at a lightning speed and get amplified through multitude of news outlets. This affects the market sentiments of both buyers and sellers. It is because of this that more people are turning towards technical analysis. They prefer short-term trades as against investing for long-term. Technical analysis involves the following:

- Analysis of emotions of the market

- Supply and demand of company stock

- Look for discounted prices of a stock based on sentiment

- Study of pattern of share price movement

- Study volume trends of sales and purchases of a stock

Fundamental analysis is a must if you wish to invest for long-term - this is what Warren Buffet does best to create long-term wealth. Technical analysis, on the other hand, is more suited for short-term trading. Whether you are long-term investor or a short-term trader, it is advisable to use both the analysis methods. This will not only maximize investment returns but also reduce risk.

Outside and Inside Investors

Most people are outside investors; they make their investment decisions based on financial reports released to the public as a part fiduciary responsibility of a corporation.

An inside investor is the one who has some degree of management control of a company. He has a greater knowledge regarding the future plans and problems within a company – this knowledge is extremely important to reduce risks and increase returns.

You can become an insider either by building your own company or by buying controlling interest in a company.

Being an inside investor should not be confused with SEC definition of an "insider". According the law "insider trading" is illegal if one profits from company information that is not public.

The difference is that an inside investor has control over direction and operations of a company whereas, an outside investor does not and is therefore limited in his capacity to change things.

Concentration Vs Diversification

Study the two statements below carefully:

"Do not put all your eggs in one basket."

— Proverb

"Diversification is a protection against ignorance. It makes very little sense for those who know what they're doing."

— Warren Buffet

This is why investing can be so confusing for many investors. Your fund manager will advise you to diversify by investing into mutual funds and Warren Buffet will give exactly the opposite council to focus only on few investments; both advices are true depending on your circumstance.

"Wide diversification is only required when investors do not understand what they are doing."

— Warren Buffet

If you lack the knowledge of investing or do not have the time, then it is best to diversify by buying into mutual funds. It is best to seek advice from competent fund managers or better still, invest on a monthly plan into an index fund.

*"By periodically investing in an index fund,
the know-nothing investors can actually outperform
most investment professionals."*

— Warren Buffet

Index funds are those that track share prices and are better because they have no loading costs. It has also been found that they perform better than most fund managers.

On the other hand, if you are a knowledgeable investor with limited funds at your disposal and wish to embark on the path of accelerated wealth creation then it is best for you to focus on one or maximum two wealth creation strategies at a time. You can truly master only one of the two things at a time. You also greatly reduce risk by concentrating on few holdings.

Once you have mastered an investment technique, it takes very little of your time to repeat the process to maximize your profit. Building wealth can be a boring repetitive process once you have mastered a technique. Unfortunately, the human mind needs excitement and most people tend to lose focus as they want to try out new things. There is nothing wrong in exploring new ideas but one should not lose focus on things that are getting results.

Once your wealth grows, it is important to diversify to preserve your wealth. Concentration builds your wealth whereas diversification preserves your wealth.

We do a full circle from diversification in the initial stages when we lack knowledge to concentration for accelerated wealth creation as we become more knowledgeable, and finally go back to diversification to preserve wealth.

Copy Trading – You can combine concentration and diversification by applying strategy to 'copy funds' on social trading platform of outstanding brokers who do buying and selling of stocks, commodities and foreign exchange as a profession. They do both fundamental and technical analysis.

It is a very time consuming and needs professional knowledge to do technical and fundamental analysis of thousands of companies, foreign exchange and commodity trading platforms. If you wish to diversify for safety reasons it is humanly impossible to follow all the trends and events that shape buying and selling decisions in various markets.

Investing in mutual funds is a safe strategy but the returns are very poor. Money in stocks, forex and commodities is made when you buy low and sell high. Your growth will be minimal if you follow buy and hold strategy as there is no leveraging like in the case of property investment for accelerated growth. That why I use 'Copy Trading' strategy for accelerated growth with minimum effort.

I do not have the patience or energy to sit on the computer for several hours each day to follow market trends. My main expertise is in real estate investing. To increase liquidity and diversify my portfolio I need to invest in stocks and commodities. All I do is copy trades of smart brokers on social trading platforms. By following this strategy I have been consistently making returns from 15% to 25% annually. The best part is that it is passive income. I check my trader's performance once a month. I stop copying brokers who have not performed well and find new traders to copy based on their potential and investment risk history.

Analyzing Investments

If you wish to become a knowledgeable investor whether it is in real estate, stocks or businesses, you have master the following:

- **Financial Statements** – Become an expert in reading and understanding Financial Statements such as balance sheets, profit and loss statements. These are important to understand financial health of a company and risks involved in investing in a company.

- **Investment formulas** – These help in calculating profitability and risks involved in an investment. There are software programs and calculators that help you with the calculations but you still need to understand what they mean in relation to an investment you are analyzing.

- **Investment Vocabulary** - Mastering investment vocabulary will help you in discussions with experts when analyzing an investment.

At the end of the book we have included basic information that will help you read and analyze financial statements, important formulas and vocabulary that you will need when making investment decisions. Initially you may find them bit intimidating but they are very simple to understand once you start using them. It is extremely important to master the basics if you are serious about becoming a knowledgeable investor.

How to Generate Massive Cash flow to Fund Investments

We have seen that as an employee, there is very little money you can spare for investing after meeting your basic needs. There is a limit to how much belt tightening you can do fund your investments. After all, there is a need to live in the present. There was a suggestion to start a part-time business that will help generate not only extra cash flow but will also save you tax dollars that can be used for investing.

Becoming self-employed improves cash flow but is still not the ideal situation. Things start to change once you become a business owner. The problem we discussed earlier is that a growing business has huge cash needs to grow. Most business owners have a tendency to redeploy their capital in growing their business rather than investing. This is not a very healthy financial situation because if something goes wrong with the business they will lose everything. The only stable situation is when you stand on two strong financial legs.

To grow rich fast, you have to sell. This is the fundamental principle. You have to buy wholesale and sell retail. You have to master selling and marketing skill. Most people hate selling but without a sale there is no money. The problem is not selling but rejection that is part and parcel of selling process. Faster you overcome hesitation regarding selling, the sooner you will embark on journey to riches.

Let us examine few other creative ways to generate cash. These methods will vary depending whether you are an employee, self-employed or in business. These methods of cash generation should not be confused with investing which is creating long-term assets that provide passive income.

Flipping Real Estate – This involves buying a property below value. Making renovations or adding value by sub-division, unit titling, adding additional space etc. The last step is to sell the property for a profit. It best works with delayed settlements and early excess to the property before settling. Your cash flow will increase on how fast you can renovate and sell the property. Flipping real estate can be risky when the property market is in a downward spiral with prices going down with few takers in the market for your end product.

Buy Build and Sell Businesses – This generates far higher profits than flipping real estate but requires a higher level of skill and experience. The trick is to buy under-valued businesses at rock bottom price. Increase revenue and profitability of the company.

There will be a considerable capital gain if you sell a business with a healthy profit. Buying and selling businesses require lesser capital outlay than flipping real estate. There are loss-making businesses you can buy with no money down. The owners of such companies are at times stuck with long-term leases and just want themselves out. It takes much lesser effort and time to turn around a loss-making business caused due to poor management. All you need is an excellent jockey to run your business, change in personnel and sales/marketing effort. Quick sale of activity can be made by providing vendor finance, finding an employee with a payout, management buyouts or selling the business one part at a time.

Franchising a Business – Once you have a successful business with systems in place, it may be possible to franchise the company for additional cash flow with little or no risk. Initially, you may have to spend some money and time to set up franchise system for your business. Once this is done successfully, it costs virtually nothing to add new franchises. Your cash flow and profits increase with every addition of a new franchise.

Take Company Public – This is the secret to real wealth and riches. This is what experienced entrepreneurs do: they take their company public. Bill Gates would not have been the wealthiest man in the world had he not taken his company public. Rich sell paper assets to become more affluent – this is trading at the ultimate level! It is like creating wealth out of nothing. Now you have other people's money to grow and buy businesses and assets. You have to sell a dream to go public and once you have the money you have to make that idea become a reality. To succeed you will need excellent trust in yourself and your team.

Converting Expenses into Cash flow – Most people buy stuff like TVs, cars, expensive clothes, holiday homes, and boats etc. from income after tax. This keeps them poor all their lives. Rich people, on the other hand, buy assets that give them passive cash flow and at the same time reduce their taxes. They get extra cash flow from a refund of tax dollars and also income from the asset. They keep repeating this process every year and growing more affluent, which is an upward spiral to riches. The poor people on the other hand keep buying stuff that not only costs them money but also regular maintenance cost that keeps mounting every year. They keep sliding down the wealth ladder with negative cash flow.

Information Technology the Next Big Frontier – Today a common man has more computing power in the palm of his hand (in the form of mobile devices) than a supercomputer a few decades back. He also has access to world marketplace to sell goods, information and services through the internet. Most people waste their time playing online games, visiting social platform, forwarding useless jokes or watching movies/ TV shows. There is nothing wrong with these if done in right proportion. Unfortunately, this becomes an all time-consuming activity with zero productive output.

The internet provides a huge opportunity to change your financial outcome at minimum start-up cost. It is a source of huge cash flow. Yes, there are internet scams and ponzi schemes but with little knowledge, you can keep clear of them—you must take a look at the opportunities it has to offer.

Some of the biggest companies in the world like Amazon, Apple and Microsoft, Alibaba were launched by young people from their garages with shoestring budgets. Some of them were school dropouts. These are big stories that inspire us but also intimidate us. Fortunately, there are thousands of small new start-ups and success stories every year in virtually every part of the globe. It is over a trillion-dollar pie getting bigger each day; it depends on you how much of the pie you want to grab.

You get paid for problems that you solve. Bigger the problem that you solve, more money you will get paid. This is true irrespective of whether you are working as an employee, are self-employed or running a business. Technology helps solve problems at a much faster and cheaper rate than anything. It can be applied to solve any daily problem that you encounter. While starting out, do not try and solve a big problem or you will get disappointed. Facebook started as a social website for college students. It gradually got scaled up. Look at a niche problem in your locality and try and solve it with the help of technology. You don't have to be a computer expert to do this. You don't even have to employ anyone. On the internet, there are hundreds of websites like elance.com, fiverr.com where experts provide technical support for any work that you may have for fraction of cost of hiring someone part or full time. You have to think like a business man and solve people's problems.

Another great thing about the internet is that you don't even need to have your own product to sell. Virtually every company in the world is paying affiliates online to sell their products. If you have used a product and are passionate about it then sign up as an affiliate for the product and start marketing it on the internet.

Have you heard of drop shipping? You can tie up with a physical product manufacturer for marketing their product. Most manufactures don't have the time for marketing their product and will be most happy to pay you if you sell their product. You can make sales on the internet through Facebook advertising or Google AdWords. Once an order is received, you can collect the money and ask the manufacturer to ship it directly to the buyer. You don't need to invest in the product, own a warehouse to store them or provide after sales service. The only thing you need to learn is how to market on the internet. It costs very little but some effort is required to acquire the marketing knowledge. Anyone can do this without any expensive start-up costs.

You can start an internet business part-time even if you are an employee. Over 60% of businesses worldwide do not have a website. Large numbers of those who have websites are not mobile compatible. The majority in business do not even understand how an application can help and grow their business. Tony, a friend of mine, understood this problem and started his own business even though he was not an expert in building either websites or applications. His target was small businesses. After taking orders, he would get the websites and applications built by various experts on the internet. He would then take up annual maintenance, website hosting, social media and promotion contracts. This gave him passive income. His business grew and soon he was hiring full time virtual assistants and technical support staff from Philippines. This was at fraction of cost of labor in his country.

Aforementioned is one small example. The internet has endless possibilities. You can build websites for handyman services, plumbers, electricians, childcare services, real estate renting/buying and selling for homeowners who wish to save on commissions, selling books, old clothes, cars ... the list is endless and limited only by your imagination. But remember, you have to start with tackling a small problem in narrow niche and stay focused until you start making money. The problem with the human mind is that it always wants to start big from the beginning. There is nothing wrong in thinking big but always start small. Take a few small steps to success. This is the only and sure route to success. As you gain experience and start making money, slowly but surely expand your business.

Once you learn the skill of marketing through the internet, your cash flow problems will be over.

Convert Ideas into Money – We are fortunate to live in a knowledge driven era where ideas can be converted into money and money can buy great ideas at a fraction of their potential value. There are all kinds of talented people in this world; there are visionaries with great ideas but lack the skills to convert those ideas to money by building a profitable business around it. Then there are business builders whose time is absorbed in solving practical problems that they have no time to be creative. They are willing to pay good money to buy ideas that can be converted into money.

Bill Gates did not create any of the software that he sold. He built his Microsoft business around products and ideas that he bought from others. The genius of Steve Jobs lay in visualizing potential of product created by others and using them to build Apple the most valuable company of our times. For example, 'mouse' was never built for use with computers. He cross pollinated the idea and rest is history.

Brilliant Idea Gone Waste

This is the story of a great idea gone to waste. Russian economy was in turmoil because of the Soviet Union break-up in the early nineties. The Government was trying hard to get the economy going again and they were suspicious of the USA and the West.

A very dear friend of mine who had recently retired from the Navy had a brilliant idea: he decided to take a bold trip and explore business opportunities in Russia. His advantage was that he spoke excellent Russian and was married to a beautiful Ukrainian lady with political connections. It was a master stroke because he came back to India with a rich haul of Government contracts for supply of food, clothing, and shoes etc. that were worth millions of dollars.

Rich businessmen got whiff of the contracts and their potential. My friend was wined and dined. Businessmen were ready to offer excellent money to buy out the contracts but my friend insisted on becoming 50% partner in the deal even though he had no money. The conditions he set forth were unacceptable to the businessmen. My friend was in no position to execute the contracts as no one would give credit to him without financial guarantees. To cut the long story short, all the contracts expired without a single one being executed successfully.

It would have been wiser for my friend to sell the contract to businessmen who had the right experience and finances to execute the orders. This would have given him the finances to build the Russian business and improve his credibility with the Russian Government – a brilliant idea gone waste.

The moral of the story is selling an idea for cash flow is a great strategy if you don't have the capacity to execute it.

Converting Ideas into Money

Everyone does not have to be Bill Gates, Steve Jobs or Eon Musk to become rich. Even small ideas have potential of making decent money; each one of us has great ideas! We face problems in life that need solution: we are angry with the government and local bodies not doing things that have common sense solutions. Sometimes, we get inspired by a new thought or idea but let it pass. We put it off for another day or think that someone else may have thought of it … the idea dies a natural death.

If we tap into even a few of those ideas, nurture them and find practical solutions we can become rich. Sometimes, an idea may be too big for you to execute. You have to then sell your idea to others. But before you start selling your idea or product, you must protect it by filing intellectual property rights. You have to show some intent, only then will venture capitalists fund your idea. You can also license your intellectual property to create passive income.

Final Thoughts

It takes very little money to start investing. After a short time, compounding effect starts to take place. You will be surprised at how fast you have the potential to grow if you take the first step.

There are thousands of creative ways to generate cash flow required for investing. We have discussed few of these opportunities in this commandment. The internet offers great opportunity to those with bright ideas and little start-up capital – the world is flushed with money! Investors are looking to invest in the next new idea. Can you focus your energy and concretize your great idea into practical existence? I assure you, if you can, money will never be an issue ever again.

Investing is the second leg of your financial stability, whether you are an employee, self-employed or in business. Investment for passive cash flow brings solidity to your financial well-being.

Preserving wealth is as important as creating wealth. There is no point in creating your financial well-being after working so hard—only to lose it by not giving adequate thought to protect your wealth. We shall study this important subject at some depth in the next commandment.

Thou Shall Preserve Thy Wealth

> *"It's not how much money you make, but how much money you keep, how hard it works for you, and how many generations you keep it for."*
>
> — Robert T. Kiyosaki

What do world heavyweight champion Mike Tyson ($400 million), Rapper 50 Cent ($155 million), Icelandic billionaire Bjorgolfur Gudmundsson ($1.1 Billion), Sean Quinn, richest man in Ireland ($6.5 Billion), tennis champion Boris Becker ($35 million), Hollywood actor Nicholas Cage ($150 million) have in common? They all went bankrupt despite having a net worth of millions/ billions of dollars at some stage in their life.

Why did that happen? If you read the stories of these famous and rich people, you will find a common trait. They lacked the financial intelligence that was needed to keep what they earned. They simply forgot *"The best way to make money is to avoid losing it in the first place."*

Shakespeare rightly said, "***Fool and his money will be soon parted.***" Fools trust others with their money and make little or no effort to educate themselves to be financially wise.

The most important part of long-term wealth creation is to learn how to control risk. The process of wealth creation involves taking risk; there is no success or growth without it. The enlightened wealth creator knows how to control risks. Generational wealth is created and sustained by implementing correct risk control methods in business and finance.

Preserving wealth throughout your lifetime and passing it onto future generations entails protecting what you have created in times of political and economic turmoil, changing technology environment, investing in assets that are resistance to inflation etc. It involves not only withstanding external turmoil but also internal turmoil of stake holders. The greatest risks to wealth preservation are future generations that are not prepared to sustainable wealth.

Let us examine in depth on how some of these problems can be overcome.

Nature of Risk

Only fools think that there is no risk and take no measure to protect them against risk. Simply look at the world around you – it is constantly in a flux and change. Even as you read this book, galaxies are collapsing and new ones being created. Days turn into nights and seasons change, empires come and go and our bodies grow from young to old and finally go back to dust: our whole universe is in a state of constant change. Everything around us is changing even as we breathe. Therefore, it is unwise to think that any business or investment on which our financial wellbeing depends will last forever.

Life Cycle of Businesses and Investments

Every business and investment has a lifespan – some have longer lifespans whilst others have relatively shorter lives. Eventually, even the best businesses and investments will die … you have to protect yourself from this eventuality!

For instance, land as an investment may have a long lifespan as compared to improvements on the land. Buildings or improvements don't last forever but give higher cash flow when compared to bare land. Similarly, businesses like education, health, hospitality, energy have longer lifespan when compared to technology companies. In the past 70 years, we have witnessed a transition of the music industry from records, LPs, tape recorders, CDs to downloadable music on your iPhone and iPad. Even iPods, after their short glory, have become extinct. Although it must be said that high-tech companies that are known for shorter lifespans have higher profitability margins.

If you invest and sleep over your investment thinking that it is long-term then one day, you will wake up and find that your money is gone. To succeed financially, it is important to be aware of what is happening in the world around you and how it is changing. Regularly monitoring your investment is important.

It is the matter of your strategy and temperament on where to invest. Some people like to make quick gains and invest in high technology businesses and stocks. On the other hand, Warren Buffet likes to invest for long-term into blue-chip brick and mortar companies with solid and recognizable products with longer lifespans. Both investment strategies are fine as long as you know what you are doing. A good investment is a function of focus and your financial intelligence. No one individual can master everything. One of the functions of financial intelligence is to understand risk and your capacity to deal with the risk.

Entry and Exit Strategy

Having understood the lifecycle of business and investments, it is important to plan entry and exit strategies. The best entry point is just before a business is about to mature and exit once it hits the peak and starts to roll off, it is easier said than done and needs a deep understanding of the company, industry and economic climate.

We tend to get impressed by stories of how someone had invested only a few thousand dollars in Google or Apple in the early Eighties that are worth millions of dollars today. What people forget are numerous failures when investing in new start-ups. There is nothing wrong with investing in new start-ups if you know about the company and have additional cash that you can invest long-term without any returns. Investing in new start-ups is not only risky but also requires specialized knowledge. The rewards can be huge if you are willing to risk and wait.

Smart investors have an exit strategy in place even before they invest. Let me give an example: a friend of mine was building a resort in a popular holiday destination, which was his first venture into the tourism sector. His previous experience was in residential and commercial property investments. He had done his calculations but was not completely sure because of a lack of experience in the hotel industry. He planned his hotel development around two-bedroom apartments with dual keying system. The two-bedroom apartment consisted of a single room studio unit with a small kitchenette (sleeping two) and a one-bedroom apartment with a living room and full kitchen (sleeping four) with an inter-connecting door. The two units could be rented out separately or as a single unit for larger families when running as a hotel. His exit strategy was to sell individual units as two-bedroom, one bedroom or studio apartments to owner occupiers or investors if the hotel did not provide the forecasted returns.

Financial Intelligence and Human Factor

In the constant flux and change in the universe, only one thing is permanent and that is your financial intelligence. It is intangible and therefore less susceptible to destruction. If you have the intelligence, you will always find an optimal solution to a problem. Each financial situation is different and only a well-educated mind can find the right solution to the problem. In times of economic collapses, when others find themselves helpless, people with financial intelligence make fortunes.

Financial intelligence is like riding a bicycle. Once you know how to ride it, you never forget. A person with a high FI can be down and out but will always bounce back – Donald Trump went bankrupt but within a decade he was back to become a billionaire.

When people are driven by greed, they tend to become oblivious to the risks involved in an investment. They will either not do proper research or turn a blind eye to the signals indicating risk. On the flipside, fear freezes people into not taking action when an opportunity presents itself – they will focus only on the dooms day scenario.

To protect and grow your wealth, there has to be a level of emotional detachment when making financial decisions – it requires mental discipline to develop this attitude. Awareness is the key. One has to be aware of external opportunities and threats and also monitor emotions of greed or fear within. As your awareness grows, you will instinctively recognize risks and rewards in a deal.

One simple way is to avoid taking hasty decisions: let the moment pass and take a pause. Don't be rushed by the salesmen into taking a hasty decision that you will regret later. Take time to think and analyze. Discuss with knowledgeable experts regarding possible upsides, risks involved, tax implications, legal issues, government regulations, future trends, financial accuracy of reports; seek proofs of data presented to you etc. Keep seeking information till the time you are fully satisfied. If you do your due diligently in a methodical manner, chances of making mistakes will greatly reduce.

Creating and preserving wealth is not only a function of financial intelligence but also fair measure of emotional and spiritual intelligence. You have to constantly look after your physical, emotional, mental and spiritual bodies. If you fail to balance these critical aspects of your wellbeing of your wealth will suffer.

Diversification of Wealth

> *"Diversification may preserve wealth, but concentration builds wealth."*
>
> — Warren Buffet

When you are young and starting out, mastering one process of wealth creation and focusing your effort on that process is the key to your success. However, in your later years when you have amassed wealth and do not have the luxury of time to start all over again, it is wise to diversify your portfolio to preserve wealth. Every investment and business has a lifespan as discussed earlier – this problem has become more acute with rapid changes in technology. It is therefore wise to diversify your portfolio when you have wealth or as you grow older. As one ages, it becomes difficult to keep up with the changes. Diversification will help you protect your wealth even if few of your investments go wrong.

Asset Protection

Why Is Asset Protection so Important?

Creating profit from business and investments is not always the bottom line; you must be capable of securing yourself against lawsuits and claims. Some of the risks you might face include obligations of mortgage and debts to vendors and third parties, claims regarding damages your employees are responsible for, issues of consumer-protection, and professional or product liability. These risks when mishandled often lead to business and financial losses that may extend to the loss of even personal assets. Being conscious of the risks you face and having the ability to effectively evade their potential effects gives you an assured opportunity to successfully run your business.

Every comprehensive plan for asset-protection is aimed at significantly strengthening the prevention of risk so as to guarantee optimum security for private and business assets from claims that can possibly be made by creditors. Ideal asset-protection plans constitute legal strategies for protecting your assets from seizure after court judgment or even restraining potential claimants from the very beginning.

Strategies employed in the planning of asset-protection comprise of arrangements or separate legal structures like partnerships, corporations, and trusts. The types of assets owned by you and the creditors from whom you are most likely to receive claims play a huge role in the best Asset Protection structure(s) for your business.

Entities differ from country to country but their purpose is to protect your wealth from risks and failures which are part and parcel of any business or investment. You have to seek legal advice as to which entity is best suited for your purpose.

You should never put all your eggs in one company failure of which can bring down your entire financial empire. Create different entities for different businesses and investments. These can be inter-linked but independent to insure failure of one does not impact the safety of the other. Expert legal advice is needed to set these up correctly.

You should control everything but own nothing: this is the best situation to be in. No liability or failure should be able to affect you personally.

Types of Claims

There are generally two types of claims that businesses can face. It is vital to have a clear understanding of the difference in relation to the protection of assets:

- **Internal claims** – These types of claims come from creditors with remedy restricted to a specific entity's assets like the assets of a corporation. An example can be someone slipping and falling on a real estate property of your corporation. The injured person can only pursue claims limited to the assets of your corporation (i.e., the real estate property). All this is dependent on you not directly causing the injury.

- **External claims** – These claims can go beyond the entity's assets, extending to your personal assets. If in the same instance above, your corporation owns a truck that is driven negligently by you into pedestrians; all injured parties could make law suits against both you and your corporation so as to get double judgment compensation from your personal and corporate assets.

Types of Assets

Getting explicit knowledge of the types of claims that you could possibly face provides a good platform on which your plan for the protection of your assets from seizure or garnishment. Similarly, important is the understanding of how susceptible different asset types are to claims. Assets referred to as dangerous assets, are naturally more liable to substantial risk. Common dangerous asset examples include commercial property, rental real estate, and business assets, like motor vehicles, equipment, and tools. On the other hand, assets that present very low inherent liability levels are termed Safe assets. The ownership individual bank accounts, bonds, and stocks incorporate no risk in relation to their existence.

Since safe assets generally carry low-risk probabilities, they can be owned by the same entity or individually.

It is not advisable to combine dangerous assets with safe assets. By ensuring ownership of dangerous assets as separate will help to reduce the risk of losing the assets individually.

Asset-Protection Vehicle Types

There are several types of asset protection vehicles that can help you protect your assets. These include; corporations; partnerships; and trusts.

Corporations

Corporations refer to business organization types that are formed as per state laws. The shareholders of every corporation control its legal ownership as seen with stock shares. All shareholders normally participate in the election of a board of directors tasked with running and managing the corporation. The officers including the president, treasurer, and secretary are then elected by the board of directors who give them the authority to direct the daily business activities of the corporation. A single individual is permitted in many states, to occupy all the corporate offices while serving as the sole director.

There exist many different corporation types used for the protection assets: C or business corporations, S corporations and LLCs (limited liability companies.)

C or Business Corporations

The limited liability corporations provide to its shareholders, directors and officers (principals) an ideal tool for the protection of assets. Corporate principals are not personally exposed to risks of contract breaches, corporate debts, or injuries caused by the corporation, agents or employees to third parties. The liability of corporations' even when responsible limits creditors to the pursuit of strictly corporate assets in order to compensate claims: corporate principals' assets are not subjected to seizure or claim for corporate debts. The clear difference between corporations and the other entities like trusts or partnerships is the personal liability protection it provides to its corporate principals.

Additionally, the availability of a corporation's liability protection depends on whether the corporation is carried as a distinct and separate entity in clear isolation from its individual officers or shareholders. Creditors often resort to trying to prove that corporations are not functioning as distinct and separate business entities especially when they seem to possess no significant assets. They can attempt to highlight the fact that the corporation is just the alter ego of its shareholders or officers – this strategy is known as piercing the corporate veil. It provides the creditor with extended reach to the assets of corporate principals when successfully proven.

S Corporations

S corporations and C corporations are similar with the exception of it being qualified for IRS special tax election that allows taxing at just the level of shareholders with business corporate profits. In addition to affording the liability protection applied in C corporations, there are other required qualifications for S corporations relating to shareholder numbers and types, profit and loss allocation between shareholders, and the stock types issued by the company to investors.

Limited Liability Corporations (LLC)

This new entity affords liability protection similar to that offered by C corporations to corporate principals in addition to the tax treatment (pass-through) of S corporations without LLC associated restrictions and formalities. It evolved from the introduction of additional formalities on S corporations.

General Partnership

A general partnership describes an association between two or more persons in agreement to perform the activities of a business together. Partnership agreements can be oral or written. As a tool for the protection of assets, the usefulness general partnership is minimal since every partner is individually susceptible to liability for all partnership debts without excluding those incurred on behalf of the partnership by other partners. Partners have the ability to account actions on behalf of the others with or without their consent.

This unlimited liability feature directly contrasts what is enjoyed by corporation owners (limited liability.) In addition to being liable for contracts negotiated by other partners, every partner is exposed to the risk offered by the negligence of the others. Also, partners are individually liable for whole amounts of partnership obligations.

Limited Partnership

Authorized by state law, a limited partnership (LP) is comprised of at least a general partner and a limited partner or more. Though there must be at least two legal entities, a single person can represent both the general and limited partners like the same person or corporation can be both the general and the limited partner. The responsibility of managing the affairs of the partnership is on the shoulders of the general partner whose personal liability for partnership obligations and debts is always unlimited.

Limited partners in limited partnerships are not susceptible to personal liability for the obligations and debts of the partnership which exclude their contributions. Limited partners exercise little or no control in the daily management of the partnership so as to afford this protection. Assuming an active management role can lead to a limited partner losing his/her limited protection from liability and changing status to a general partner. The value of shares for limited partnership is highly diminished, thanks to this restricted control and contribution in the management of the partnership business.

Trusts

A trust is a document between the trust creator (known as the settler, grantor or trustor) and the person tasked with the responsibility of managing the assets inside a trust called the trustee. Trusts beneficiaries are people or institutions who will receive some or all benefits from the trust.

The trust document spells out the rules in regard to assets held in the trust. Trusts are designed to protect assets inside the trust and reduce estate tax liabilities.

Once an asset goes inside a trust, it takes a new identity. Trusts certify the transfer of certain assets from the grantor to the trustee, allowed to hold and manage the trust assets for someone else's benefit (the beneficiary). It now has the immunity from estate taxes and resistance to probate.

When a trust is created in the lifetime of the grantor, it is known as a living trust, while a testamentary trust refers to trusts created at the grantor's death or through a will or living trust.

There are basically two basic types of trusts: revocable and irrevocable. The grantor in a revocable trust reserves the right to amend the trust with alterations or revoke it through the dissolution of a part/the entire trust. In an irrevocable trust, the grantor reserves no such right. This lack of control makes the irrevocable trust an incredibly powerful tool for asset-protection. It is impossible to get sued for assets you don't own or control anymore.

Picking the Ideal Asset-Protection Vehicle

After gaining knowledge on the popular structures for asset-protection, let's take a look at the particular asset types and their ideal vehicles.

Owning a professional business or practice, specifically, implies your liability for claims and risk of loss is high. This business type is, therefore, a dangerous asset. Getting your practice or business incorporated has long been regarded as ideal strategy for the prevention of seizure and liability of your personal assets that could arise from claims or lawsuits against your business. C Corporation is, however, being quickly replaced by the limited liability company as the best asset-protection entity.

LLC, while offering similar protection to C Corporation, offers more flexibility, efficiency and has lower setting up costs.

If the business entity lacks the ability to protect you personally, seek protection in other entities like: a family limited partnership (FLP), LLC, or a trust for your personal assets. In situations where you get personally sued, some or all of your personal assets would be protected within some single or multiple entities making it pointless for creditors to pursue them.

Finally, professional business or practice owners should prioritize incorporation with either an LLC or a C corporation. These business entities, though not an assurance of protection against claims of malpractice, they provide you with shelter from corporate financial obligations unless the debt is personally guaranteed by you. Another benefit is the possible protection against other business claims

Praveen Kumar & Prashant Kumar

without direct relations to your professional actions like claims of suppliers, employees, tenants or landlords.

Is it advisable to Ever Participate in a General Partnership?

The response to this is an unequivocal "no" almost always. Being a co-partner means you are responsible for your partner's actions and partnership debts regardless of your knowledge or participation. As part of a general partnership, the liability of your personal assets is greatly expanded for all claims related to your business relationship.

If you are in a general partnership then use other methods for protection of your personal assets. Without an ideal protection plan, you risk losing everything for merely being in association with partners who may not be as prudent as you are.

There are numerous vehicles for asset protection—there is no single perfect plan that will suit everyone because each individual's circumstances are different. It is advisable to use services of a professional in asset protection like a financial advisor or an attorney in the development of the ideal asset-protection plan for your business and investments.

Insurance

These days it is possible to insurance virtually everything, which may include your life, health, property, business, income, travel, goods, services, etc. The downside is that there is a cost attached to insurance which pinches especially when you are starting out and struggling to make your ends meet. Once you have the cash flow and funds, insurance decisions are easier. Insuring risks is very important part of wealth protection because an uncovered risk can ruin you for life.

There are myriads of insurance products. It is important to qualify and quantify your risk and shop around for the correct policy that covers your risk at minimum out of pocket cost.

Over insuring is equally bad for your finances as is under insurance; prudence is the key. Fine judgement is needed when taking out insurance policies. Your premiums can come down dramatically depending on the excess amount (this is the amount you are willing to pay from your pocket in case of an accident).

You have to also see if a policy is important or not in the first place. For instance, if your children are grown up and well settled, and you have adequate assets for your retirement then there is no point in taking out a life insurance policy. If, on the other hand, you have a young family dependent on your income, then it is extremely important for you to take out an insurance policy protecting your life and income.

Transfer of Wealth

"Always understand that wealth isn't something you possess, but a flow which has found a temporary parking place under your stewardship. Eventually this stewardship will move to others as all things must pass (including you.)"

— Emperor Magazine

For wealth to be preserved, it must pass from one generation to the next smoothly and with minimum loss. It is also incumbent on each successive generation not only to preserve wealth but also to enhance it.

There are several important aspects to transfer of wealth that we shall examine in succeeding paragraphs.

Financial Education of Loved Ones

A person who works hard, creates wealth values and preserves it is better than those who inherit it without much effort. For this reason alone, financial education of children becomes paramount.

It is not only important to send children to the best colleges and universities but to also educate them on financial matters from a very young age. They must be groomed into business and investing because this education is not readily available in schools. It is important to pass experience and wisdom through practical application by family members who have created wealth and have the experience of managing it.

Rockefellers have managed, not only to build enormous wealth but also, to sustain it through multiple generations in large part because of sustained financial education of younger family members. Rockefeller use to give each of his young children an allowance of 25 cents to teach them how to handle money. If they wanted more money, they had to earn it by working. The children were required to account for the money they were given. This is a great example of practical lessons we need to pass to our children to create sustainable wealth.

If a family does not have adequate experience then children should be sent to attend investment seminars and made to interact with professionals like financial advisors, tax professionals and lawyers.

There is nothing more fascinating than stories; tell your children how their grandpa rolled up his sleeves and through sheer hard work and persistence lay the foundation of family wealth they now enjoy! This will excite and inspire them to emulate their family heroes. If you do not have any in your family, read them stories of other wealth creators with whom they can relate. Teach them about delayed gratification and what stewardship of wealth for greater good means. Proper handling of wealth is a great responsibility. It can be put to great use if handled correctly but can be a destructive force when given to people with untrained minds.

Strategic Joint Decisions

> *"Families that share and learn together tend to work well together, growing their financial, intellectual and social capital."*
>
> — James Hughes, Author

Every new generation will have new ideas about money and what values they attach to it. They will have their views on how best it can be grown and used to enhance their lives and those around them. You may not always agree with your kids but it is important to give them chance to participate in family decisions that have impact on their lives. Such discussions are essential not only for the education value but also promotes openness, trust and brings harmony within a family. It leads to better understanding of family values and teaches conflict resolution skills.

Avoiding conversation regarding money matters as they are sensitive is one of the most common mistakes in family. You can not reveal everything to a young child and burden them with information that they are not prepared to process. As they grow, the level of their participation can be increased gradually.

Your bank balance and accumulation of assets accounts to nothing if you do not properly prepare the next generation to handle money. Your true wealth lies in collective human and intellectual capital within a family.

Children must be given the opportunity to solve their financial problems. Even if you have the money, do not bail them out just to show your care and concern. Once children learn to solve their problems, they will have the tools to succeed in life.

Make a Will

It is extremely important to make a will or the State will decide who will receive the money. In some countries, estate duties can be excessive if there is no will in place.

A will is also important for smooth transfer of assets to your loved ones. In absence of a will, there will be lack of clarity that can result in ugly and very expensive legal fights within family members, which will result in dilution of your wealth.

Drafting a will is a very responsible thing to do to preserve your financial legacy. The best part is that it does not take much money to do so. A good lawyer will charge you only a few hundred dollars to make a will.

Online Will - These days there are online services that allow you to make a will. Online wills are suitable when wealth tax is not involved. In case of complex holdings, it is wise to get a lawyer to draw out the will. Online Will costs are much lesser than using services of a lawyer. In addition, you can do this within half an hour or so sitting in comfort of your home. The software used in creating the will in most cases is very user friendly. It will ask you a few questions and your responses will create a final will document. It is also easy to revise your wills online. Wills are living documents! You will need to revisit them time and again as your circumstances change with marriages, divorces, new births or deaths in your family.

Online wills are normally filed with local probate court and will become public document. If privacy is a concern to you then use a lawyer or a living trust.

Caution - One important thing to check about your will is how much it will cost to execute the will. Some services are free upfront but will cost you substantial amount of money at the time of execution of the will. In some cases, they take a percentage of the estate. It is always wise to read terms of service before making a will whether online or through a lawyer.

Once the will is made, you should make several copies and keep them in a safe place. A copy should be given to executor of your will or at least he should know where to find the will. Executor can be your lawyer or an impartial member of your family whom you can trust.

How to Beat Inheritance Tax

Inheritance tax can be huge in some countries. They can dilute your wealth assets substantially when passed from one generation to the next. For instance, on the death of a person the assets will pass to the surviving spouse who may be equally aged. There will be payment of inheritance tax. Within a few years, the assets will be taxed again as the property passes from the surviving spouse to the children.

Through proper planning, inheritance tax liabilities can be reduced or eliminated altogether.

Joint Holdings – In jointly holding assets, there is nothing to transfer when one of the joint holders dies, which also reduces income tax liabilities when the joint holders are alive.

Transfer Estate to Your Loved Ones when still Alive– You can transfer money and assets to your nominees before you die. There are limits to how much you can gift each year. The amount you can transfer will differ according to laws in each country and you must consult your accountant before transferring money or assets.

Leave Something to Philanthropy - Anything you leave to philanthropy is free of Inheritance Tax so it can be a helpful method for lessening your Inheritance Tax burden – at the same time, giving money for a noble cause.

Put your Life Insurance Cover in Trust – If you do this, payout from the life insurance will go into the trust directly. Your beneficiaries will get the money without paying any inheritance tax. You simply have to inform your insurance company and they will do this free of charge.

Set up a Trust in your Will – This kind of a trust comes into existence only when a person dies. It facilitates transfer of assets to surviving spouse through sale of shares in return for an IOU. When the second person dies the loan is repaid thereby saving inheritance tax. This is a very complicated trust and needs to be set up by experts.

Pension Arrangement – Lump-sum payments on death like insurance should be paid into a trust so that they can be transferred to beneficiaries with paying inheritance tax.

Tax Saving Investments – There are several investments that are exempt from inheritance tax and you may consider investing in them in time. A word of caution: you should not invest in such schemes blindly simply because they are tax efficient. You must look at each investment on merit after taking into account tax benefits. There is no point in buying a bad investment simply to avoid paying tax.

Final Thoughts

"The rich man is a fool who dies without arranging his affairs to assure that his wealth does well during his lifetime and after his passing."

Arraigning your affairs means that you should start taking actions when you are still in your prime and not leave it for too late in life. You can put your wealth to great use in your lifetime and with proper planning, ensure that it continues to be productive long after you are gone. These include educating all stake holders, using proper asset protection vehicles and planning transference of wealth to the next generation.

Wealth has a spiritual dimension. In the tenth and final commandment, we shall examine how we can transcend wealth and create something that is indestructible.

Thou Shalt Give Thy Wealth Away

> *"The meaning of life is to find your gift.*
> *The purpose of life is to give it away."*
>
> — Pablo Picasso

Have you ever wondered why Bill Gates has pledged 95% and Warren Buffet 99% of their wealth away to charity?

Have you also wondered why Bill Gates continues to be the richest man in the world after having donated over $38 billion to his foundation? His wealth continues to grow at an ever-increasing pace even as he donates.

Bill Gates and Warren Buffet are not alone; there are other billionaires who have pledged to give a major part of their wealth to charity. These include Microsoft cofounder Paul Allen, Manoj Bhargava the founder and CEO of 5-Hour Energy, Spanx founder Sara Blakely, Patrice Motsepe founder of the mining company African Rainbow Minerals, Virgin Group founder Richard Branson, The chairman of Indian consulting and IT company Wipro Azim

Premji, Facebook founder and CEO Mark Zuckerberg. The list of these great individuals is simply too long to include here.

This brings us to the question "Is there a co-relation between giving money to charity and becoming richer?" Have these billionaires found some secret to wealth creation that we don't know. Can we apply the same principles to increase our net worth?

We don't learn this from wealth creators alone. Every religious book that I have read or spiritual leader I have met teach that in act of giving we truly receive. We can be cynical about religion or spiritual practices but we simply cannot deny the teaching or the evidence.

The charitable give out the door and God puts it back through the window.

— Traditional proverb

Every wealth creation book that I have read, seminars I have attended or knowledge gained from mentors emphasize the fact that giving leads to wealth creation. I certainly know this from my experience in life: whenever I gave, I received and whenever I was stingy, some misfortune happened in my financial life.

Let us examine some research findings on this subject.

Research

Logically speaking it does not make any sense as to why giving away your hard-earned money should result in increase of wealth. However, research on co-relation between giving and increase in wealth by Arthur C. Brooks of American social scientist and president of the American Enterprise Institute shows that there is connection between the two.

Arthur analyzed data from SCCBS *(The Social Capital Community Benchmark Survey)*. The data included a survey of about 30,000 people of different education background, race, age, religion in over 40 communities in the U.S. They were also from various socio-economic backgrounds. The survey revealed the following:

- The people who gave money to charity made more money than those who did not.

- Giving increased by 7% when wealth increased by 10%. This means as a person got richer he could give more.

- People who volunteered for social causes made more money than those who did not.

- Charitable impulse of volunteering made these individuals donate more money than others.

- Giving is about charitable impulse and not only about money. You can get the same results by donating time, sharing knowledge, giving food or for that matter blood.

In his final Analysis, Arthur found that regardless of income, a family who gave away $100 more than another family, in the same earning bracket, earned on an average $375 more than the other family as a result of generosity. He found that this was also true for the organizations and countries that gave away money to charity. In the past 50 years, the per capita of Americans has risen by 150% with an increase in donation of 190% within the same time frame.

This finding is supported by that of data from ***Statistical Abstract of United States.*** $100 in giving away resulted in an increase of GDP by more than $1800. America being one of the most charitable nations has benefited by being one of the richest.

Sir John Templeton, investor and one of the greatest pioneer of mutual funds of 20th Century stated *"I have observed 100,000 families over my years of investment counselling. I always saw greater prosperity and happiness among those families who tithed than among those who didn't."*

There seems to be some logic in these findings after all! Statistical evidence bears witness to the fact that giving leads to more wealth. But we still need to explore as to why this happens.

Why Giving Leads to Wealth

There are various reasons as to why giving leads to wealth. Some are intuitive and others supported through research.

Sense of Wealth Increases through Act of Giving

Zoe Chance of Yale University and Michael Norton of Harvard Business School, in their research 'I Give, Therefore I Have,' observed the act of giving increases the giver's 'Sense of Wealth.' The giver psychologically feels wealthier than they actually are through the act of giving. This change in mind-set leads to more wealth. Winston Churchill intuitively supported this theory *"We make a living by what we get, but we make a life by what we give."*

Please check out what some of the donors say in their words:

Ted Turner, the founder of CNN: *"Being generous always made I feel great, and it seemed like every time I gave money away, I somehow made that much more."*

Ackman hedge fund billionaire: *"Over the years, the emotional and psychological returns I have earned from charitable giving have been enormous. The more I do for others, the happier I am. The happiness and optimism I have obtained from helping others are a big part of what keeps me sane."*

Mobile phone entrepreneur John Caudwell: *"Philanthropy gives me far more pleasure and satisfaction than making money. In fact, making money is now largely driven by the knowledge that I will be able to leave even more wealth behind for charitable causes when I go."*

Hedge fund billionaire Tom Stayer: *"Surely the pleasure we derive from... consoling, understanding, loving, giving and pardoning far outweigh any selfish and passive pleasures of owning, having, or possessing."*

Michael Bloomberg, founder of Bloomberg: *"Making a difference in people's lives – and seeing it with your own eyes – is perhaps the most satisfying thing you'll ever do. If you want to fully enjoy life, give."*

Hedge fund billionaire John Arnold: *"There is no more worthwhile work and no greater mission [than philanthropy]."*

Here's a quote from the book "Start Late, Finish Rich" by David Bach:

"Over the years, I've spent a lot of time studying the rich and the superrich. The more I've learned, the more I've become convinced that most people who achieve great wealth have at least one thing in common – giving.

When I first heard the billionaire investor and philanthropist Sir John Templeton make this point, I wondered if it could really be true. Could the secret to being rich really be as simple as "give more and more will come back to you"? Does giving really attract wealth?

Some 10 years later, I can say that I am certain of it. Time and again, I've come across examples of superrich individuals who made a point of donating a portion of their earnings to charity – even before they became rich. Indeed, virtually every self-made billionaire I've ever studied echoes Templeton in declaring that tithing or giving was a principle of their life well before they had any money.

As a result, I've come to believe that giving of your time or money to help others is more that the "golden rule." It is the golden magnet. I have seen this happen in my own life and in the lives of hundreds of people around me. It's a simple, observable fact: Those who give lead more abundant lives.

This sums up my thoughts, beliefs, and experiences as well. In fact, I've commented that in the years that I've given the most, I've seen the largest increases in my net worth. It's not a coincidence in my opinion.

This doesn't mean that we give to get more. Really, our motivation should be to help others and that's why we should give. Then, as we're blessed even more financially, that allows us to give even more – and the cycle goes on and on this way."

Increase in Happiness Index and Productivity

The act of giving to under-privileged leads to inner fulfilment which in turn increases the happiness index of a person. Statistics have shown that a happy person is more productive. When a person is more productive it leads to higher levels of earning and wealth.

Studies show that act of giving lowers stress levels. People with low stress levels are more productive and successful. A relaxed person generally has better health, happiness index is higher and they're more successful. Giving creates strong communities. A charitable person will eventually profit from it even though he did not desire it.

Highest of human motivation, according to Maslow's hierarchy, is self-actualization. This is taught in every business class. Just before Maslow died, he put self-transcendence one step beyond self-actualization. According to him, the greatest fulfilment comes when a person seeks a benefit beyond what is personal. He called it self-transcendence – when one's own needs are put aside for service to others, which provides the ultimate fulfilment and happiness. This level of motivation leads to highest productivity.

When we do any good to others, we do as much,
or more, well to ourselves.

— Benjamin Whichcote

The act of giving creates psychological changes within a person. Researchers have found that the act of giving stimulates parts of your brain associated with fulfilment of basic needs and primal instincts. Once the brain feels that our fundamental needs are met, it becomes more productive; our decision-making skills, including financial decisions, improve.

Studies also show that giving stimulates empathy and compassion. You tend to become more confident as a person. These subtle changes in personality traits are observed by people around you. They will perceive you as a kind and gentle human being. They will invariably gravitate towards you. They recognize leadership qualities in services to others. Servant leadership is the new mantra to success whether one plans it that way or not. When people see you giving, it inspires them – they cannot help but help you. You will be viewed as a natural leader amongst people and your voice will be heard. These are simple by-products of act of giving and will indirectly result in making you a happier and successful person.

Giving Starts the Receiving Process

The act of giving starts the receiving process. Have you ever tried to receive money with your fists closed? This is simply not possible. If you are hurt after a broken relationship and shut down your heart for fear of pain then you are not in a position to receive love from even the most beautiful and loving person on the planet. You have to open your heart in spite of fear of pain to receive love again. Similarly, if your mind is closed then you are not in the right frame to receive wonderful thoughts that may transform your life forever. The act of giving not only opens your hands, but also your mind and heart. Once you give, you are in a position to receive great wealth. You have to keep your heart, mind and palm open to receive great gifts of life.

"The more doors you open, the more you will allow the universe the opportunity to bring something to you and in ways you could never have imagined."

— Anonymous

This is something I can share from my own experience of life: whenever I was stingy, it invariably led to some financial catastrophe in my life. When I observed this fact repeatedly in my life, I forced myself to give even when I found myself in most difficult financial situations. I never wavered in my support of under-privileged children I was educating or refuse anyone who asked me for help in worst of financial times. Providence would always come to my rescue. This magic has never failed.

There is always an ebb and flow of money in our lives. Give when you have cash in hand. Give even more when you are low in money and see the magic happen. I can't prove it scientifically, but it happens. Just try this simple recipe and it will do wonders to your financial health. In every action we take in our lives there is an element of luck involved. Ask any successful person; once you get into the habit of giving the element of luck for some strange reason will favor you.

Law of Cause and Effect

Whether it is physics that explains the law of cause of cause and effect, or spiritual laws of karma that say *"We reap what we sow,"* no one can escape it. David Cameron Gikandi rightfully says *"Give cheerfully and freely. It is the energy behind giving that matters so do not give grudgingly. The law of cause and effect guarantees that you shall receive plenty for what you give."*

Pitanjali, an ancient Indian philosopher, explained this fact a bit differently. He said that there is no linear motion in this universe—everything moves in a circle: planets rotate around the sun, the moon circles the Earth, the Earth rotates around its axis, water rises from the seas becomes cloud, the rain water forms rivers and flows back into the sea completing the full circle. A tree rises from the earth and when it perishes, it goes back to the earth. Man is formed from five elements of the earth and goes back to those elements after death. Good or bad, deeds come back to us in some form whether we realize or not. Similarly, when you give money away it will always come back to you – this is the universal law of nature that no one can escape. Sometimes in our greed, we fail to see the implications of this law. Most enlightened wealth creators understand this basic fact and act according to this law.

Giving Increases Size of Your Network

Although giving is not done with an aim of any monetary benefit, it generates goodwill in hearts and minds of people. It is like a certificate of good health and many people and businesses will like to partner or associate with you.

Bill Ackman, hedge fund billionaire has stated that *"While my motivations for giving are not driven by a profit motive, I am quite sure that I have earned financial returns from giving money away. Not directly by any means, but as a result of the people I have met, the ideas I have been exposed to, and the experiences I have had as a result of giving money away. A number of my closest friends, partners and advisers I met through charitable giving. Their advice, judgment and partnership have been invaluable in my business and in my life. Life becomes richer, the more one gives away."*

There is also inherent fun and joy in giving that brings people together. Ask this question to donors, activists and volunteers and they will tell you about the sense of happiness and camaraderie that happens when people work together for a nobler cause than personal gain. By giving your time, effort or money you increase your circle of influence. You meet diverse and interesting people. As your network grows, so will your wealth.

How Much Money to Give Your Children?

This question is relevant to wealthy parents. How much money to leave to your children?

Most wealthy parents are concerned about the impact of too much unearned wealth on lives of their children. They want their children to lead significant, meaningful and productive lives. They don't want their wealth to come in the way to hurt them. They want to help their children and provide them with adequate financial security but too much wealth can hurt their productivity – it is a very fine and difficult balance.

Most of the super-rich are leaving only fraction of their money to their children. Warren Buffett when asked this question offered a good rule of thumb: *"enough money so that they would feel they could do anything, but not so much that they could do nothing."*

Other rich parents take a completely different view. "Shark Tank" investor and self-made millionaire Kevin O'Leary's has taken a more severe approach. According to him, ***"I'm not planning on giving my kids any of my wealth. They know when their education is over; I'm pushing them out of the nest. You want to prepare your children for launching their own lives. I tell wealthy parents that if they don't kick their kids out of the house and put them under the stresses of the real world, they will fail to launch."***

How much money to leave to the kids is a very philosophical question which each parent has to address individually depending upon their situation? No single rule is applicable. One has to understand the nature and capability of their children. Are they wealth creators? Can they handle money? Will they put money to good use or destroy your hard-earned wealth? Will too much money have a corrupting influence or will they use it wisely to enhance their lives and those around them? Parents have to ask these questions of them before deciding on amount of wealth they leave to their children.

Best Way to Give Wealth Away

The best way to give charity is to not make the receiver feel belittled in any way. A self-respecting person can feel humiliated when receiving handouts. The idea is to help a person overcome their problem so that they do not have to be supported for long.

A plant can never grow in shadow of a big tree. Your help should be to make the receiver stand in the sunlight of success. They should never feel beholden to you for help.

There are eight levels of charity.... The highest is when you strengthen a man's hand until he need no longer be dependent upon others.

— Maimonides

The aim of charity should be to help a person become strong so that they become capable and no longer dependent on others. Help should be given without destroying their self-respect.

Monetary help given without proper advice or support is never long lasting. For example, one of the most popular charities is paying for educational support of under-privileged children in third world countries. This is because education changes lives and is the biggest leverage to success. Educating a girl child is even more effective because it changes not only one person but affects the lives of an entire family. However, giving money for child education support is not effective without involving the parents, community and environment around the child.

Andrew Carnegie, one of the richest men of all time (1835 – 1919), gave away 90% of his fortune – around $350 million – to charities, foundations and universities. He did not recommend wealth to be distributed in small quantities as it resulted in waste. Carnegie suggested supporting larger projects such libraries, schools and foundations which he felt brought greater good to humanity.

Carnegie also strongly recommended the rich to live modestly, provide moderately to dependents and use surplus wealth in ways that bring good to community. He spent the last eighteen years of his live devoted to administering charities.

Whenever you decide to give to charity, you must thoroughly research the project; there are many charitable projects that are total waste of your money. In some cases, the administration costs of a project are so high that very little benefit reaches the beneficiary. The charitable organization becomes an end in itself. There are also fraudsters who are only in it to make gain for them.

The best way to give your money is to become involved in the charity of your choice so that you can make a difference. In case you do not have the time, at least make the effort of analyzing the charity and getting feedback from reliable sources before donating money. Giving money away is not as easy as it looks – it takes knowledge, time and effort.

One way is to be sensitive to people and the environment around us. You will be able to find people who need your help. We can't change the whole world but we can definitely influence a few lives within our sphere of influence.

"Wealth is your servant, and you are a servant to your wealth. Money is little more than a tool that comes with a responsibility to use it wisely."

Charity also means taking responsibility for the wealth we create. It should be created without exploiting people and by giving them a fair wage for their work. It also involves taking care of schooling of children of the staff we employ, providing them with housing and health insurance. Also, in the process of creating wealth, we should not cause damage to the environment, which is the immediate sphere of influence. It is charity if we are sensitive and take care of our sphere of influence.

Transcendental Wealth

Most enlightened wealth creators understand that wealth flows, and nobody can block its flow. We are mere custodians of money for a short span of time. It invariably passes through our hands to those of others. No one has been able to take their wealth with them. We pass it to our loved ones or give it to charity. Some fools try and guard it closely only to leave legacy of legal battles when they die. Wealth continues to flow whether we like it or not.

What we do with the wealth when we are custodians for a limited period of time is what matters. Wealth is a privilege and great responsibility. It takes much lesser effort and knowledge to make money than to spend it wisely. It needs great wisdom to use the power of wealth correctly. When used with restraint and wisdom, wealth can help us to become greater than ourselves. Acts of giving and kindness help us to connect with a large suffering humanity and in the process raise our consciousness.

> *"Giving frees us from the familiar territory of our own needs by opening our mind to the unexplained worlds occupied by the needs of others."*
>
> — Barbara Bush

What benefactors like Warren Buffet and Bill Gates are trying to do is transcend wealth itself. They are not consumers of wealth; they lead very modest lifestyles in comparison to their wealth. They understand the transcendental nature of wealth and simply choose to give it away willingly. In the process, they become larger than themselves and will outlive their wealth. Their legacy will continue long after their wealth has vanished. They will live in the hearts of men, women and children whom they have helped.

> *"What we do for ourselves dies with us. What we do for others and the world remains and is immortal"*
>
> — Albert Pine

Some will ask as to why we should make an effort to create wealth if the end purpose is to give it away. The answer to that question is: the process of wealth creation evolves you as a human being. It normally starts with a selfish motive but in the end, it transforms you into something bigger than your narrow self. It transforms your family and other human beings who come in your contact. You understand its transitionary nature once you possess it – its possession gives you the freedom to explore and understand new things, and the chance to help others and in the process, help yourself.

Wealth is never an end in itself: it is a means towards the greater good. Some unfortunate people lose sight of the real purpose of wealth and get consumed by greed. Ultimately, such people get destroyed by their greed. Wealth built on the foundation of greed never lasts.

It does not matter how much you give—it is the principle of giving that is important. The very act of sacrifice in order to help others who are in more need than you is transformative. It sets into motion laws of karma that will open the universe of riches to you. The act of giving is a necessity and not a luxury if you want to be truly successful in life.

The purpose of this book will be served if it helps in educating and help morph enlightened people who create wealth the right way, preserve wealth the right way and ultimately, use their wealth for the greater good of humanity. This process leads to seeking a higher purpose in life and its fulfillment. I hope and pray that to some extent, that purpose is served. If you have read to this point, I thank you with gratitude in my heart and hope you succeed in creating true wealth that helps not only you and your family but entire humanity.

If you liked the book and gained some knowledge that will be useful to you in life, then please leave an honest review to help others find this book. It will be a small effort on your part, but an act of charity that may help in changing few lives for the better. I thank you in advance for your help.

This book is about fundamental principles of wealth creation that can be applied to any business or investing strategy. At Wealth

<u>Creation Academy</u>, we teach multitude ways to generate passive income, which includes: real estate investing, digital publishing, affiliate marketing, multi-level marketing and investing in forex, commodities, and shares by copying experienced traders that need very little of time. You may like to get started with some of the strategies depending on your budget and time.

Montgomery

Other Books by the Author

Praveen Kumar & Prashant Kumar have authored several bestselling books. Please visit their website http://praveenkumarauthor.com/ for more information

About The Authors

Praveen Kumar was abandoned by his father at the age of fourteen and joined the Navy at tender age of fifteen where education, roof and free food were guaranteed.

In order to understand the root cause of suffering he turned towards philosophy and religion. After 10 years of soul searching and meditation he understood that 'life is 'and material and spiritual world are closely interwoven. You cannot live in one without the other.

Praveen was highly successful in the Navy, where he successfully commanded submarines, sailed around the world in a yacht and received gallantry award for his contribution to the Navy.

Despite his success in the Navy, Praveen realized that lack of financial security for his family was one of key root causes of his suffering, resulting from his childhood deprivation. To improve his financial standing, Praveen took pre-mature retirement from the Navy to build his financial future through investing in Real Estate. The decision to educate on financial matters paid off, and today he and his wife are comfortably retired on six-figure passive income.

His aim is to help others create wealth in an enlightened way and empower them to live a healthy and happy life. He dedicates his time to write books and articles on financial and spiritual matters.

Prashant graduated with distinction from Auckland University as a computer engineer and later completed his MBA from the world's leading institution - INSEAD. During his successful corporate career, he worked for the most reputable consulting firms in the world - BCG & Deloitte - and represented New Zealand on Prime Minister-led trade missions to South East Asian countries.

After successfully generating income through his passive investments in property and stocks, Prashant decided to team up with his father to help people transform their lives through the leverage of financial education.

Their website http://wealth-creation-academy.com/ is devoted to teaching people how to create Multiple Streams of Passive Income through investing in real estate, online marketing and creating digital products.

Financial Statements

Investors rely on financial reports is due to the fact that these reports provide detailed information on the status of a business and its current financial stand position. It is important to remember that it is businesses that publish the report and not independent impartial reporters or organizations. When reading financial reports online or in magazines it is important to keep this fact in mind.

FINANCIAL STATEMENTS

There are basically three primary types of business financial statements.

- **Income statement:** This statement carries the summary of sales revenue including any other income and expenses including any losses during a particular time period. At the end of every income statement is the bottom line profit during that period also called the net income or net profit. The profit performance statement is commonly referred to by businesses as the *P&L* or *profit and loss report.*

- **Balance sheet:** This statement is a summary of the financial condition of a business. It is a summary of assets and liabilities of a company and the equity of owners at the end date of the period of the balance sheet. The formal name for a balance sheet is ''the statement of financial position/ condition''.

- **Statement of cash flows**: This statement is a report on the net increase or decrease in cash during the period. It is based on net income or net profit reported in the income statement. The statement of cash flows also summarizes sources of cash and how the cash has been used for investment and financing activities.

These three statements constitute the vital building blocks that constitute a financial report. A combination of the primary statements above, their financial footnotes and other relevant content are summarized and distributed to the investors and lenders of a company to help them keep updated on the financial and health performance of the business. As per the law, in most countries, public companies are required to distribute abbreviated versions of their quarterly reports in addition to the annual report. Though not required by the law, most private companies also distribute interim financial reports.

RELEVANCE OF FINANCIAL REPORTS

Financial reports are designed to provide answers to many popular and basic financial questions:

- How much profit or loss is the business making if any?

- How comparable are the assets and liabilities of the business?

- What is the source of income for the business and how is this capital being used?

- What is cash flow during a period and is it sufficient to meet current needs of the business?

- How much of the profit is being reinvestment and what portion is being distributed to the owners?

- Has the business enough and sustained capital for growth in the future?

- The main <u>purpose of financial reporting</u> can be summarized as the fulfillment of the obligation to deliver required business details to the shareholders and lenders of the business. Financial reporting is a key feature of the agreement made between investors/lenders and a business.

- It is the way of businesses stating that provide us with funding and we'll offer accountability through information on our activities with your money.

- The common statutory law controls financial reporting – which is also subject to ethical standards. Financial reporting, however, is sometimes used in methods contrary to set ethical and legal standards.

When studying the parameters of any business with the desire of making investments in it, going through the financial reports of the business is imperative. This is not to say, you are required to read the entire annual report. The vital sections alone provide enough insight into the business dealings. Taking a look at the annual report together with the other financial statements filed by a corporation to the Securities and Exchange Commission (SEC) could provide information needed to determine liquidity and profitability ratios that make cash flow a lot more understandable.

THE IMPORTANT PARTS OF ANNUAL REPORTS

It can be a challenging task going through annual reports and anyone would be relieved with the knowledge of not needing to scrutinize every single page. The important parts below will give you an ideal view of the entire report:

- **Auditor's report:** Reveals challenges faced by business the accuracy of the numbers while indicating whether or not there is a need for skepticism in the context of future business operations.

- **Financial statements:** The statement of cash flows; the balance sheet (statement of financial position) and the income statement; these statements carry the actual annual financial results.

- **Notes on Financial Statements:** These are details about possible problems with the numbers and derivative methods used to arrive at those numbers.

- **Analysis and Discussion of the Management:** The financial report analysis by the management including other issues discussed affecting the operations of the company.

READING FINANCIAL REPORTS FOR PROFITABILITY RATIOS

Financial reports are read to provide us with insight into the financial position of a company while understanding a sense of its viability in the market. You can make investing decisions by testing financial viability of a company with the use of the important formulas outlined below:

- **Price/Earnings ratio** draws a comparison between the stock price and its earnings. This determines what returns you can expect from a company if you purchase a stock at the current market value.

  Price/Earnings ratio = Market value for every share of stock / Earnings for every share of stock

  A ratio of 10 will imply that a stock of $10 per share can

expect to earn $1 from the company earnings for every share. This does not mean that you will get a cash return of $1 because some of the profits may be reinvested in the company.

- **Dividend pay-out ratio** presents a figure of the earnings of a company given to its investors. It can be used to calculate the accurate amount of cash return an investor can expect to earn from owning a share of stock.

  Dividend pay-out ratio = annual dividend per share/Earnings per share

- **Return on sales** indicates the efficiency of a company's management at controlling and carrying out its operations. It involves profit measurements for every dollar worth of products sold.

  Return on sales = Net income before taxes/Sales

- **Return on assets** indicates how effective company assets are being used. A relatively great return on assets value reflects the high efficiency levels employed by the company in the management of its assets.

  Return on assets = Net income/Total assets

- **Return on equity** is a measure of how effective a company is at earning money for its investors'.

  Return on equity = Net income/Shareholders' equity

- **The gross margin** provides understanding on the amount of revenue left after the subtraction of the total cost of production and marketing of the product.

  Gross margin = Gross profit/Net revenues or sales

- The operating margin represents the efficiency of a company in its control of costs, and the factoring of expenses without direct relation to a specific product's production and the marketing.

- Operating margin = Operating profit/Net sales

LIQUIDITY RATIOS AS BASIS FOR FINANCIAL REPORT READING

A company finds itself on shaky ground when it happens to lack ready cash to finance its daily operations. The formulas stated below can be used to determine whether or not a company is in possession of sufficient liquid assets (easy to convert to cash):

- **The current ratio** provides information on a company's ability to comfortably settle bills due for 12 following months with on hand assets.

  Current ratio = Current assets/Current Liabilities

- **Quick ratio or acid test ratio** gives a clear idea on the ability of a company to settle its bills strictly with cash which is due from receivable accounts or cash on hand. This excludes anticipated money from inventory and other sales.

  Quick ratio = Quick assets/Current Liabilities

- **Interest coverage ratio** gives insight on whether or not a company is earning money enough to pay the interests on its outstanding debts no matter the value.

  Interest coverage ratio = EBITDA/Interest expense

  Note - Earnings before interest, tax, depreciation and amortization (**EBITDA**) is a measure of the company's operating performance.

CASH FLOW FORMULAS AS BASIS FOR FINANCIAL REPORT READING

Having an interest in a particular company definitely implies you have interest in going through its reports (financial). This part covers the testing whether or not viable operations are bringing in enough cash required to sustain the company.

- **Free cash flow** brings to note the amount of money earned from the operations of a company which can be kept for future use in an account for savings.

  Free cash flow = Cash from business operations – Cash dividends – Capital expenditures

- **Cash return on sales** focuses directly on the amount of cash a company is earning from sales of its products.

  Cash return on sales = Cash from business operation / Net sales

- **Current cash debt coverage ratio** provides knowledge on whether or not a company has the ability to cover its needs within a short period with the cash it has.

  Current cash debt coverage ratio = Cash from business operation / Current average liabilities

- **Cash flow coverage ratio** checks for the ability of a company to pay its bills while financing its growth.

  Cash flow coverage ratio = Cash flows from business operations / Cash requirements

APPENDIX 2

Real Estate Formulas

To be successful in <u>real estate, it is important to understand the</u> math and finance behind investing. This includes knowledge of formulas and ratios. These may look complex at first but are relatively easier to understand and master. The good news is that there are investment calculators that will do the grunt work and give all projections for sound decision making. Calculations apart you still need to understand what each terminology means to know the value and returns of an investment.

Gross Scheduled Income (GSI)

Gross Scheduled Income is the rental income collected in a year assuming the property is 100% tenanted and all rents are collected. Rents of vacant units are included at their reasonable market rent for the purpose of calculation.

Gross Scheduled Income = Rental Income (actual) + Vacant Units (at market rent)

Gross Operating Income (GOI)

Gross Operating Income (GOI) is calculated after subtracting from the GSI income from vacancies and adding income derived from other sources such as coin-operated laundry facilities. GOI can be considered as actual income the investor collects from the rental property.

Gross Operating Income = Gross Scheduled Income - Vacancy and Credit Loss + Other Income

Operating Expenses (OPEX)

OPEX function on annual costs associated with keeping a property in service and fully operational. These include body corporate fees, property taxes, insurance, routine maintenance and payment of utilities. Payments made for mortgages, capital expenditures or income taxes are not included in OPEX.

Net Operating Income (NOI)

Net Operating Income is arrived after subtracting OPEX from the Gross Operating Income.

Net Operating Income = Gross Operating Income - Operating Expenses

NOI is an important indicator to a property investor to arrive at a price he is willing to pay for an income stream. It determines the property's market value.

Cash flow before Tax (CFBT)

Cash flow before Tax is the income a property generates in a given year before tax after deducting all expenses.

Cash flow before Tax = Net Operating Income - Debt Service

Cap Rate

Cap Rate or Capitalization Rate is the ratio between the net operating income and a property's market value. It is a very popular term used to calculate a property's estimate of market value.

Cap Rate = Net Operating Income ÷ Market Value

Or,

Market Value = Net Operating Income ÷ Cap rate

Note of Caution – You can arrive at totally different and wrong market value by applying wrong Cap Rate. Great effort should be taken to find out the correct Cap Rate for a particular type of property in a given area.

Cash on Cash Return (CoC)

Cash-on-cash return is used in real estate to calculate the cash income earned vis-a-vis cash invested in a property.

Cash on Cash Return = Cash flow Before Taxes ÷ Initial Capital Investment

Most investors usually look at cash-on-cash as it relates to cash flow before taxes during the first year of ownership.

Calculating the Cash-On-Cash Return

For example, a real estate investor invests in an industrial warehouse that does not produce monthly income. Let us say the total purchase price of the property is $1 million. The investor puts 10% ($100,000) down and borrows $900,000 from the bank. In the first year, the investor pays maintenance and insurance costs of $10,000 out of pocket.

In the first year, the investor pays $25,000 in loan payments which includes $5,000 is principal repayment and $20,000 towards interest. This will imply that the investor's total out of pocket cash outflow during the first year is $135,000

After one year, the investor sells the property for $1.1 million. After repaying debt owed to the bank of $895,000, he is left with a cash inflow of $205,000.

In this case, the investor's cash-on-cash return is: ($205,000 - $135,000) / $135,000 = 51.9%. This is a very healthy return in one year. In case the property was rented, CoC would have been higher.

Cash-on-Cash return can also be used to forecast future cash earnings from an investment. It is an estimate of what an investor may expect to receive over the life of the investment.

Operating Expense Ratio (OER)

Operating Expense Ratio is the ratio between a real estate investment's total operating expenses dollar amount to its gross operating income. It is expressed as a percentage.

Operating Expense Ratio = Operating Expenses ÷ Gross Operating Income

Higher OER is matter concern when a commercial property is vacant. The owner will need to pay OPEX out of pocket that can considerably bring down rate of return from a property.

Debt Coverage Ratio (DCR)

Debt Coverage Ratio (DCR) is the ratio between annual net operating income and debt service (includes both principal and interest loan payments.)

Debt Coverage Ratio = Net Operating Income ÷ Debt Service

What DCR ratios indicate?

- Less than 1.0 – Net Operating Income will not cover debt servicing requirement.

- Exactly 1.0 – Net Operating Income will just about cover the debt requirement.

- Greater than 1.0 – There is adequate Net Operating Income to cover the debt

Break-Even Ratio (BER)

Lenders use BER to calculate ratio between the cash out flow to cash inflow from a property to determine how vulnerable the investment is to defaulting on its debt obligations. BER is expressed as percent.

Break-Even Ratio = (Operating Expense + Debt Service) ÷ Gross Operating Income

BER analysis:

- Less than 100% - expenses are less than income. Investment is in healthy shape.

- Greater than 100% - expenses are more than income being generated. This is matter of concern to lenders as the investor may default in case they do not have alternate sources of cash flow.

Loan to Value (LTV) or Loan to Value Ratio (LVR)

Loan to Value is the ratio between the loan amount to property's selling price or appraised value (whichever is lesser.) LVR is the lending criteria that financial instructions apply when approving a loan. It depends on their policy and type of property against which the loan is being given. LTV determines the leverage that an investor can use when purchasing an investment property. A higher leverage can result in higher returns but can also be risky.

Loan to Value = Loan Amount ÷ Lesser of Selling Price or Appraised Value

Annual Depreciation Allowance

Annual depreciation allowance is the annual tax deductions allowed on an investment property. It varies depending upon the tax code of a country.

Depreciable Basis = Property Value x Percent Allotted to Improvements

Next step:

Annual Depreciation Allowance = Depreciable Basis ÷ Useful Life

Taxable Income

Taxable income is the amount which the owner has to pay based on taxable income derived from the property which is calculated as per the formula below:

Taxable Income = Net Operating Income - Mortgage Interest – Depreciation - Capital Additions - Closing Costs + plus Interest earned in bank or escrow

To arrive at the tax payable by an investor, Taxable Income is multiplied by marginal tax rate.

Tax Liability = Taxable Income x Marginal Tax Rate

Cash flow after Tax (CFAT)

Cash flow after Tax. as the name suggests, is the cash flow accruing from a property after paying tax.

Cash flow after Tax = Cash flow before Tax - Tax Liability

This is the money that an investor can spend to either support their lifestyle or to make future purchases.

Time Value of Money

The value of money is dependent upon the time we need it for. Time of receipt of money, at times, may be more valuable than the amount we receive. This is an important consideration in real estate investing that may at times be hard to liquidate. It is the reason why some people sell their assets below value.

Present Value (PV)

Present Value (PV) shows what future cash flow is worth in terms of present value of dollars. We calculate PV by "discounting" future cash flows by applying "discount rate."

Future Value (FV)

Future Value (FV) – as the name suggests – is the cash flow in the future at a specified time. FV is calculated by applying a given "compound rate" forward in time.

Net Present Value (NPV)

Net Present Value (NPV) tells an investor whether the investment is achieving a target yield based on initial investment: it is the difference between the PV of future cash flows after applying a particular discount rate minus the initial cash invested in purchasing those cash flows.

Net Present Value = Present Value of all Future Cash flows - Initial Cash Investment

NPV Analysis:

- Negative – means the required return on an investment is not met

- Zero – the required return is met as per plan

- Positive – achieved higher than the required return

Internal Rate of Return (IRR)

The internal rate of return (IRR) for an investment property is the percentage rate earned on each dollar invested for each specified period of investment. IRR is also another term people use for interest or yield.

The internal rate of return (IRR) for an investment property is an estimate of the return it generates for each dollar invested during the time frame in which you own it. In simpler terms: IRR is the percentage of interest you earn on each dollar you have invested in a property over the duration of period you hold the property.

For instance, you purchase a retail shop to for a period of 10 years. The compounded interest earned over the 10-year period would represent the IRR.

IRR is a great way to estimate a real estate investment's profitability over a period of time. Unlike Cap Rate, IRR looks beyond the property's net operating income and its purchase price. It gives a clearer picture of expected returns on an investment from start to finish. This is a great tool to analyze profitability of an investment if you are planning to hold it for a long duration.

Formulas for calculating IRR are complex and it is advisable to use an investment calculator or software.

Escrow and Real Estate

Escrow accounts are funds held by a reliable third party to enable the buyer to preform due diligence on a property, assuring the seller they have the capacity to close deal at the end of the stated period. Once the conditions on the sale, such as building inspection or getting satisfactory valuation report are fulfilled, the escrow account holder will release and transfer the payment to the seller. The title of the property is transferred to the buyer.

How to Calculate Rate of Return (ROI) for Real Estate Investments

There are various methods of calculating Return on Investment or ROI of an investment property. In the succeeding paragraphs, we will discuss some of the important ones.

The most common method of calculating <u>Return on investment</u> (ROI) is by using the simple formula:

The above equation may look easy to calculate but care needs to be taken to get accurate figures on variables such as repair and <u>maintenance costs,</u> interest on loans, rates, insurances, etc. ROI will be higher if your initial purchase price for the investment is low. Apart from the initial purchase cost, finance cost is another important factor in determining ROI. You must shop for the cheapest loan. Even a small amount of variation in interest rate can have a major implication on ROI.

The Cost Method for Calculating ROI

In the cost method, ROI is calculated by dividing <u>equity in the property</u> by all costs incurred (these include the initial purchase price plus cost of improvements.)

As an example, let us assume that we buy an investment property for $100,000. Let us say that it costs additional $50,000 to carry out repairs and make improvements to the property. On completion of the upgrade, the property valuation comes to $200,000. The investors' <u>equity</u> position in this example will be $50,000. This is arrived at by subtracting the initial purchase cost of $100,000 plus $50,000 repair cost from the revalued price of $200,000.

$200,000 - (100,000 + 50,000) = 50,000$

ROI from the cost method is arrived at by dividing the equity by all the costs related to the <u>purchase,</u> the upgrade and the repairs in the property.

ROI, in this example, works out to 33% ($50,000 divided by $150,000 multiplied by 100).

The Out of Pocket Method

The Out of Pocket method is very similar to Cost Method but in calculating ROI, only out of pocket cash is taken into account.

Using the same numbers in the example for Cost Method, let us assume that $100,000 purchase was financed taking out a loan in which the <u>down payment</u> was only $20,000. Out of pocket expense in this case will only be $70,000, which includes a down payment of $20,000 plus $50,000 for repairs and upgrade. If the property after rehab is valued at $200,000, the equity will be $130,000.

200,000 - (20,000 + 50,000) = 130,000

The ROI, in this case, will be whopping 185% ($130,000 equity divided by $70,000 out of pocket expenses expressed as a percentage).

The increase in ROI is attributable to leverage applied to the loan by only 20% down payment.

Real estate investors prefer the out-of-pocket method for achieving higher ROI results by applying leverage by putting minimum down payment for the property.

Note of Caution - When calculating ROI, cited in the above examples, care should be taken in adding costs of marketing and brokerage associated with selling. It is also prudent to remember that properties don't always sell at market value. The actual ROI in all probability will be lesser than shown in the example.

ROI will increase if part of the property is tenanted during the rehab process. Rents will add to the cash flow and income.

ROI will also be affected by payment of interest rate during the period of rehab or if the property is refinanced.

The calculations in some cases can become very complex. It is advisable to use investment software /calculators or services of an accountant to arrive at the correct figure.

Investment Vocabulary

Annuity

This is a sum of money invested in the hope of gaining an interest which is paid annually.

Arbitrage

The act of purchasing particular things, like company shares or currencies from an area, and selling them out in a different one within the same time frame in order to make profit.

Blue chip

Is a very secure investment or a company with excellent credentials that has a track record of reliable returns to investors or business partners.

Bond

A document carrying the promise of payback with interest provided to anyone having invested in a company or a government.

Capital

The start-up property or money for any business invested to return profit.

Capital gains tax

This is a tax requested on your profit gotten from invested money or property sales.

Capital-intensive

A business or activity earns the appellation Capital-intensive when it requires the investment of huge sums of money.

Contrarian

Anyone who makes investments contrary to popular trends, like buying shares from companies currently in bad shape or when the market sentiments are down. These actions are usually driven by the hope that things will change in the nearest future resulting in higher profits.

Debenture

An official agreement between an individual and a company wherein the company promises to pay the fixed-rate interest payment to the individual on the money invested by him/her.

Derivative

A type of investment that experiences gain in value whenever a product's price changes as predicted.

Disinvestment

A situation where money is being taken from an industry, country or business, and is invested somewhere else.

Divestment

It is the process of withdrawing your invested money or selling your shares/assets in a company.

Drawdown

A fall in value of an investment.

Equity capital

Funds raised for a business by saving some of the income made by the business or selling shares of the business.

Fund

Is a financial organization that manages money on behalf of others by making investments with it.

Fund manager

An individual employed by a financial organization to manage funds and help in the organization's investment.

Futures

These are agreements that involve the buying or selling of goods, shares or currency at agreed prices with clearly stated future delivery periods.

Gilt-edged

This describes investments often recognized as being extremely safe and reliable.

Hedge fund

A company or a financial organization making investments in high risk ventures like new start-up companies that presents exceptionally large profit potential when successful.

Investment bank

Is a bank specializing in buying and selling large securities.

Investment trust

An organization or company that invests money raised from its customers for a specific purpose.

Inward investment

An investment made in a country by a foreign organization or person.

Junk bond

Is a high-risk bond that pays a high interest rate and reflects the risk.

Limited liability

Is a legal position that protects a person to pay just a small proportion of the debts of an organization they have investments in.

Margin

Money provided by you to a stockbroker to cover possible losses on the investment they made for you.

Maturity

It is the time when profits or interest on invested money have to be paid back.

Offshore

Involving or related to the investment of money in a foreign country.

Pay out

Paying out of interest or profits at the end of a specific period or in instalments over a period of time, as per the terms of investment.

Performance

The success rate of an investment producing income or capital gain for you.

Portfolio

The total investments made by a company or an individual in various entities.

Private equity

Investments made in private organizations having shares that cannot be purchased on the stock exchange market.

Prospectus

A document that provides the details of a proposed business to people who may be interested in making investments in the company.

Pump-priming

An investment made in a project to promote or develop it. Demonstration of putting money is to urge others to invest money in the project.

Reinvest

It is the process of putting profit made in a business back into the business as an investment.

Return

It is the profit made on an investment.

Rollover

A case where the profit made from an investment is being invested again in a similar business.

Savings

Saved or invested budget for future use.

Share

One of the many equal parts of a company that can be bought as an investment.

Short-selling

The process of selling borrowed securities and repurchasing them at a lower price.

Simple interest

The earnings from money invested, calculated annually on the principal investment

Stake

Part of a business owned by you in proportion to the money invest is what is termed as your stake in the company.

Stakeholder

Is an organization or individual owning part of a business because of their investments in it.

Supply-side economics

Tax reducing economic policies aimed at encouraging more investments from people and companies.

Tax shelter

A place or entity to invest money where the profits will not be taxed.

Tracker fund

Invested money in companies found on a specific list.

Trust

This is an agreement through which an organization or a person is given the responsibility of managing properties or money belonging to someone else.

Trust fund

An invested sum of money managed by either an organization or an individual for someone else (usually a child.)

Venture capital

Is the money invested in a new business where outcome of success is not known.

White knight

Is a company or an individual who makes an investment in a company so as to prevent it from being bought by a bigger company.

Yield

Is the profit on total money invested in a business or venture.

References:

1. *DeRoos, D. (2004). Real Estate Riches: How to Become Rich Using Your Banker's Money. John Wiley & Sons.*

2. *Sugars, B. J. (2006). Billionaire in training. New York: Mc-Graw-Hill.*

3. *Kiyosaki, R. T., & Lechter, S. L. (2002). Rich dad, poor dad. employee, self-employed, business owner, or investor - which is the best quadrant for you?* London: Time Warner.

4. *Hansen, M. V., & Allen, R. G. (2009). The one minute millionaire: the enlightened way to wealth. New York: Three Rivers Press*

5. *Hill, N. (2014). Think and grow rich Napoleon Hill: annotated classic. S.d.: Classic Good Books.*

6. *Carlsen, R., & Willis, D. A. (2007). Society for Information Technology & Teacher Education International Conference annual: March 26-30, San Antonio, Texas, USA. Chesapeake, Va: Association for the Advancement of Computing in Education.*

7. *Allen, R. G. (2013). Multiple streams of income: how to generate a lifetime of unlimited wealth. Hoboken, NJ: Wiley.*

8. *Eker, T. H. (2008). Secrets of the millionaire mind: think rich to get rich. London: Piatkus.*

www.ingramcontent.com/pod-product-compliance
Lightning Source LLC
Chambersburg PA
CBHW020912210326
41598CB00018B/1846